CW00829795

SELF-HYPNOSIS
The Chicago Paradigm

The Guilford Clinical and Experimental Hypnosis Series
Michael J. Diamond and Helen M. Pettinati, Editors

SELF-HYPNOSIS
The Chicago Paradigm

ERIKA FROMM, Ph.D.
STEPHEN KAHN, Ph.D.
The University of Chicago

Foreword by Martin T. Orne, M.D., Ph.D.

THE GUILFORD PRESS
New York　　London

© 1990 The Guilford Press
A Division of Guilford Publications, Inc.
72 Spring Street, New York, NY 10012

Printed in the United States of America

This book is printed on acid-free paper.

Last digit is print number: 9   8   7   6   5   4   3   2   1

Library of Congress Cataloging-in-Publication Data

Fromm, Erika.
    Self-hypnosis: the Chicago paradigm / Erika Fromm, Stephen Kahn.
       p.   cm. —(The Guilford clinical and experimental hypnosis
series)
    Includes bibliographical references.
    ISBN 0-89862-341-3
    1. Autogenic training.   I. Kahn, Stephen, 1950–   II. Title.
III. Series.
    [DNLM: 1. Hypnosis.   WM 415 F932s]
RC499.A8F76   1990
154.7—dc20
DNLM/DLC
for Library of Congress   90-3167
                                             CIP

Acknowledgments

Earlier versions of Chapters 3, 4, 6–11, 14, and 15 have appeared in journals and as book chapters. We are grateful to the following for letting us republish them:

Lars-Eric Uneståhl, editor of *Hypnosis in the Seventies*, and the Veje Förlag for the "Autohypnosis and Heterohypnosis: Phenomenological Similarities and Differences" section of Chapter 3; *Psychotherapy: Theory, Research and Practice* for the "Characteristics of Self-Hypnosis," "Some Differences between Self-Hypnosis and Heterohypnosis," and "The Fading of Motivation with Time" sections of Chapter 3; the *International Journal of Clinical and Experimental Hypnosis* for Chapters 4, 7, 10, 11, and 15; D. Waxman, P. C. Misra, M. Gibson, and M. A. Basker, editors of *Modern Trends in Hypnosis*, and the Plenum Press for Chapters 6 and 8; *Imagination, Cognition and Personality* for Chapter 9; and the *American Journal of Clinical Hypnosis* for Chapter 14.

Foreword

Perhaps the greatest single advancement made in the scientific study of hypnosis has been the realization that the ability to enter hypnosis is largely a skill of the patient, combining elements of focused attention, fantasy, and suspended disbelief. The role of the therapist working with a patient to use his or her hypnotic ability is to provide a context in which the patient can willingly express aspects of this cognitive skill. Further, it is important to guide the patient's hypnotic engagement in a direction that helps him or her therapeutically while inviting the patient to be active in the therapeutic process. Not only can the patient benefit from hypnosis during therapy, but self-hypnosis, once learned, can be used effectively outside the therapist's presence.

Recognizing the advantages inherent in the use of self-hypnosis has resulted in its increasing use by therapists to extend the benefits of treatment. Further, the patient's role in self-hypnosis is consistent with the ethos generally shared by most of us—that the patient rather than the therapist should take control of the process.

Beyond the therapeutic potential of self-hypnosis, it also challenges our understanding of the hypnotic experience. Already before the turn of the century, Coué argued that there is no suggestion other than self-suggestion and that all hypnosis is really self-hypnosis. Although such a view is now even more tenable than in the past given the demonstrated importance of the individual's ability and willingness, it may be equally true that all self-hypnosis can be conceived of as heterohypnosis to the extent that its success and continued usage seem to depend on an actual or implied relationship with a therapist. When used intensively in therapy, the line between self- and heterohypnosis fades further as the process seems to live at the interface of the patient–therapist relationship.

Clearly, there is a need to clarify the interaction between heterohypnosis and self-hypnosis, and to understand the ways in which self-hypnosis links to a wide range of meditative disciplines as well as to autogenic training and biofeedback. There are therefore many questions about the nature of self-hypnosis.

This volume excels in addressing some of the most fundamental of these questions, including investigations of the phenomenological differences between hetero- and self-hypnotic experiences, and the characteristics of these two modes of hypnosis. The volume is especially welcome because there is a plethora of books directed at the lay public instructing them on how to use self-hypnosis, and texts for therapists as well, but this marks the first to provide an understanding of self-hypnotic processes that is both empirically based and clinically useful.

The book has its foundation in the many years of study that Dr. Erika Fromm and her students and collaborators have conducted on self- and heterohypnosis developing "the Chicago paradigm." As Clinical Editor of the *International Journal of Clinical and Experimental Hypnosis*, Professor Fromm has been at the forefront of expanding our understanding of the therapeutic use of heterohypnosis as well as the systematic study of self-hypnosis. This text culminates those efforts and is a major advance for hypnosis researchers and therapists alike. The creative studies in this volume provide exciting new avenues for continued research on the one hand and novel and effective clinical approaches on the other. Self-hypnosis develops a true collaboration between therapist and patient, challenging the creativity of both. Once again, Professor Fromm has inspired us all to rethink the concept of self-change and how hypnosis and self-hypnosis can be used to facilitate this process.

MARTIN T. ORNE, M.D., Ph.D.
University of Pennsylvania and
The Institute of Pennsylvania Hospital

Preface

In the early 1970s Erika Fromm, the senior author of this book, became aware of the fact that while a great deal of research had been done since the late 1950s in experimental and in clinical hypnosis, the field of self-hypnosis lay barren and open. Hardly any research on self-hypnosis existed, and nothing was in a planning stage. She therefore decided to do some experiments in self-hypnosis and to collect phenomenological data, based on her subjects' introspections.

Grants for phenomenological research were practically impossible to get at that time. Behaviorism still reigned supreme. Fromm did not get the grants needed to support the scope of this research. But she was fortunate enough to collect around herself a group of truly devoted students who assisted her in setting up the project, collecting and working through the data, and coauthoring papers with her. Only rarely, when a small grant came in, could some of them be paid. It was an extraordinary group of students, some starting on the project early, some coming into the group later. Some left the group after receiving their Ph.D.'s and finding positions in other cities; some stayed on even after receiving their Ph.D.'s. One of Fromm's collaborators, Stephen Kahn, became the coauthor of this book. The others were Daniel P. Brown, Lisa S. Lombard, Stephen W. Hurt, Andrew M. Boxer, Joab Z. Oberlander, Sarah H. Skinner, Marlene Eisen, and Gary Pfeifer. Their devotion both to science and to this project and their real joy in tackling difficult conceptual problems, have been sources of great satisfaction to us.

Others who helped us screen subjects and collect data for shorter times, or who critiqued drafts of various papers, were Mary Helen Barcellos, Laurie Brandt, Stephen Coyne, Mary Hallowitz, Betty Johnson, Linda Lewis, Kerry Poethig, Blanche Schulz, Cynthia Shambaugh, Daniel Sinnott, Michael Sossi, and Francesca von Broembsen. Blanche Schulz also compiled the index. To all of them, as well as to our subjects (who could not be paid either), go our warmest thanks.

The book consists of 17 chapters. Seven of them—Chapters 1, 2, 5, 12, 13, 16, and 17—are new chapters not published before. Earlier versions of Chapters 3, 4, 6–11, 14, and 15 were published before as journal articles or book chapters. Footnotes to these chapters give the names of the original authors, our collaborators, and the journal or book in which the earlier version of the chapter was published.

This volume addresses itself mainly to experimental researchers, and with it we hope to stimulate more research in self-hypnosis as well as in heterohypnosis. But the book addresses itself also to clinicians. For one can only be a good clinician if one is aware of research developments and modifies one's clinical techniques according to unfolding relevant research findings. We hope that this book will stimulate young experimental and clinical researchers to answer questions we have asked here, to ask questions not yet posed, to test ideas as yet untested, and to examine facts about self-hypnosis that so far have not been investigated.

ERIKA FROMM
STEPHEN KAHN

Contents

SELF-HYPNOSIS
The Chicago Paradigm

PART ONE

INTRODUCTION AND THEORETICAL FRAMEWORK

CHAPTER 1

Review of the Literature

HISTORY: THEORIES AND DEFINITIONS

In our culture, some individuals consider hypnosis to involve a total loss of both control and consciousness, with complete power given over to the hypnotist. Others, at the opposite end of the spectrum, conceive of hypnosis as an active rather than a passive state, with power and will located squarely within the individual. Hypnotists as well as subjects differ in their views of the hypnotic experience. Until the end of World War II, hypnotists maintained an authoritarian stance vis-à-vis their subjects. The style, the content, and the very wording and intonation utilized reflected this stance. The hypnotic subject or patient believed that to be hypnotized meant surrendering one's will to the hypnotist. Since World War II this view has changed, and permissive hypnosis has evolved. The hypnotist now views himself as the patient's collaborator, who simply facilitates the hypnotic experience for the patient. The capability and the skill for creating and maintaining the trance reside in the patient or subject. The more sophisticated subject whose contact with hypnosis has gone well beyond that of stage hypnosis or depictions in movies realizes that he is the repository of talent for the experience, and that the hypnotist merely provides direction and enhancement for this capability.

There are two forms of hypnosis: "heterohypnosis," the more prevalent form, in which a hypnotist hypnotizes someone else, and "self-hypnosis." Heterohypnosis usually is subdivided into experimental hypnosis done for scientific-investigative purposes, and clinical hypnosis employed for therapeutic ones. A great deal of serious research has been done on heterohypnosis, particularly since the 1950s (for overviews, see Fromm & Shor, 1979; Brown & Fromm, 1986, 1987), but not much on self-hypnosis.

Although there is a plethora of books on self-hypnosis written by laypeople for the general public, the scientific literature on self-hypnosis is still sparse. Early in 1970, for the "Quo Vadis" chapter in her and Shor's book on experimental hypnosis (Fromm & Shor, 1972), Fromm (1972a) conducted a survey of the research in hypnosis that was then either in progress or in the planning stage. She found that serious research was being conducted only in the area of heterohypnosis. A review of the literature revealed this to be characteristic of the whole 19th century and the 20th century up to 1970. With a few exceptions—Liébeault (1889), Coué (1922), Salter (1941), and Weitzenhoffer (1957)—the literature on self-hypnosis had been produced by quacks and laypeople. It was within the context of the paucity of scientific research on self-hypnosis that Fromm and her students began to plan and execute the studies collected in the current book.

At the same time, Ronald E. Shor (1970), independently, had also started to do some research on self-hypnosis. Together with his student Easton (Shor & Easton, 1973), he developed two variations of Weitzenhoffer and Hilgard's (1959) heterohypnotic Stanford Hypnotic Susceptibility Scale, Form A (SHSS:A), the Inventory of Self-Hypnosis (ISH). The ISH is an adaptation of the SHSS:A to be used as a self-hypnotic induction procedure. The difficulty with the Shor and Easton scales is that subjects have to *read* to themselves the text for each subtest verbatim, and thus have to open their eyes 11 times during the induction and deepening procedures. We question whether this continuous changing between reality awareness during reading and the trance state is advisable.

Self-Hypnosis versus Heterohypnosis

In 1975 Ruch, a student of E. R. Hilgard's, published a paper in which he compared self-hypnosis in the presence of a hypnotist with heterohypnosis. His subjects were given only one experience of heterohypnosis and one of self-hypnosis,[1] on consecutive days. His findings were as follows:

1. Untrained subjects were as effective in self-hypnosis as in hetero-hypnosis. That is, they achieved the same scores on the Harvard Group Scale of Hypnotic Susceptibility, Form A (HGSHS:A) and Form C of the SHSS (SHSS:C), regardless of whether the experimenter hypnotized them or they administered hypnosis to themselves in the presence of the exper-imenter).

2. Initial self-hypnosis facilitated heterohypnosis on the next day.

3. Conventional heterohypnosis experienced on the first day inhibited self-hypnosis on the second day.

Ruch concluded that self-hypnosis is the primary phenomenon; hete-rohypnosis is "in effect a form of guided self-hypnosis" (1975, p. 296). He also confirmed the hypothesis that more visual imagery and idiosyncratic fantasy arise in self-hypnosis than in heterohypnosis. This hypothesis was

---

[1] Whether what Ruch did really qualifies to be called self-hypnosis is discussed in Chapter 4.

originally proposed by Fromm, Litchman, and Brown (1973) in a paper read at the annual convention of the Society for Clinical and Experimental Hypnosis.

E. R. Hilgard (1977) believes that *all* hypnosis is really self-hypnosis and that heterohypnosis is "merely aided self-hypnosis" (p. 229).

In 1976 Johnson and Weight conducted a study comparing self-hypnosis with heterohypnosis. This study showed that in inexperienced subjects, not selected for high hypnotizability, the subjective experiences for the two types of hypnosis are generally similar and that the total behavioral scores are comparable, too. As Fromm's (1975a,b,c—see Chapter 3) research has shown, this is particularly true for subjects with low and medium hypnotizability, and not necessarily for highly hypnotizable people. Johnson and Weight concluded that self-hypnosis and heterohypnosis are similar in most behavioral and phenomenological aspects. However, they did find that heterohypnosis evoked more feelings of unawareness, passivity, and loss of control in their subjects, whereas self-hypnosis evoked more feelings of activity, awareness, and being in control of one's feelings. In 1979, Johnson confirmed Ruch's finding that inexperienced subjects are as capable of hypnotizing themselves as of being hypnotized by someone else.

In their self-hypnosis research, Shor and Easton (1973), Ruch (1975), Johnson (1979), and Johnson and Weight (1976) have been primarily interested in quantitative aspects of self-hypnosis. In their experiments the hypnotist was present and even told each subject what to say to himself. Fromm, on the other hand, examined the qualitative phenomena of the autohypnosis to explore what it was like for a subject to induce and experience a hypnotic state on his own. She also endeavored to find the personality characteristics that enable a person to be a good self-hypnotic subject. In her experiments the subject was alone; no hypnotist/experimenter was present.

The Chicago Paradigm[2]

In the mid-1970s, in order to stimulate more research in self-hypnosis and also in order to distinguish self-hypnosis clearly from other altered states of consciousness (such as meditation, daydreaming, and the relaxation response), Fromm—in her capacity as the clinical editor of the *International Journal of Clinical and Experimental Hypnosis*—invited a number of researchers to write articles on self-hypnosis or on the similarities and differences between self-hypnosis and other altered states of consciousness. The articles were published in a special issue of the *International Journal of Clinical and Experimental Hypnosis* (July issue, 1981).

---

[2] We thank Lynn Johnson for coining the name "the Chicago paradigm" for our research—a name that we have now used as a subtitle for this book.

The first article in this issue, written by Fromm and her students (Fromm, Brown, Hurt, Oberlander, Boxer, & Pfeifer, 1981), represents our basic experimental research into the phenomenology and characteristics of self-hypnosis. This article, in somewhat revised form, appears as Chapters 4 and 7 of the current book. An interesting discussion and critique of this Fromm et al. paper, by Lynn S. Johnson (1981), follows it.

In an excellent article in that same journal issue, Singer and Pope (1981) point out several features self-hypnosis and reverie have in common—namely, the capacity for intense absorption and the capacity for experiencing vivid imagery. They describe daydreaming and imagery skills as predisposing capacities for self-hypnosis. Benson, Arns, and Hoffman (1981) state that the induction procedures for hypnosis and their "relaxation response" appear to be similar. But they fail to make a real comparison between self-hypnosis and the relaxation response. Paul Sacerdote (1981) and Gail Gardner (1981) were invited to contribute to this journal issue on self-hypnosis because they were well-known clinical teachers of self-hypnosis. Contrary to Ruch (1975) and E. R. Hilgard (1977), Sacerdote (1981) does not believe that self-hypnosis is the primary phenomenon, and therefore teaches his patients self-hypnosis during or after heterohypnosis by direct or indirect posthypnotic suggestions. Gardner's paper is discussed in the section on teaching, below.

In the last article of this journal issue, Orne and McConkey (1981) stress the importance of investigating self-hypnosis for reasons of clinical application as well as of further conceptual clarification. They feel that self-hypnosis must convergently be assessed through behavioral and phenomenological techniques, and that the consequences and dangers of its private, unsupervised use must continue to be investigated.

CLINICAL INVESTIGATIONS AND PRACTICE

The first two hypnotherapists who, in the 19th century, systematically instructed their patients to use self-hypnosis were the two Frenchmen A. A. Liébeault (1889) and Émilie Coué (1922). Coué told his patients to say to themselves, several times a day for half an hour, "Day by day, in every way, I am getting better and better." Patients were supposed to say this sentence to themselves over and over again with ever-increasing speed, in order to prevent any idea that they might not get better from coming into consciousness—so fast that the words would slur into each other and be indistinguishable from each other. Then the whole mind, Coué felt, would effectively be taken up by the suggestion of getting better, and no time would be left for any negative thought or doubt to enter the mind.

We wonder whether what Coué did was really teaching people self-hypnosis, and whether it was not more like teaching them a form of concentrative meditation (e.g., something akin to the beginning levels of Tibetan meditation or of transcendental meditation). In these forms of meditation one concentrates on the mantra and strictly keeps all other contents from entering into awareness. Coué's prescription sentence, "Day by day, in every way, I am getting better and better," is like a mantra, and all attention is so totally focused on it that everything else is kept out of awareness. In (self-) hypnosis people allow all kinds of thoughts, emotions, memories, and the like to drift into their consciousness.

Coué's method, invented in the later 19th century, became so well known in Europe that its use amounted to a popular fad between 1910 and 1930. Since then many hypnotherapists have taught their patients how to utilize self-hypnosis, particularly those patients who suffer from physical pain. Some clinician/researchers have done scientifically controlled studies. Various patient populations have been used in these researches in order to test systematically the efficacy of clinical self-hypnosis. The studies outlined below represent some of the better research on clinical self-hypnosis.

J. R. Hilgard and LeBaron (1984) studied 34 young patients (aged 4 to 19) suffering from cancer pain, and helped them with heterohypnosis. Although these authors did not really study the effect of self-hypnosis on the patients, they made some statements about self-hypnosis—namely, that self-hypnosis permits the individual to be in charge and therefore helps the patient to get out of the role of the victim who suffers and into the role of the person who masters or attempts to master her pain. Through practicing self-hypnosis, patients can learn to isolate the feared pain that accompanies many a medical intervention; they can productively dissociate themselves into a position in which they can enjoy pleasurable fantasies and memories, away from the negative aspects of their current reality.

Spinhoven (1989) did some elegant empirical research on hypnotic and self-hypnotic headache control and on self-hypnosis in the management of low back pain on large patient populations.

Wakeman (1988) studied 50 patients who had suffered extensive third-degree burns; they were recovered from the burns, but still found it difficult to be at work in high-temperature environments. Half of the group received heterohypnotic therapy for 16 weeks, 2 hours per week, and were taught self-hypnosis. The other 25 did not get any hypnotherapy or self-hypnosis. The hypnosis/self-hypnosis group made a much better recovery than the control group.

Katz, Kellerman, and Ellenberg (1987) taught self-hypnosis to part of a group of 36 children with acute lymphoblastic leukemia who needed to undergo bone marrow aspirations. In diminishing fear and pain, it worked as well as but not better than relaxing play activities engaged in prior to the painful procedure.

D. Spiegel and Bloom (1983) investigated the pain and mood disturbances of 54 women with metastasized carcinoma of the breast over the course of

1 year. Those who were taught self-hypnosis in addition to group therapy fared best.

Wark (1989) used "alert" self-hypnosis techniques to help seven students improve their reading comprehension. They were taught how to induce an alert trance, and in addition were encouraged to generate their own personalized self-suggestions for improvement in reading comprehension.

Aronson (1986) developed an interesting, highly structured hypnotherapy program for adolescent psychiatric inpatients, in which each adolescent listened to her own tape-recorded voice for the induction and deepening procedure, and then the therapist took over and suggested ego-strengthening themes. His procedure put the adolescents in control of their inductions and thus shifted them from external to internal control.

In a scientifically well-conceived study, Swirsky-Sacchetti and Margolis (1986) investigated the effects of a comprehensive self-hypnosis training program for helping severe hemophiliacs. Those who used self-hypnosis as directed were more successful in reducing Factor VIII (the coagulant deficiency of hemophilia A).

Kohen, Olness, Colwell, and Heimel (1984) treated 505 pediatric patients suffering from a variety of problems (enuresis, pain, obesity, anxiety reactions, habit problems, encopresis, headache, fear of pelvic examinations) with relaxation and mental imagery methods that were defined to them as self-hypnosis. In about half of all of their patients, the authors found a high percentage of improvement.

Anderson, Basker, and Dalton (1975) had promising results with a group of migraine patients who were taught to use self-hypnosis and to imagine the blood vessels in their heads becoming progressively less dilated.

Hammond, Haskins-Bartsch, Grant, and McGhee (1988) compared self-directed and tape-assisted self-hypnosis in 48 inexperienced subjects. They found that the tape-assisted experiences were more gratifying to the subjects and convinced them more fully that they had been in an altered state. However, the authors state that over time subjects usually moved from tape-assisted self-hypnosis to self-induced self-hypnosis (i.e., from training to mastery).

A good number of single-case studies or studies on two to five cases employing self-hypnosis have been published. We mention only a few here. A paper by Dane and Rowlingson (1988) describes the management of a case of postherpetic neuralgia; a paper by Smith and Balaban (1983) outlines a multidimensional approach to pain relief in systemic lupus erythematosus. There is a paper by Epstein and Deyoub (1983) on the hypnotherapeutic control of exhibitionism; a paper by Feinstein and Morgan (1986) on self-hypnotically learning to regulate bipolar affective disorders; and one by Young and Montano (1988) on teaching three children who suffered from Gilles de la Tourette's syndrome to control their symptoms and increase self-efficacy.

A famous single-case study is that of Milton Erickson (Erickson & Rossi, 1977), who spontaneously used autohypnosis from the age of 6 on throughout his lifetime. He employed it to master the many problems in his life associated with various congenital physical anomalies and infirmities, dyslexia, and pain. After polio struck him late in his teenage years, in trance he used memories of what it was like to run until he temporarily learned to use his legs again. And he recalls that he learned to give himself posthypnotic suggestions within self-hypnosis to help him accomplish various other tasks that would have been almost impossible to accomplish without self-hypnosis. Furthermore, as a therapist, he frequently put himself into a self-hypnotic trance in order to make his sensitivity to a patient's productions maximally operative.

On the more clinical-theoretical side, Araoz and Sanders should be mentioned. Like E. R. Hilgard (1977), Araoz (1981) thinks that all hypnosis is self-hypnosis. He has also introduced a new concept, that of "negative self-hypnosis." According to Araoz, individuals with little self-confidence, courage, and initiative engage in many unconscious and conscious combinations of perceptions of and script making for themselves to keep their (sexual) lives ungratifying. He applies the label "negative self-hypnosis" to these activities. By using this framework to define the problems of patients, Araoz has been able to devise a technique using self-hypnosis, heterohypnosis, and a cognitive–hypnobehavioral approach to work with individuals and couples and help them undo the emotional difficulties that are so painful to them. Consciously directed self-hypnosis is an essential part of his sex therapy, aimed at undoing what he conceives of as negative self-hypnosis.

Sanders (1987) defines self-hypnosis as an altered state of consciousness, self-induced, similar in many ways to heterohypnosis. She divides orientations to clinical self-hypnosis into five different categories: (1) behavioral, (2) eclectic, (3) psychoanalytic, (4) physiological, and (5) "other." She classifies self-hypnotic induction techniques into the physiological ones (eye fixation, relaxation, breathing, eye roll), the ideomotor self-hypnotic induction techniques (clenched fist, counting backwards), imagery techniques (stairs, comfortable place to go to), and the kinesthetic techniques (arm levitation, arm drop, blowing out cheeks).

In her book *Clinical Self-Hypnosis: The Power of Words and Images*, Sanders (1990) discusses the history of clinical self-hypnosis, the areas of its use, specific techniques, and goals, as well as the uses of guided imagery and the fine-tuning of wordings for the patient.

TEACHING OF SELF-HYPNOSIS

Besides the publications mentioned above in connection with the 1981 special issue of the *International Journal of Clinical and Experimental Hypnosis* (Gardner, 1981; Sacerdote, 1981), Soskis's (1986) book is perhaps so far the best book on the teaching of self-hypnosis. It is a thoughtful, step-by-step manual that shows the beginning hypnotherapist how to teach self-hypnosis to patients. Soskis clearly specifies the types of patients and behaviors to whom self-hypnosis should or should not be taught. He also outlines very specific protocols and ways of teaching self-hypnosis to patients, and the requirements the patients must fulfill in order to be successful.

Gardner (1981) discusses the necessary skills that young children must have to benefit from hypnosis (such as some language development and the capacity to follow posthypnotic suggestions); indications and contraindications; patient resistance; and parental involvement. She also describes her three-step method of teaching hypnosis to children. Since the 19th century, when Liébeault (1889) used it therapeutically to help children (as well as adults), child hypnosis had rarely been used until Gardner revived it in the 1970s. Gardner and Olness (1981) have pioneered teaching self-hypnosis to children, with the emphasis on giving tools for mastery, particularly mastery of pain.

Alman's book with Lambrou (1983) addresses itself both to the layperson and to the professional. It is a self-help book, and teaches the reader relaxation and the use of guided imagery for developing self-hypnotic trances for various self-developmental and therapeutic purposes, without having to see a professional hypnotherapist. Appropriate precautionary remarks are made, and the book basically is a sound book. But to us it seems unwise to encourage people to practice self-hypnosis for therapeutic purposes, without having a professional make at least an initial assessment of their ego strength and ability to handle strong affect.

Van Dijck (1988) uses an initial heterohypnotic session to teach his patients self-hypnosis by means of a posthypnotic suggestion, for the purpose of stimulating them to find new ways for looking at their own problems.

Citrenbaum, King, and Cohen (1985) also teach their patients self-hypnosis in the very first heterohypnotic session, for habit control—for instance, in order to lengthen the time between reaching for a cigarette or to silence the inner voice that is urging them on to smoke.

Soskis, Orne, Orne, and Dinges (1989) taught self-hypnotic relexaation to 21 executives in a single 1½-hour group session, and found that this brief procedure sufficed to initiate self-directed self-hypnosis for stress reduction. However, telephone follow-up calls showed that the use of self-hypnosis among their subjects steadily declined during the first 6 months, from 90% to 42%.

In their books covering a wide range of topics in the field of clinical hypnosis, Weitzenhoffer (1957, 1989), Dengrove (1976), Udolf (1981), Crasilneck and Hall (1985), Watkins (1987), and Brown and Fromm (1987) also discuss techniques, advantages, caveats, and purposes of teaching self-hypnosis to patients.

The main purpose of teaching self-hypnosis to patients is to help them relax and to relieve tension and anxiety as well as pain. It has probably been taught most frequently to patients who are suffering from physical pain. The hypnotist cannot be with these patients at all times when they are in pain, and the patients need to have a tool by means of which they can learn to control and master it, or at least be able to live with reduced pain. Frequently, particularly in the beginning, a tape is made for a patient. Whether the patient's listening at home to a tape made by the hypnotist can truly be called self-hypnosis is, as we have said above, questionable to us (see also Chapter 4). However, after a while, when the patient has gained more familiarity and security with hypnosis, it often leads him to induce trance by himself, and then it becomes true self-hypnosis.

ACKNOWLEDGMENT

We wish to express our gratitude to Mary E. Hallowitz for collecting and abstracting most of the literature covered in this chapter.

CHAPTER 2

The University of Chicago Research on Self-Hypnosis

For a long time it has been assumed that the phenomena of autohypnosis must be the same as those in heterohypnosis, and that theoretically and in essence there is no difference between the two. Fromm questioned this assumption and hypothesized that in heterohypnosis the subject's ego divides into two parts (experiencer and observer), while in self-hypnosis it divides into three parts (the "director" who gives the hypnotic instructions, the "experiencer" or the directed part, and the "observer"; see Chapter 3). In self-hypnosis, after all, the subject must be both hypnotist and subject. Fromm further hypothesized that although there are many similarities between the two hypnotic processes, there may also be important phenomenological differences in such areas as surrender versus control and mastery; spontaneously arising visual imagery and idiosyncratic fantasy; depth of hypnotic state and ease of achieving it; cognitive activity; and general reality orientation, including time perception.

Thus, what prompted us to undertake the research for this book were questions such as these: What is the phenomenology of self-hypnosis? What are the similarities and the differences between self-hypnosis and hetero-hypnosis? Can we as clinicians assume (as we ordinarily do) that a good way to teach our patients self-hypnosis is to model it by means of hetero-hypnosis—that is, to tell them after they have experienced heterohypnosis a few times that they can induce effective self-hypnosis by proceeding along the same lines, using the same techniques we have employed to help them become hypnotized by us? Do people who go into deep heterohypnotic trances also go into deep trance states *self*-hypnotically? What are the personality characteristics of those who are highly susceptible to self-hypnosis? Are they different from those of people who are susceptible to heterohypnosis? These are the questions we have endeavored to answer over the last 17 years through research into self-hypnosis conducted at the University of Chicago—research that came to be known as "the Chicago paradigm" (Johnson, 1981).

In the beginning our interest was focused on finding the similarities and differences between self-hypnosis and heterohypnosis. As time went on, we became more fascinated with just exploring the phenomena of self-hypnosis, their structure and content. Later we realized that not all those who were highly susceptible to heterohypnosis were also good self-hypnotic subjects. Our interest then turned more and more to finding the personality style that enables a person to be or to become a good self-hypnotic subject. Furthermore, it was possible that specific personality characteristics could contribute to varying kinds of experiences in self-hypnosis differentially. Fortunately, we had built into our original design a number of personality tests, which were administered before the actual self-hypnosis experiment started. This enabled us to answer a number of questions about the effects of personality. In our research, we defined "self-hypnosis" as hypnosis in which the subject guides his own experience of induction and trance without the physical presence of a hypnotist, and initiates his own suggestions.

METHODS AND PROCEDURES

The sample for all subsequent chapters of this book except Chapters 3 and 14–15 consisted of the same volunteers. The data for the two pilot studies described in this book (Chapter 3) were collected by Fromm and her students in January 1972, and in May 1973 (Fromm, 1975a,b,c). The data for Chapters 4–13 were collected between 1974 and 1976. Most of the volunteer subjects were University of Chicago undergraduate students, aged 18 to 21 years. Some were graduate students, and three were professionals, the oldest participant being 45 years of age. Only highly hypnotizable, emotionally healthy subjects were selected to participate in the study. Hypnotizability was considered to be suitable if a subject scored 9 or above out of a possible score of 12 points on the Harvard Group Scale of Hypnotic Susceptibility (HGSHS:A; Shor & Orne, 1962) and within the same range on the Stanford Hypnotic Susceptibility Scale, Form C (SHSS:C; Weitzenhoffer & Hilgard, 1962). Prior to participating in the month-long experiment, all applicants were given the Minnesota Multiphasic Personality Inventory (MMPI; Hathaway & McKinley, 1967; Dahlstrom, Welsh, & Dahlstrom, 1972, 1975) and the Rorschach test (Rorschach, 1949, 1954), as screening tests to exclude individuals with psychopathology from the sample.

Originally, 425 subjects had been screened, and a sample of 58 heterohypnotically highly susceptible volunteers was obtained. Only a bit more than half of them (33 subjects) finished the demanding task of practicing self-hypnosis daily for a full hour on 28 consecutive days, alone in a barren room and without remuneration. This group of 33 formed the basic pool of subjects. Selection of subsets of this basic sample were made for the various research endeavors undertaken in the 1980s (Chapters 4–13).

Prior to participating in the experiment, all subjects chosen for the study were given Weitzenhoffer and Hilgard's (1967) Revised Stanford Profile Scales of Hypnotic Susceptibility, Form I (SPSHS:I) to give them some familiarity with the range of phenomena that can occur in deep (hetero)hypnosis. Because we also had an interest in finding out whether heterohypnotizability would improve with continuing practicing of self-hypnosis, Form II of the SPSHS (SPSHS:II; Weitzenhoffer & Hilgard, 1967) was administered midway through the self-hypnosis experiment (after 2 weeks), and the SPSHS: I was given once again at the completion of the experimental run (i.e., after 4 weeks). Another procedure consisted of an assessment of the subjects' personality characteristics. For this purpose, Jackson's (1974) Personality Research Form (PRF), Shostrum's (1972) Personal Orientation Inventory (POI), and the Differential Personality Questionnaire (DPQ) by Tellegen and Atkinson (1974)[1] were administered prior to the subjects' initial self-hypnotic experience.

At the outset, subjects were instructed to make daily journal entries after each session describing the content of their self-hypnotic experience. From these instructions and from uniform training sessions in heterohypnosis to standardize their understanding of hypnosis, the subjects knew how to induce and deepen trance. They were permitted to use any of these learned techniques, but were also encouraged to invent their own induction and deepening methods with which to explore their internal experiences in trance. The diary entries included the subjects' self-suggestions; their descriptions of the phenomena they experienced in each self-hypnotic session; and the subjects' testings of their own trance depth (via the Extended North Carolina Scale (ENCS; Tart, 1972, 1979). At the end of the month-long experiment they were given three extensive questionnaires, the results of which are described in Chapters 4 and 5.

Some of our subjects occasionally failed to make the required daily journal entries or omitted personality data. As a result, the number of cases involved in a particular analysis in Chapters 7–13 can vary from 27 to 33 subjects.

We have organized our presentation of the research as follows. Chapter 3, the final chapter of this introductory section, presents descriptions of our pilot studies and theoretical speculations derived from them. In Part II, Section A (Chapters 4–6) presents analyses of the three questionnaires mentioned above and the conclusions we draw from these analyses; Section B

---

[1] Unfortunately, the DPQ was added only after we had already started the experimental procedure with about one-third of our subjects. This was due to the fact that we became aware of Tellegen and Atkinson's work only a few years after it had been published.

(Chapters 7–13) provides a similar treatment of the subjects' diaries. Part III (Chapters 14–15) describes clinical applications of self-hypnosis. Finally, the two chapters of Part IV (Chapters 16–17) present our overall conclusions and thoughts for directions in future research.

THE PHENOMENA: QUALITATIVE SAMPLES

To give the reader a flavor of the phenomena of self-hypnosis, we present some excerpts from our subjects' diaries here in order to exemplify the various levels of "success" our subjects achieved, the changes in control of both inductions and deepening experienced, the strength of affect and vividness of imagery accomplished, and finally changes that occurred in the ego modes and attentional processes. All diary entries were made by the subjects immediately following each session. Practically all of our subjects adopted individual styles of inductions and trance that suited their tastes and needs. Some found their experiences more satisfying and meaningful than others, but, except for the poorest self-hypnotic subjects, all found the experiment with self-hypnosis interesting and successful over the 4 weeks of practice.

Objectively, all subjects in this study had high scores on the standard heterohypnotic susceptibility scales administered in preliminary screening. Notwithstanding this, the journals enabled us to divide the subjects into three groups, based on their self-perceived overall success in self-hypnosis: (1) the highest group, containing those subjects who had unusual and remarkable self-hypnosis sessions; (2) the middle group, containing those subjects who felt they were successful; and (3) the lowest group, containing those subjects who defined their self-hypnosis experiences as unsuccessful.

The journals of most of our subjects were imaginative. Some even illustrated their journals with elaborate drawings made during their self-hypnotic experiences. Susan,[2] one of our three most hypnotizable subjects, wrote on Day 1:

> "I went down to first grade on a day when I was visiting my kindergarten teacher. She taught me how to write my name in script, so I drew a picture for her (I still have it in my art book). With my art book and pencil I brought myself back up to 18 [Susan's current age] and drew another picture, this time of me swinging, in a sort of fantasy world. I seemed to draw it and be in it at the same time. The drawing came quickly and easily, and it was a real pleasure to do it.
>
> "After I put my drawing book down, I was in a trance for 5 minutes or so. I then began to have a conversation with myself. 'Susan, what do you want to

---

[2] Here and throughout the book, all names used for subjects are pseudonyms.

be?' 'I don't know.' 'Be a snail.' So I became a snail for a little while. 'I don't want to be a snail.' 'What do you want to be?' 'A bird.' 'No, no, you can't be a bird yet, you have to start out on the ground.' 'I'm not going to be an ant.' 'All right, then be a log.' So I became a log. My arms were two stiff, dead branches and my feet the old roots. 'I don't want to be a log any more.' 'All right, then it is time to wake up.' So I came out of the trance and then completely out of hypnosis.

"The whole experience was really interesting. Being able to make suggestions to myself and letting myself slip through dreams and memories and become the persons in the dreams and memories was really good. I enjoyed that experience a lot more than the others where it was just a matter of bending your arm, or having it get heavy, etc."

The great majority of our sample—that is, 22 of the 27 subjects who made daily journal entries—fell into the second group, which we have called the "successful" group. On Day 3 Robert, a subject from this middle group of "successful" subjects, reported:

"I went very smoothly into a trance by imagining sliding slowly down a spiral. First suggestion: that a force was repelling my hands from each other. This was successful. Then I imagined a force was attracting them: also successful. Imagined that my right hand would feel no pain: successful (I pinched it very hard, repeatedly).

"Then imagined I was sitting in a flying cape (like the one in the story of *The Little Lame Prince*) and that it rose and started flying. Then I had a dream: first, in it I was stretching my hands towards the sky and rain was running down my fingers. Then I was sitting in a warm cave/den with a friend in front of a fire. Next, I became a panther (the one that lived in the cave) and walked around over the rocks. This dream was fairly successful—parts were very natural, but here and there I had to will it to continue.

"Next I traveled back to my boarding school—St. Paul's. Went over all details of the area around my dorm. Went in the back door—very aware of surroundings—visited my room as it was in the fall of senior year, and the rooms of my two roommates, recreating the details perfectly. Then put on clothes such as I would have worn at that time, went out for a bike ride—rode my accustomed route."

The third group, consisting of only two subjects, had many difficulties entering the self-hypnotic state. They did not get into the deep states they had experienced in heterohypnosis. They either became tense and frustrated because they felt "nothing happened," or they fell asleep. On Day 19, Joe wrote into his diary:

"Another session of nothing happening. Nothing. Maybe some sleep. It's frustrating."

Changes in control of both induction and deepening took place over time. For most of our subjects, induction of self-hypnosis became an automatized procedure after the first few days, quickly bringing them into trance. On Day 13, Bruce wrote:

"I used the relaxation induction procedure of concentrating on the nail of my left forefinger. I gazed on that until I felt so tired that my eyes closed automatically. This may have taken 30 seconds at the most."

After 2 weeks of practice all our subjects, except for the two unsuccessful ones, were able to "flow" with the self-hypnotic experience relatively easily. However, being able to control their experience was an issue of concern to all of them—even to the most successful subjects—in terms of both trance induction and deepening. Debbie, a representative of the large middle group of successful subjects, wrote on Day 22:

"Induction is no problem any more. Deepening is not a problem up to a point. I don't seem to get *very* deep."

One of the most important features of the journals written by our successful and highly successful subjects—that is, by 25 out of 27 subjects who faithfully kept their diaries—is the vividness of imagery and the strength of affect. Here is an example from Jennifer's diary, Day 21:

"Today I decided to become something. First I became a different person. A woman. As I let the character come, it turned out that I was a woman accused of being a witch. I was very frightened. I began to tremble. I kept denying the charges but knew I was going to be burned. It was very upsetting. Then I became a mole. I was very irritated at the humans tromping over my home— I was a very irritable mole. Then I became a siren. First I dreamt being on a rock surrounded by the sea. It was green, gray, and dark. I was singing. As I dreamt I started to become the part more and more. I let down my hair and began to sing quietly. Quietly, but it seemed the tune could be heard distinctly by someone else. I was terribly sad. Very, very lonely. I knew that as a siren I lured men to their death, but that didn't seem to be right or wrong. It was inevitable. I could only sing unendingly. It was rather sad being a siren.

"Letting myself become several things or people in one hour puts me through a variety of emotions each very different from the last. It can be quite tiring but very interesting."

The subject became emotionally so absorbed in her hypnotic fantasy that the reality of her being a 20th-century student sitting alone in a room faded into the background of her awareness. She began to tremble and became very frightened, or felt herself to be an irritable mole in a hole underground. The various affects were powerful, and the imagery was felt to be very real.

The subjects in our successful and highly successful groups experienced alternations of attentional processes and often went back and forth between ego-actively *deciding* to focus their attention on performing a specific task and ego-receptively *letting* thoughts and imagery float into awareness without giving themselves any specific instructions. Such a switch can be from Ego Activity to Ego Receptivity or from Ego Receptivity to Ego Activity. A switch from Activity to Receptivity is characterized by a concrete suggestion, followed by the spontaneous emergence of materials that are consciously or unconsciously thematically related to the original suggestions. A switch from Receptivity to Activity represents an interruption of free-flowing materials by voluntary mental activity such as stopping anxiety dreams when they become too unpleasant. Jennifer, in the excerpt above, made this quick shift from Ego Activity ("I decided to become something") to Ego Receptivity ("As I let the character come, it turned out that I was . . ."). Our results show that both Ego Receptivity and Ego Activity are highly important factors in self-hypnosis. Alternations between Ego Activity and Ego Receptivity can occur quickly and can follow one another in rapid succession. At the beginning of her self-hypnotic experience, Susan also described this phenomenon (Day 2):

> "I went into a trance. The first scene I saw was of an Indian woman getting into a canoe. Then a scene of me waiting for the bus flashed in. Quickly the woman in the canoe came back into the picture. She had an errand [to do]. So did I in the scene of me taking a bus. The Indian woman seemed to be me. We looked very different but were the same person. Then I went into a quiet trance, without pictures, so I decided to draw. I let my pen and hand start the drawing with no idea of what it would do. I started to draw a woman—tribal woman. As the picture developed, it appeared that she was holding a spear in one hand, and a child was holding onto her other hand. An Amazon, I finally decided. Then I put more women with spears behind the first one. One of these women was pregnant. I started to feel like an Amazon. Really tough, fighting for survival, a little angry. Then I woke up."

The times when things seem to happen to Susan were punctuated by periodic decisions she made and suggestions she gave to herself.

In our self-hypnosis studies, 64% of our subjects experienced greater Ego Receptivity in self-hypnosis than in their pre-experimental exposures to heterohypnosis. It also appears from their journals that our subjects were more receptive to *internal* states, to imagery and fantasy that welled up from the inside.

Although these alternations in ego modes occurred often, there were times when subjects were simply ego-active and gave themselves suggestions or commands.

> "I suggested that my left leg would feel lighter . . . that I would taste a specific candy bar . . ." (Kevin, Day 1)

At other times they were ego-receptive only.

> "I felt that I was released from my surroundings and traveling or moving in a vacuum. Various colored images came into my mind, quite abstract without reference to meaning and without my asking for them." (Fred, Day 26)

> "Later, quick images: saw self in maroon suit, meeting my boyfriend for the first time, at a dance. Scene shifted to Orthodox High Holiday service, so different, so interesting! All the men shouting arguments at the rabbi, and the women gossiping in the balcony. Then back to his [the boyfriend's] house to prepare dinner. Everything smelled like onions fried in chicken fat. Horrible smell—I knew I could never become a part of that world. Fascinated, but felt like an observer in a strange land. Later, quick images riding horseback in Rockies, sorority meeting, just visions of heads thrown back, laughing." (Louise, Day 23)

As demonstrated in the excerpts given in this section, our heterohypnotically highly hypnotizable subjects did experience various degrees of success in self-hypnosis. The more successful subjects experienced more affect-laden and powerful imagery, more control over their inductions and deepening, and more time spent in Ego Receptivity and in alternations between Ego Receptivity and Activity.

QUANTITATIVE DATA

In the next chapter of this book (Chapter 3), we describe the two pilot studies we conducted on the similarities and differences between self-hypnosis and heterohypnosis, as well as on the phenomena of self-hypnosis when it is practiced regularly over some time. We learned from these studies (1) that only highly hypnotizable subjects could give us worthwhile information about the phenomenological similarities and differences between self-hypnosis and heterohypnosis; and (2) that imagery is quite idiosyncratic and very rich and vivid in self-hypnosis.

The quantitative data on self-hypnosis described in this book from Chapter 4 onward were derived from two sources. The first source consisted of the structured self-reports of the self-hypnotic experience obtained after the 4-week experimental period. Subjects were asked to complete three questionnaires. In one questionnaire, the Comparative Questionnaire (CQ), the first week of self-hypnosis was compared with heterohypnosis (a total of three screening, one interim, and one final session). In the Longitudinal Questionnaire (LQ), self-hypnosis was studied over time (4 weeks); and the Self-Hypnosis Proper Questionnaire (SHPQ) dealt specifically with the phenomenon of self-hypnosis. The three questionnaires were given to each subject only at the completion of his or her 4-week experiment, in order to avoid the risk of making subjects aware of phenomena they had not been aware of before and thus inadvertently altering the experimental conditions.

The second source of quantitative data was derived by systematically analyzing the diaries and creating specific categories for the phenomena the subjects experienced. The journals represented an ongoing day-by-day account of the self-hypnotic experience, whereas the questionnaires involved a retrospective approach. The ratings of the diaries were performed on each of the daily journal entries and then summed for each subject across the 28 days of the experiment.

We came to see that the fading of the General Reality Orientation and Absorption set the stage for hypnosis per se, heterohypnosis as well as self-hypnosis. The General Reality Orientation and Absorption are essential characteristics of both. The two other structural characteristics—expansive, free-floating attention and Ego Receptivity to stimuli coming from within—differentiate self-hypnosis from heterophynosis, according to our subjects' self-reports on the questionnaires. They are state-specific for self-hypnosis, while concentrative attention and Ego Receptivity to stimuli coming from a single outside source (the hypnotist on whom the subject or patient steadily focuses his attention) are state-specific for heterohypnosis.

Chapters 4 and 5 are based on analyses of the three extensive questionnaires we gave to our subjects at the end of their month-long practice with self-hypnosis. These chapters, particularly Chapter 4, form the core of our whole experimental work on self-hypnosis.

In the analyses of the CQ and the LQ reported in Chapter 4, we separated the questions into two broad categories. One category of questions dealt with what we called the structural dimensions of the hypnotic experience; a second category of questions focused on the content of the sessions. The Structural Category embraced the following areas: Concentrative Attention, Expansive Attention, Ego Activity, Ego Receptivity, Ego Passivity, Absorption/Fascination, fading of the General Reality Orientation, and Trance Depth. The Content Areas we analyzed were Imagery, Strong Affect, Age Regression, Personal Memories, Dreams (usually induced by self-suggestion), Working

on Personal Problems, and Self-Suggested Phenomena (such as sensory phenomena or motor activities).

Results of the two questionnaires showed that Concentrative Attention
invariably went hand-in-hand with Ego Activity, and Expansive Attention
with Ego Receptivity. The CQ showed that Absorption/Fascination and fading
of the General Reality Orientation were characteristic of both heterohypnosis
and self-hypnosis. The differentiating characteristics lay in the areas of Attention
and Ego Receptivity. Expansive, free-floating Attention and Ego Receptivity
to stimuli coming from *within* were state-specific for self-hypnosis, whereas
Concentrative Attention and Ego Receptivity to stimuli coming from one
outside source—the hypnotist on whom the subject concentrated his
attention—were state-specific for laboratory-defined heterohypnosis. Other
results from the CQ showed that attempts to produce Age Regression and
positive or negative hallucinations were markedly more successful in heterohypnosis. On the other hand, Imagery was reported as much richer in
self-hypnosis than in heterohypnosis.

The LQ made it clear that self-hypnosis requires adaptation to the state.
In the beginning, subjects reported a good deal of anxiety and self-doubt.
As the subjects began to feel more comfortable in the self-hypnotic state,
they spent less time worrying about failures in self-suggestion. Their ability
to enter trance quickly and easily increased. So did Trance Depth, Absorption,
and the fading of the General Reality Orientation.

In 1982 our focus changed somewhat. We became less interested in
comparing self-hypnosis and heterohypnosis, and more fascinated with the
phenomena of self-hypnosis itself, regardless of whether they were the same
or were different from those occurring in heterohypnosis.

Chapter 5 focuses on results from the Self-Hypnosis Proper Questionnaire
(SHPQ). Overall, these results, like those of the other two questionnaires,
indicated that the self-hypnotic experience was characterized by fading of
the General Reality Orientation and by Absorption. The focus of attention
generally alternated between Ego Activity and Ego Receptivity. Visual imagery
represented a core aspect of the experience, with most subjects finding their
imagery quite vivid. Time distortion almost always occurred, and personal
memories (age regressions and hypermnesias) were explored by most of the
subjects. The need to include the waking state as a standard of
comparison—not only in the examination of self-hypnosis generally, but in
particular in the areas of modes of attention and imagery—is discussed in
this chapter.

Whereas Chapters 4 and 5 are based on the analyses of the three questionnaires, Chapters 7–13 are based on the analyses of the diaries. (Chapter
6 summarizes the conclusions we draw from Chapters 4 and 5.) Chapter 7
is a slightly revised version of that portion of our major 1981 paper having
to do with the diaries (the bulk of this paper has become Chapter 4). It

presents our preliminary findings and serves as an introduction to our more detailed analyses.

Chapter 8 examines intraindividual changes in self-hypnotic experiences, based on the written journal narratives, and compares them to the questionnaire findings of Chapters 4 and 5. As noted earlier, the journals permitted us to divide the subjects into three groups: (1) those who had unusual and remarkable self-hypnosis sessions; (2) those who felt they were successful; and (3) those who defined their self-hypnotic experiences as unsuccessful. (Objectively, of course, all subjects in this study had scored highly on standard heterohypnotic susceptibility scores in the prescreening process.) Intraindividual change is examined through the sequences of daily reports in three subjects' journals (one subject from each group), with special references to the specific self-suggestions made, how they succeeded, and what the accompanying phenomena and states of consciousness were.

Chapter 9 presents analyses of the diary entries of 30 subjects with regard to manifestations of four ego modes: Ego Activity, Ego Receptivity, Ego Passivity, and Ego Inactivity. Results showed that Ego Activity (decision making, structuring of the experiences) and Ego Receptivity (openness to stimuli rising from within) were essential elements in subjects' self-hypnosis, whereas Ego Inactivity ("nothing happens") and Ego Passivity (feeling overwhelmed) rarely occurred in the self-hypnotic experiences of our healthy subjects. Ego Receptivity is central to self-hypnosis. It is strongly positively related to vivid imagery, absorption, and self-hypnotic trance depth, as well as to heterohypnotic susceptibility. Personality characteristics of subjects who demonstrated high Ego Receptivity were a need for independence, self-reliance, and trust in one's own unconscious. On the other hand, a greater preponderance of Ego Activity in self-hypnosis was found in subjects who had a need for structure, certainty, and control in their lives. These subjects could not allow themselves to let imagery emerge naturally or to become deeply absorbed in the self-hypnotic process.

Chapter 10 deals with imagery produced in self-hypnosis and its relationship to personality characteristics and gender. Each day of each subject's diary was coded for imagery in two ways—namely, either as being reality-oriented or as being fantastic and having primary-process qualities. Levels of imagery production remained virtually the same over the 4-week period. Self-hypnotic imagery, particularly primary-process imagery, was significantly greater for the female subjects than it was for the male subjects. When imagery scores were standardized to allow for differences in verbosity, female subjects still produced significantly more primary-process imagery than male subjects. Personality characteristics (assessed by standard personality inventories) were examined in relation to self-hypnotic imagery. A factor we called "Impulse Expression" was positively related to primary-process imagery for the female subjects. "Outgoingness" was positively related to primary-process imagery for the entire sample, and especially for the female subjects.

Chapter 11 investigates the relationship of self-reported self-hypnotic depth to heterohypnotic susceptibility and to the kinds of imagery produced during self-hypnosis. The journals were coded for imagery production by scoring for both reality-oriented and primary-process imagery. Subjects had been taught to monitor their hypnotic depth using a slightly revised version of Tart's (1972, 1979) Extended North Carolina Scale (ENCS). Tart's ENCS previously had been used only with heterohypnotic subjects. The self-reports of depth correlated highly with hypnotizability (SPSHS:I) and with imagery production. Results of this study demonstrate that the ENCS depth scores are a valid indicator not only of heterohypnotic depth but also of self-hypnotic depth among highly hypnotizable subjects. Furthermore, they show that both heterohypnotic susceptibility and imagery production are related to self-hypnotic depth, but that the association between imagery and hypnotic susceptibility is due to the relationship each of them has to self-hypnotic depth. (The sample for this study, 22 subjects, was smaller than that for the other chapters because the ENCS and SPSHS:I had outliers that were dropped.)

So far in the literature Absorption has been measured as a *trait*, one that can be manifested in many waking situations as well as in trance-like conditions. In Chapter 12 we have examined the state of Absorption by assessing it directly, *in the state of self-hypnosis itself*. Raters' judgment of Absorption was based on the report of the self-hypnotic experience as chronicled in the diaries of 30 subjects. Our measure of self-hypnotic Absorption/Fascination was positively related to other aspects of self-hypnosis (Trance Depth, Imagery, and Ego Receptivity) and to personality traits, including a measure of the ability to become imaginatively absorbed in the waking state (Tellegen & Atkinson, 1974). Results indicate that those who have the capacity to be imaginatively involved in their waking activities tend to use this capacity to become absorbed in self-hypnosis. Further, it was established that self-hypnotic phenomena like Imagery, Depth, and Ego Receptivity are likely to be present when one is absorbed in the self-hypnotic trance. Absorption/Fascination is more than the backdrop for self-hypnotic phenomena; it is a powerful facet of the state itself. It is found when core aspects of trance are present in self-hypnosis.

This study also demonstrates that absorption in self-hypnosis is clearly related to hypnotic susceptibility. The most important findings of this study demonstrate that a certain personality style is conducive to becoming absorbed and fascinated during self-hypnosis. The results paint a portrait of a self-actualized individual who takes risks, has a high tolerance for ambiguity, needs little external validation and support, and is open to experience. The implication of this study for treatment is that self-hypnosis as a therapeutic technique may be used most effectively with those who are self-reliant and self-actualizing. For the more dependent, less self-actualized individual, heterohypnosis may be more effective until such time as the patient's confidence and self-actualization can be enhanced.

Chapter 13 explores the relationship of four different self-hypnosis variables to one another and to the whole set of personality traits. The sample consisted of the same 22 subjects examined in the chapter on Depth (Chapter 11). Depth, Ego Receptivity, Absorption/Fascination, and Imagery—four variables examined individually in previous chapters, but not related to one another as a group—were now interrelated in order to determine the relative strength of each in self-hypnosis. Then these variables were combined into a Composite Self-Hypnosis variable. Results indicated that Ego Receptivity and Imagery represented the most powerful aspects of the self-hypnotic experience. With respect to achieving a *deep* self-hypnotic trance, Imagery exerted an influence beyond that laid down by the structure of the experience as measured by Absorption/Fascination and Ego Receptivity.

Personality traits affected the general self-hypnosis experience, and certain traits influenced specific aspects of self-hypnosis. A linear combination of four personality variables (Outgoingness and Impulse Expression from the PRF, the Actualized Personality Factor from the POI, and Hypnotizability) correlated strongly with the Composite Self-Hypnosis variable. Further analyses revealed that the Actualized Personality Factor and Impulse Expression predicted primarily how absorbed/fascinated an individual became in trance, while Hypnotizability predicted the general aspects of the trance itself (i.e., Depth and Imagery). The personality trait of Outgoingness was more closely related to heterohypnotizability than to any aspects of self-hypnosis.

CLINICAL APPLICATIONS
AND GENERAL CONCLUSIONS

Chapters 14 and 15 provide two examples of how self-hypnosis can be used clinically. In Chapter 14 we present a clinical case report showing—through excerpts from daily diary entries—how a woman who had lost her husband worked through her mourning in self-hypnosis. The woman was a subject in our self-hypnosis research. Mourning has three phases that must be worked through, and this usually takes a total of 1 to 2 years. Intensely and creatively, the subject worked through the three phases of mourning for herself in the self-hypnosis project. At the end of the 4 weeks of daily self-hypnosis sessions, she felt liberated from her deep grief and could start a productive and happy new life again.

Chapter 15 presents our method of interweaving heterohypnotic psychotherapy and self-hypnosis. In the heterohypnotic sessions, the hypnotherapist acts as a dependable parent figure who is supporting and available when that is desirable, but who also encourages and fosters the patient's efforts to develop her inner resources and ability to function autonomously. Self-hypnosis is utilized for its rich idiosyncratic imagery. The hypnotherapist uses and elaborates on this rich, affect-loaded imagery. At other times the therapist takes a guiding role in producing therapeutic metaphors of positive valence. The patient uses and enlarges on these during self-hypnosis between the weekly therapeutic hours. In addition, the hypnotist may counteract any strong negative self-hypnotic images during heterohypnosis. Self-directed self-hypnosis allows patients to experience openness and receptivity to internal and unconscious processes against which they may defend themselves in the interrelationship with the therapist. For patients struggling with issues of control and for patients fighting their own regressive pull toward dependency, this mode of therapy appears to be particularly effective. The emphasis in this chapter is on imagery and on the intertwining of the two modalities, therapeutic heterohypnosis and self-hypnosis.

The results of nearly all of our studies indicated that Ego Receptivity and Imagery are the most important aspects of self-hypnosis. Indeed, they may be considered to be markers of the self-hypnotic state itself. With regard to Imagery: Both vivid realism of imagery as well as the fantastic, creative quality of imagery emerged as key features. In addition, it became clear that "effortless experiencing" (P. G. Bowers, 1982–1983) is part and parcel of Ego Receptivity. Our results confirm Bowers's finding that it is highly conducive to the creative process.

In Chapter 16 we discuss what conclusions can be drawn from our experimental findings with regard to therapy and the teaching of self-hypnosis to patients. This chapter emphasizes the importance of personality factors in deciding to whom and how to teach self-hypnosis with the prospect of good success. Chapter 17 presents a new model for self-hypnosis based on all of our self-hypnosis research, and discusses directions for future research.

CHAPTER 3

The Pilot Studies on Self-Hypnosis: Results and Speculations

AUTOHYPNOSIS AND HETEROHYPNOSIS: PHENOMENOLOGICAL SIMILARITIES AND DIFFERENCES

In the first of our two pilot studies, begun in 1972, we wanted to shed light on the varieties of experiences in self-hypnosis. It was our intention to examine various qualities of the autohypnotic experience and to compare them to those of an experience induced by another (heterohypnosis).

Method

Subjects were 18 male and 18 female students at the University of Chicago, randomly selected from a list of volunteers. They varied in age from 18 to 41, with the median being 22.

PROCEDURE

All subjects were given an hypnotic and a self-hypnotic session, each lasting for about 90 minutes. Half of the subjects had the heterohypnotic experience

An earlier version of the "Autohypnosis and Heterohypnosis: Phenomenological Similarities and Differences" section of this chapter was published under that title in 1975 by Erika Fromm, in Lars-Eric Uneståhl (Ed.), *Hypnosis in the Seventies* (pp. 24–28). Örebro, Sweden: Veje Förlag. Reprinted by permission of the volume editor and publisher.

Earlier versions of the "Characteristics of Self-Hypnosis," "Some Differences between Self-Hypnosis and Heterohypnosis," and "The Fading of Motivation with Time" sections of this chapter appeared as part of a paper titled "Self-Hypnosis: A New Area of Research," published in 1975 by Erika Fromm in *Psychotherapy: Theory, Research and Practice, 12*, 295–301. Reprinted by permission of the journal editor.

first, half the self-hypnotic one. In order to keep the heterohypnotic induction constant from subject to subject, a tape of the Harvard Group Scale of Hypnotic Susceptibility, Form A (HGSHS:A; Shor & Orne, 1962) was used individually for each subject.

In the autohypnotic experience, subjects had to read a standardized instruction booklet written by Ronald E. Shor, entitled *The Inventory of Self-Hypnosis* (Shor, 1970). This contains step-by-step instructions for performing the same induction and challenge items as those contained in the HGSHS:A.

All subjects were interviewed by Fromm for roughly 1 hour within 1–2 weeks after the conclusion of their second testing. In this interview, subjects were asked to sum up the autohypnosis and heterohypnosis experiences, illustrate similarities and differences between them, and note any facets that had been particularly enjoyable. Subjects were then asked to describe the expectations they had had. The interviewer kept running notes. All interviews were intentionally kept rather free-floating and unstructured, like clinical interviews. At the end of each interview, subjects were asked to summarize the salient points in 10 minutes. These 10-minute statements were tape-recorded and transcribed verbatim. The transcriptions, together with the interviewer's notes of the whole interview, provided the source of data for the phenomenological and qualitative comparison of autohypnosis and heterohypnosis.

Results

SIMILARITIES BETWEEN SELF-HYPNOSIS
AND HETEROHYPNOSIS

For 12 of our subjects (i.e., one-third of the group), phenomenologically there were no differences between heterohypnosis and autohypnosis. Four of them had expected this a priori. All of these subjects scored between 2 and 8 on the HGSHS:A, with a median of 4.5 (i.e., they all were relatively poor subjects). The other 24 subjects ranged in their scores on the HGSHS:A from 4 to 12, with a median of 9.0. They (i.e., the good subjects) experienced the differences between self-hypnosis and heterohypnosis with which the remainder of this section of the chapter concerns itself.

Discussion

Very clear-cut, unequivocal differences were found in two areas: spontaneously arising imagery, and divisions of the ego. For all our good subjects, much more idiosyncratic imagery suggested itself in self-hypnosis than in heterohypnosis. In self-hypnosis, fantasy and thought have more primary-process quality—they "occur" playfully, effortlessly, rather than being actively or willfully "produced." The adding of personal instructions (to those already given in the booklet of directions) "just comes up." As one subject said: "One does not tell oneself, 'Now let fantasies or imagery come up.' They just kind of happen." The organism is in a receptive mode of consciousness (Deikman, 1971) rather than in an active mode.

EGO DIVISIONS

In heterohypnosis, the operator is the director; the subject is the one who is directed, who experiences the phenomena, and who may watch himself experiencing them—often with a good deal of amusement or awe. In self-hypnosis, the subject is the director *and* the directed simultaneously. We asked ourselves: Does the ego in self-hypnosis split into three parts—the instructor/speaker, the listener/experiencer, and the observer? By contrast, in heterohypnosis does it divide only into the listener/experiencer and the observer (Fromm, 1972b, p. 579)?

Our subjects confirmed unanimously that there are more ego splits in self-hypnosis than in heterohypnosis. They described that in self-hypnosis they felt they were "the speaker, the listener, and the experiencer," while in heterohypnosis the instructor/speaker role was that of the outside hypnotist.

Some subjects experienced a four-way ego split in self-hypnosis and a three-way ego split in heterohypnosis, with the additional part being the doubter or the voice of resistance. Some said that they had to use "more energy" in autohypnosis because "in self-hypnosis the ego splits into more parts, all of which have to be kept going simultaneously."

With regard to other ego functions, there was more of a dichotomy. In all categories that follow below, some of the subjects stated they experienced certain phenomena more clearly or more deeply in self-hypnosis, others in heterohypnosis. We suspect that personality factors play an important role here.

EGO PASSIVITY VERSUS EGO ACTIVITY:
SURRENDER VERSUS CONTROL

Fromm (1972a) pointed out that it is necessary to differentiate Ego Activity and Passivity in hypnosis from behavioral activity and passivity. Ego Activity involves either masterful coping or protecting; Ego Passivity means going along with a demand or being overwhelmed by it. Unwilling surrender to authority—that is, going along with the hypnotist's demand when this demand is felt as being ego-dystonic (unpleasant, disliked, violating one's integrity, causing embarrassment or shame)—is characteristic of Ego Passivity. Be-

TABLE 3.1
Ego Activity and Ego Receptivity in Heterohypnosis and in Self-Hypnosis

	More in heterohypnosis	More in self-hypnosis
Ego Activity		
Smooth, masterful control	3	9
Decision to submit or let things happen	8	5
Defensive activity (resistance to hypnotic instruction)	2	0
Ego Receptivity		
Going along or allowing things to "happen"	11 + 8[a]	3 (to own needs)

[a] The same 8 subjects are accounted for twice here because for them it was a two-step process—first Ego Activity (making the decision), then Ego Receptivity (allowing things to happen).

haviorally it is often very active. Consider, for instance, a stage hypnotist's performance in which the hypnotic subject is told he is a wild horse and—to the subject's own embarrassment—feels compelled to stampede neighing around the room. In contrast, an example of Ego Activity with behavioral passivity might be the subject who, after being asked to open his eyes while remaining in a deep trance and to get up and walk to the other end of the room, decides to stay put in the chair and keep his eyes closed, in order not to risk getting into a lighter hypnotic state. It is the decision the subject makes that marks this as Ego Activity.

Comparing heterohypnosis with self-hypnosis, the majority of our subjects described that they felt their egos to be in a more active state, making more decisions in autohypnosis; in heterohypnosis, more Ego Passivity (Receptivity) prevailed.[1] This is not to say that they felt that heterohypnosis was fully passive, and autohypnosis was fully active. It was a question of more or less.

We found three types of Ego Activity in hypnosis (see Table 3.1): (1) smoothly functioning, masterful control, which consisted of the subject's giving himself the hypnotic instructions effectively; (2) the decision to submit or to let things happen; and (3) defensive activity—resistance to the hypnotist's or (in autohypnosis) the subject's own suggestions. Ego-active control in self-hypnosis was exemplified by such statements as the following: "I liked self-hypnosis better than being hypnotized by another person because I am more in control in self-hypnosis"; or "I am more willing to follow my own instructions."

---

[1] Most of what we called Ego Passivity in 1975, when this was written, we later found out is really Ego Receptivity (see Chapter 9).

Most, but by no means all, of our deeper subjects felt that autohypnosis was more active, whereas heterohypnosis was more passive, more receptive.

The Ego Activity in self-hypnosis can be experienced as exciting or joyful, or as difficult and effortful, probably depending on the subject's personality makeup and/or inner conflicts about active and passive yearnings.

A few subjects controlled the heterohypnosis by giving themselves instructions along with the hypnotist, and thus, à la Coué, changing the heterohypnosis into another self-hypnosis.

Summary

Results of this study on the similarities and differences between hypnosis induced and deepened by an outside hypnotist and self-induced hypnosis separate into those for the poor and those for the good subjects. The poorer hypnotic subjects saw no or hardly any phenomenological differences between their heterohypnotic and their autohypnotic experiences. Findings for the group of better subjects were as follows:

1. Unequivocally, there was more idiosyncratic, primary-process-type, visual imagery in self-hypnosis than in heterohypnosis.

2. Unequivocally, there were more ego divisions or splits in self-hypnosis than in heterohypnosis, the added disassociated part being "the speaker."

3. With regard to several other ego functions as well as with regard to depth of trance, differences were found, but they were not unequivocal. The same or nearly the same phenomenon that some subjects would experience much more frequently in heterohypnosis would be experienced much more frequently by others in self-hypnosis.

We expect individual personality factors to account for these differences. Some people may let themselves go more easily when led by what they perceive to be a kind but strong hand (leader, father, or mother figure), others when they are alone or do things for themselves.

After the completion of this pilot study, we began further research on similarities and differences in self-hypnosis and heterohypnosis, which shed more light on the variables of personality differences. Chapter 4 discusses this research.

CHARACTERISTICS OF SELF-HYPNOSIS

Our second pilot study on self-hypnosis, begun in 1973, produced very exciting results. In the first study, subjects had been given only one self-hypnotic and one heterohypnotic experience, and we learned that only the more deeply hypnotizable subjects were able to experience enough to become aware of differences between self-hypnosis and heterohypnosis. Now we wanted to explore these differences in greater depth. Also, we wondered whether a single autohypnotic session was sufficient to enable a subject to experience and explore the really significant phenomena of self-hypnosis. And we wanted to find out whether special skills had to be developed, or adaptations had to be made to the self-hypnotic state.

Methodology

Accordingly, six new subjects were selected for further self-hypnosis experiments, three males and three females. These were subjects who had proven to be deeply hypnotizable by means of heterohypnosis but had had no autohypnotic experience.[2]

As eventually we hoped to find some correlation between personality characteristics and the capability for self-hypnosis, the subjects were given personality tests before starting the experiment: a Rorschach test (Rorschach, 1949, 1954) with the Holt type of inquiry (Holt, 1970), a Minnesota Multiphasic Personality Inventory (MMPI), and a Personal Orientation Inventory (POI; Shostrom, 1972). The instructions for the month-long autohypnotic experiment simply consisted of our telling the subjects to induce self-hypnosis and go as deeply as possible, once a day for a full month. They were to use whatever induction and deepening methods they found most compatible, either those learned in heterohypnosis or new methods of their own invention.

At three points in the experiment, the subjects were given a heterohypnotic experience: at the start of the month of autohypnosis, Weitzenhoffer and Hilgard's (1962) Stanford Hypnotic Susceptibility Scale, Form C (SHSS:C); after 2 weeks, the same authors' (Weitzenhoffer & Hilgard, 1967) Revised Stanford Profile Scale of Hypnotic Susceptibility, Form I (SPSHS:I); and at the end of the month, the SPSHS, Form II (SPSHS:II). Each subject was instructed to keep a diary on his autohypnotic experiences with daily entries; every few days an examiner telephoned each subject and encouraged the subject to describe the phenomena he had experienced.

Initial Motivation

All the subjects were University of Chicago students and were volunteers. The names given to them, like those given to subjects throughout this book, are pseudonyms. The subjects' motivation for wanting to participate in the

---

[2] The subjects were intentionally not given an intellectual framework of what to expect, so as not to bias the results (Fromm, 1975b).

extended and demanding experiment were curiosity, fascination with hypnosis, an exploratory spirit, and the desire to learn something about themselves. For three of the subjects, an additional motivation was perhaps a positive transference to their teacher, Fromm.

Phenomenology

Naomi described self-hypnosis as follows:

> "The self-hypnotic state usually feels like a transition to something concentrated but effortless—where the surroundings slip away; an intensive trip into the self, imagination, vivid memory—a removal or aloofness."

And Sabrina reported:

> "I seemed to float in and out; where I was, I'm not sure. . . . At times when I am deepest, it feels like I am asleep, but upon reflecting, it seems as if I was thinking all the time."

Developing Skills and Adaptation to the Self-Hypnotic State

As our subjects' ability to induce self-hypnosis increased, the hypnotic process became more and more *automatized* as a skill. They needed only to give themselves a cue—a set—and they went into trance. On Day 16, Sabrina wrote in her notebook:

> "Going into trance becomes more and more spontaneous, fortunately, because it is less of a hassle. . . . [In the beginning] induction was the most frustrating thing. . . . Now all I do is say 'relax' and I'm on my way."

For some subjects, this process of giving themselves a cue was a more active, conscious process. For others, the skill consisted of developing a more passive/receptive, nonvoluntary attitude of allowing themselves to "let things happen." Such subjects would close their eyes, for example, and give themselves the set that as soon as the first eidetic imagery came up, they would go into a deep state of trance. On Day 18 Ezra wrote in his diary:

> "The thing I am noticing about the second round of self-hypnosis is that I'm less anxious to explore and try new things, and to experiment with each suggestion in four or five different ways. I don't do that as much as I used to.

What I do this time—I noticed I'm a lot more passive in the hypnotic state. I just want to enjoy the state and I'm just behaviorally passive—not wanting to do much. This is quite a shift. I want to clarify this. On the one hand I'm not doing too much—not giving myself any active suggestions. On the other hand, I'm being more acutely aware or mindful to internal processes such as imagery, such as muscle tonus and movement of muscles, such as the action of my digestive tract, my breathing—things like that."

On Day 1 this same subject, one of our three most introspective subjects, had already stated:

"The more passivity, the deeper I feel. As soon as I start an ideomotor item, I feel in a lighter state. When passive, I not only lose my surroundings and generalized reality orientation, but all sense of a reality, including body awareness."

What Ezra was describing was really Ego Receptivity, not Passivity. In Ego Passivity the subject feels overwhelmed, not calm and contented.

Some of our subjects developed spontaneous age regression or hypermnesia without having given themselves any instructions to that effect. Suddenly they would see or feel themselves to be in a childhood situation, with all its concomitant affects; or long-forgotten or repressed memories would come into awareness. These skills of age regression and hypermnesia did not appear in the beginning, but rather in the later phases of the self-hypnosis experiment.

Another manifestation of developing skills and adaptation to the self-hypnotic state was in the area of *concentration*. Subjects generally reported that as time went on, it became progressively easier to concentrate.

Sometimes subjects (Gwen, Ezra, and others) concentrated on their imagery, letting it unfold. This represented a combination of concentration and the passive/receptive ego processes. Intense concentration is not incompatible with receptive spontaneity; however, it more closely resembles alertness or vigilance than the active, effortful kind of attention that we employ, for example, in the waking state in an examination situation. In self-hypnosis, it seems that subjects after a while develop this vigilant type of attention with regard to watching their imagery, whereas the more effortful type of attention is more often involved when subjects attempt to do automatic writing, positive hallucinations, or other dissociations of a difficult nature.[3]

---

[3] We believe that both increased automatization and concentration in self-hypnosis are closely connected with acquiring the skill of going into the preconscious, whereas dissociation states are connected with going into the unconscious (Fromm, 1975b).

Dissociative States

Some subjects used dissociative methods from the very beginning of the self-hypnosis experiment. On Day 1 Ezra wrote in his journal:

> "Induction by arm levitation surprised me. . . . I found myself saying, 'That's not your hand,' spontaneously. At other times, when the arm would falter while rising, I found I had to focus my attention intensely on some other part of my body in order that it would rise further. Seems as if the more I could forget about the arm, the more it could just rise. Seems like I dissociated the arm. I went off into a fantasy and forgot about the arm while it was up in the air. It didn't get at all tired. I wonder if I can do this a different way without dissociating. Felt a little apprehensive having to give up my arm. Pardon the pun, but I am sort of attached to it."

Ezra then experimented with three dissociative methods: (1) purposely forgetting about the arm while concentrating intensely on a point on his left knee; (2) humming a complex song (meanwhile, the arm was rising "by itself"), and (3) speaking to the arm in a dissociated personified way (e.g., "Arm, I command you to rise"). All three methods worked; the first two—which also could be labeled as withdrawing attention from the arm—were the most effective.

The ego splits into "speaker" (or director), experiencer, and observer that our first pilot study had revealed to be characteristic of self-hypnosis were confirmed by our second group of subjects. Although we had not spelled out our hypotheses to our subjects, on Day 1 Naomi dreamt an autohypnotic dream that clearly illustrated this three-way split; it is so lovely that we want to share it with our readers.

> "Dream: I'm standing at the top of a lighthouse overlooking the ocean. Very colorful. Suddenly I am clearly looking through binoculars. I see a boat with me in a bathing suit waving at me at the lighthouse to come to the boat. I indicated I don't have a way to get to the boat. Me on the boat indicates to swim. Suddenly we see a boat. I, smiling, agree to take the boat. The way down is very long, by stairs and by rope, down a tree, around a path, deep. I realize in fact that it is not the same me as that behind the binoculars who gets to the boat (and give up trying to force the issue of the same one). So I get into the boat, join the other me in the sun on the boat, a third arm also behind binoculars, watching. We all shrug about how there can be three. The two on the boat enter into an active conversation about 'do you remember'—a feeling of oneness comes—that is, a sense of watching the two from the tower recede; and feeling focus is much more on the interchange between the two on the boat.
>
> "I tell myself the dream is over and to stay deeply hypnotized.

"I walk along a path to a garden. I smell a rose (faintly but clearly). I sit on a white lattice bench. Another me sits down and discusses two issues which I explain are intertwined and which I will work on with hypnosis: (1) Staying on a diet and not eating unduly. (2) Working efficiently and with clarity and without approaching an avoidance hangup on my Ph.D. proposal.

"I relate food intake to anxiety around avoiding work which needs to be done.

"I told myself to enjoy the garden [i.e., self-hypnosis]. I felt myself in a hammock, rocking pleasantly and surrounded by red camellias, lovely gardenias, and lush green leaves.

"I said the rocking would stop. Count up steps: 100—75—25—then count up to 1, awake.

"I liked the dream. I liked the idea of using experience with purpose. I enjoyed the experience—especially the new dream content with a sense of exploration; clear splits of observing and experiencing; and the idea of remembering experiences. I feel refreshed and awake. I am curious to see how the suggestions hold. I am closer to hallucinating the smell of the rose than before.

"The hypnotic dream seems self-explanatory and very useful."

SOME DIFFERENCES BETWEEN SELF-HYPNOSIS AND HETEROHYPNOSIS

In comparing heterohypnosis and self-hypnosis, most of our second group of subjects found that certain tasks could be more easily accomplished in heterohypnosis: positive hallucinations, profound age regressions, and role playing. You cannot role-play in self-hypnosis. To whom do you play? To yourself. And that just doesn't work, because, as Kevin said,

"You divide yourself, and one part is observing. That observing part knows whether you are role-playing or not. If you are, it also knows you have not succeeded in hypnotizing yourself yet."

Another difference our highly hypnotizable subjects brought out between heterohypnosis and self-hypnosis also became apparent. An outside hypnotist, in an experimental situation, is rarely as finely attuned to the subject's wishes and needs as is the subject who hypnotizes himself. Said Kevin in the final group interview—and others nodded approval:

"In heterohypnosis the subject is actually, in a way, forced—due to the set, due to the conditions—to go along with what the hypnotist says. And if the subject feels like doing one thing, he can't blurt out, 'Let's do this'—it's not called for, it's not the proper thing to do in that situation, I guess. And that's one thing I enjoyed about autohypnosis: There's constant interaction between the different parts of me doing the thing. And the other part of me was that which was saying, 'Do this, do that.' I always knew what both parts wanted done. And so I was always doing exactly what I wanted to do."

Our subjects also felt that a great advantage of self-hypnosis was that one could give oneself enough time. The subject always knows how much time he needs in order to feel comfortable with or to complete a suggestion, an instruction, a fantasy. The outside hypnotist can make an educated guess; he can observe the subject carefully and try to pace himself to meet the subject's needs. The excellent hypnotist succeeds in that. However, no one knows as well as the subject when he needs more time, or less. If the subject is both the hypnotist and the hypnotized, the matter of timing can be handled to his full satisfaction.

With regard to Generalized Reality Orientation (Shor, 1962), there was a rather elusive difference between autohypnosis and heterohypnosis. The subjects found it difficult to describe because "there isn't anything like it in our language." As in many other altered states of consciousness, some phenomena are state-bound and hard to describe in the rational, secondary-process language of the waking state.

Imagery

Our deeply hypnotizable subjects in the second pilot study confirmed what we had found in the first pilot study: Imagery is more idiosyncratic, richer, and more vivid in self-hypnosis than in heterohypnosis. For some people the imagery is visual; for others it is auditory. Kevin experienced "a constant flow of words, and a lot of hearing, a lot of phrases, a lot of conversation, a lot of ideas going through my head." Only one subject, Sabrina, reported lack of imagery; instead, she had increased cognitive activity.

In a later chapter, we say more about the bountiful imagery produced by our subjects in self-hypnosis and give other revealing excerpts (see Chapter 10). Suffice it to say here that the imagery was *much* greater in self-hypnosis than in heterohypnosis. However, we must not forget that all our hetero-hypnosis experiments in both pilot studies consisted of the administration of various forms of the Weitzenhoffer–Hilgard scales or the HGSHS:A. This is, the Demand Characteristics of the particular heterohypnotic situations we employed perhaps did not allow as much expression, and as many varieties of imagery and fantasy, as did the totally free situation we set up for the self-hypnosis experiments.

THE FADING OF MOTIVATION WITH TIME

A striking and initially disconcerting result of the month-long self-hypnosis experiment was the fading of the desire to keep daily self-hypnosis sessions after 2–3 weeks. This occurred in all six pilot subjects in our second group—in some of them so strongly that they had to be urged and cajoled to finish the experiment.

We believe that this fading of motivation can be explained by what has come to be called the "Schachter effect." Schachter and Singer (1962) found that emotional states have two determinants: (1) a state of physiological arousal; (2) a cognitive factor appropriate to the arousal level, by which the subject interprets the physiological alteration as a specific emotion (e.g., fear, joy, etc.). Subjects not having an interpretative scheme appropriate to an experimentally induced physiological change tended to suppress the change in arousal or to remain unaware of essential experiential elements concomitant to the change in arousal. These subjects also tended to search the social environment for any available scheme and apply it to the physiological change, whether or not it was appropriate.

Schachter's concepts have since been applied to a variety of states of consciousness. They also seem to apply to self-hypnosis. As noted earlier, our subjects were intentionally not given an interpretative scheme, so as not to influence the results through experimenter bias. As the subjects had neither an initial interpretative scheme nor a means of finding such a scheme in their immediate social environment, their only recourse was suppression of essential aspects of the experience and the resultant loss of interest in the phenomena over time. It should also be pointed out that most subjects tended to evolve their own interpretative scheme toward the end of the experiment, a finding consistent with the concept of adaptation to altered states of consciousness.

Initially, all six subjects had entered into the experiment enthusiastically. All wanted to learn autohypnosis. However, after they had developed the skill to go into an autohypnotic state easily, and after they had experimented with some techniques, experienced interesting phenomena, and achieved their own goals, they came to a point where they "didn't know what else to do" or what to expect, and their enthusiasm waned.

Another reason for the subjects' drifting off after a while into doing less and less self-hypnosis is what for the time being we wish to call "diminishing transference." Perhaps it should rather be called "prolonged self-hypnosis as a diminishing interactive phenomenon." Initially, a number of these subjects had fantasized an outside hypnotist sitting with them and giving them hypnotic suggestions. As time went on and they became more skillful in inducing autohypnosis, the use of this fantasized outside hypnotist diminished; so also did the reliance on other techniques they had been given as possible helps for self-induction, such as knowledge of arm levitation and other motor techniques. Eventually they were using almost exclusively methods of their own invention. However, in the end, all of the subjects said that an outside hypnotist could have been useful for them, provided he would not have structured their experience. They wanted to create this structure for themselves. Thus, they seemed to be longing mildly for a very permissive hypnotist—someone who was fully attuned to their needs and who would be there to help them occasionally, especially someone who could bring them new skills and give them new areas to explore. Since practically all of the subjects were between 20 and 30 years old, one must consider that this phenomenon could be a reflection of a late adolescent conflictful wish for independence in the face of dependency needs.

If subjects build the newly acquired skill of self-hypnosis into their life style, they will continue to use it as a valued tool; otherwise they will soon drop it. For most of our subjects, after the novelty of the experiment had worn off, the daily autohypnotic sessions became a bore. However, two of the subjects found that self-hypnosis could be useful in their lives and decided to continue using it. For one of them, it became a means of relaxation, and an aid in concentration and in overcoming a writing block. In one of this subject's self-hypnosis sessions the following sensations and imagery came up: She felt her hands become light, let them be lifted up by balloons, and then pulled blocks out of her head and threw the blocks away! This subject was looking forward to continuing to employ autohypnosis whenever she felt a need for relaxation, or for new ways of creative thinking—by letting cognitive processes work with the inclusion of primary process rather than by excluding it. The other subject, too, planned to continue to use self-hypnosis for relaxation and for greater concentration in studying, and in addition for relieving herself of frequent headaches. Both young women had *very* similar MMPIs.

As noted earlier, each subject was given two free-floating interviews during which he was asked to elaborate on and discuss the phenomena he had experienced. One of these interviews was held at the midpoint (i.e., after 2 weeks), the other at termination (4 weeks). About a month after all the subjects had completed their hypnotic experiences a group discussion was held, bringing together all the subjects, the two examiners, and Fromm for a wrap-up discussion.

The analyses of the subjects' diaries (some of which were beautifully introspective), together with the tape-recorded discussions, provided a rich base for the larger research we could now undertake. The two pilot studies served to generate hypotheses that could be rigorously tested in more highly controlled studies. These researches are described in Part II of the book, Chapters 4–13.

PART TWO

EMPIRICAL RESEARCH

Methodology and Analyses
of the Questionnaires

CHAPTER 4

Self-Hypnosis versus Heterohypnosis, and Self-Hypnosis over Time: Comparative and Longitudinal Research

Previous to 1970, it had been generally assumed that the phenomena of heterohypnosis and self-hypnosis were the same, the only difference being that in heterohypnosis the hypnotic induction was performed by an outside person, the hypnotist, and in self-hypnosis by the individual himself. Clinicians believed they could teach self-hypnosis to patients by the example of heterohypnotic trance induction; the patients would learn their procedures and then apply these themselves. In the early 1970s Fromm felt a need to question whether self-hypnosis is really nothing else but heterohypnosis self-applied. In our pilot studies (see Chapter 3), we found that subjects high, but not low, in hypnotizability were able to discriminate between the subjective phenomena of self-hypnosis and heterohypnosis. We then designed a large study to chart essential landmarks of self-hypnosis.

CONCEPTUAL BACKGROUND

It is almost impossible to conceptualize self-hypnosis without taking the concept of heterohypnosis as a baseline or point of departure. This brings with it, however, methodological difficulties for the researcher of self-hypnosis:

An earlier version of this chapter was published as portions of a paper titled "The Phenomena and Characteristics of Self-Hypnosis" by Erika Fromm, Daniel P. Brown, Stephen W. Hurt, Joab Z. Oberlander, Andrew M. Boxer, and Gary Pfeifer in the July 1981 issue of the *International Journal of Clinical and Experimental Hypnosis, 29,* 189–246. Copyrighted by The Society for Clinical and Experimental Hypnosis, July 1981. Reprinted by permission of the coauthors and the journal editor.

The experimenter, by his very influence upon the subject through observation, interaction, and providing information, interferes with a genuine "self"-experience. The way to circumvent the problem is to define self-hypnosis at one of four levels and to structure the interaction and information provided accordingly. Those levels are (1) set, (2) setting, (3) suggestions, and (4) response.

Laboratory-Defined Hypnosis as Determining the Set

It is necessary to assure that subjects participating in a study of self-hypnosis indeed experience self-hypnosis and not just relaxation, spontaneous reverie, meditation, or any other altered state of consciousness. Furthermore, most naive volunteers for hypnosis research have some preconceived notions about hypnosis, reflecting cultural stereotypes and/or specific attitudes acquired through some contact with stage hypnotists or the popular press. In fact, there is likely to be a variety of intracultural differences in expectations, attitudes, and beliefs about hypnosis, many of which may be at variance with the laboratory understanding of hypnosis. Nevertheless, such attitudes affect susceptibility (Diamond, Gregory, Lenney, Steadman, & Talone, 1974) as well as the experience of hypnosis (Barber, 1979).

These differences in set pose a problem for studies of "self"-hypnosis. A conservative definition of self-hypnosis is "self-defined hypnosis" (i.e., hypnosis in which the subject, not an experimenter or clinician, uses her own attitudes and beliefs about hypnosis to guide the trance experience). It is at least theoretically conceivable to study self-defined hypnosis. An investigator may, for example, study spontaneous, idiosyncratic trance experience. He may study trance experience within a given subculture, such as a trance cult. In each instance, the trance experience is defined by the individual or small group, not by consensual cultural beliefs. By way of contrast, laboratory investigators have historically circumvented the difficulties inherent in studying self-defined hypnosis by taking a more liberal view of self-hypnosis. Hypnotic phenomena reported in the scientific literature, even self-hypnotic phenomena, are "laboratory-defined hypnosis" or "clinically defined hypnosis." Although naive subjects may differ widely in their initial attitudes and beliefs, subjects "learn" about hypnosis once they are in the laboratory—during the preinduction interview, during the often standardized trance experiences, and sometimes also during training sessions. As subjects learn about those phenomena usually considered to fall within the domain of hypnosis, they acquire a set for experiencing self-hypnosis.

The advantages of the laboratory-defined hypnosis approach for the scientific study of hypnosis are obvious. Intracultural differences are more or less standardized, so as to insure that subjects will report experiences recognizable to the laboratory investigators instead of reporting idiosyncratic phenomena. The main disadvantage pertains to the very definition of "self"-hypnosis. The trance experience, so defined, is no longer in a strict sense "self"-hypnosis (i.e., a self-defined experience), although it may still be considered "self"-hypnotic on other grounds. For our purposes, we have accepted the wording and practices of standardized hypnotic susceptibility scales as defining laboratory hypnosis, although we are aware that these routines do not fully represent laboratory investigations.

Hypnotist-Absent Self-Hypnosis

An important factor in the setting of hypnosis is the presence or absence of the hypnotist, who through direct or indirect suggestions and challenges may significantly influence the nature of the hypnotic experience. In heterohypnosis a hypnotist is, of course, present to facilitate the experience. But he need not be present in self-hypnosis. The importance of the hypnotist's presence during self-hypnosis depends on how self-hypnosis is defined. In stringently defined self-hypnosis, which we call "hypnotist-absent self-hypnosis," no hypnotist is present. In more loosely defined self-hypnosis, to be called "hypnotist-present self-hypnosis," the hypnotist may still be present, but the usual heterohypnotic verbal and nonverbal interactions have been altered. For example, a hypnotist present during self-hypnosis may remain silent; he may speak to the subject but indicate through his inflections that the words are not intended to be suggestions; or he may give suggestions in a modified or reduced form.

Historically, clinicians and researchers alike have come to varying views on the relative utility of the hypnotist's presence during self-hypnosis. To many clinicians, a patient is considered to engage in self-hypnosis when she practices hypnotic techniques alone, outside the clinical hour, although these techniques have been taught to the patient by the hypnotist/clinician. On the other hand, Coué (1922) conceived of self-hypnosis as self-motivated practice sessions while in the presence of the clinician. The same two views appear in the experimental literature. In most of the research, then, self-hypnosis has been defined as hypnosis achieved either by a subject alone in a room (Shor & Easton, 1973) or by a subject in the presence of an experimenter/hypnotist (Ruch, 1975). Furthermore, those researchers who have adopted the hypnotist-present view have differed in how they conceive the pattern of interaction between hypnotist and subject during self-hypnosis. Johnson and Weight (1976), for instance, use a silent experimenter/hypnotist, while Ruch (1975) uses an experimenter/hypnotist who is active and verbal, but gives only terse suggestions (Ruch's "thin items," 1975; E. R. Hilgard, 1975).

Self-Initiated Suggestions and Self-Directed Responses

In heterohypnosis the hypnotist gives the suggestions for the induction and also for the trance experience. He facilitates performance of certain behavioral tasks and phenomenological experiences; he defines and structures hypnotic behavior so that subjects can perform these tasks. The hypnotist may also request verbal reports and thereby select certain subjective experiences for communication. In more liberally defined self-hypnosis, a researcher may likewise assume that suggestions for induction and/or trance experience be experimenter-given. In such examples of "experimenter-initiated suggestions," the subject follows the suggestions of the experimenter/hypnotist, but usually in a modified form. For example, Shor and Easton (1973) as well as Johnson and Weight (1976) told their subjects to read item by item the Inventory of Self-Hypnosis (Shor, 1970, 1978), which is a modified form of the Stanford Hypnotic Susceptibility Scale, Form A (SHSS:A) of Weitzenhoffer and Hilgard (1959). These subjects first read experimenter-initiated suggestions and then responded to these prescribed tasks. The main departure from SHSS:A is that the subject is allowed to respond to the suggestions after reading the instructions, instead of listening to the hypnotist giving them to him; that is, the response to each suggested task is delayed until the subject has read the full instructions for the particular task, so that, theoretically, the subject can use the tasks in his own way.

In Ruch's (1975) version of self-hypnosis, the suggestions were modified further, although Ruch still used the standard hypnotic scales as a source for suggestions—the Harvard Group Scale of Hypnotic Susceptibility, Form A (HGSHS:A) of Shor and Orne (1962), and the Stanford Hypnotic Susceptibility Scale, Form C (SHSS:C) of Weitzenhoffer and Hilgard (1962). For one group the standard instructions were reworded in the first person; another group received only the gist of the standard instructions. Such approaches to self-hypnosis, which measure self-responses to experimentally defined suggestions, have been called "mediated" or "pseudo-"self-hypnosis (Weitzenhoffer, 1957, p. 324). Slight modifications in the form of response to suggestions may not sufficiently distinguish self-hypnosis and heterohypnosis. In a more stringently defined self-hypnosis, the subject would be allowed to create his own suggestions for induction and/or trance experience, thereby enacting "self-initiated suggestions."

Whether experimenter-initiated suggestion leads to genuine self-hypnosis remains an open question. It is finally a matter of definition. In such research, self-hypnosis is defined more in terms of "self-directed responses"—that is, in terms of those variables or communications that the subject produces during trance in response to experimenter-defined or experimenter-given suggestions, however modified. In the Shor and Easton (1973), and in Johnson's (1979) research, the emphasis is clearly on self-directed responses, not on self-initiated suggestions. In Ruch's research, even though modifications in the wording of suggestions are used, the experimenter nevertheless still gives the suggestions. This therefore is another example of self-directed response.

In our research, we have attempted to define self-hypnosis more stringently than other researchers did. While other writers define self-hypnosis primarily in terms of self-directed responses, we define self-hypnosis primarily in terms of self-initiated suggestions. For example, some experimenters, notably Ruch (1975), in the actual self-hypnosis experiment would say to the subject, "Now first raise your left arm to shoulder height and imagine a weight forcing it down. As you do it, it will get heavy and move down" (Ruch, 1975, p. 289). In contrast, we instructed our subjects before they embarked on their first self-hypnosis experiences, as follows:

> "You are now going to begin your four weeks of self-hypnosis. During your two pre-experimental standardized hypnotic experiences with the experimenters, you have become familiar with a good number of hypnotic procedures. You may use these as examples of what you can do in your hour of self-hypnosis each day. However, do not feel that you need to limit yourself to these. You may wish to think up suggestions for some other experiences, and then experiment with them. You may also wish at times just to remain in trance but not do anything specific."

Table 4.1 clarifies the assumptions behind the varying definitions of "self"-hypnosis. All the research (our own included) has defined self-hypnosis, minimally, in terms of self-defined responses. Our research differs from the rest by attempting to define self-hypnosis more closely to the ideal—in terms of self-initiated suggestions, given in the absence of a hypnotist. Since we were studying laboratory hypnosis, however, and not spontaneous trance, an attempt was made similar to that of other self-hypnosis research to standardize subjects' attitudes and beliefs about hypnosis by giving subjects pre-experimental heterohypnosis training sessions with standard hypnotic phenomena. Once the experiment began, however, subjects were explicitly instructed not to limit themselves to the heterohypnosis phenomena with which they had become familiar, but to explore and develop their own ideas for both induction and trance experiences in the absence of a hypnotist. The subjects were honestly told that it was not known whether self-hypnosis and heterohypnosis were the same or different, and that this question was being investigated. The subjects were also told that they, the subjects, were to be the coinvestigators on whom we depended for unbiased exploration of the phenomena the subjects would suggest to themselves, and that they would self-report. With this more stringent definition of self-hypnosis in mind, we hoped that whatever differences existed between heterohypnosis and self-

TABLE 4.1
Delineations of Self-Hypnosis

Areas of delineating self-hypnosis	Genuine (ideal) self-hypnosis	Fromm laboratory	Other researchers	
			Ruch (1975)	Shor & Easton (1973); Johnson & Weight (1976); Johnson (1979)
Set	Self-defined self-hypnosis	Laboratory-defined self-hypnosis	Laboratory-defined self-hypnosis	Laboratory-defined self-hypnosis
Setting	Hypnotist-absent self-hypnosis	Hypnotist-absent self-hypnosis	Hypnotist-present self-hypnosis	Hypnotist-absent self-hypnosis
Suggestion	Self-initiated suggestions	Self-initiated suggestions	Subject-elaborated suggestions on experimenter-proposed topics	Experimenter-initiated suggestions
Response	Self-directed response	Self-directed response	Self-directed response	Self-directed response

hypnosis would become clearer—differences that might have been obscured in more liberally defined self-hypnosis.

The absence of the experimenter/hypnotist (hypnotist-absent self-hypnosis) of course carried with it the methodological difficulty of how to measure subjects' behaviors and experiences in a minimal-interaction situation (i.e., without our being in the same room and observing the subjects). We opted for a phenomenological investigation. The subjects were allowed to create their own suggestions, to respond by carrying them out in tasks, and further to respond by reporting on their subjective experiences. Tasks and subjective experiences were assessed through journals and questionnaires, with the questionnaires serving as the primary measuring instruments, and the journals, with daily entries, providing additional idiographic data. (The journals are described in detail in Section B of this part of the book.) Our experiment was designed to assess the structure and content of the self-hypnotic experience instead of hypnotic task performance.

THE STRUCTURE AND CONTENT OF THE SELF-HYPNOTIC EXPERIENCE TO BE ASSESSED

There is a growing consensus that phenomenological investigations can reveal important aspects of states of consciousness that are not clearly established when one insists on using behavioral or psychophysiological measures only (Shor, 1979). For example, Field and Palmer (1969) constructed a questionnaire for the subjective experiences accompanying heterohypnosis, which they correlated to behavioral measures of hypnotic susceptibility. They concluded that their Hypnotic Inventory and the behavioral indices measured separate variables, and that behavioral indices alone failed to measure important aspects of the heterohypnotic experience.

Similarly, Barr, Langs, Holt, Goldberger, and Klein (1972) studied the nature of the hallucinogenic drug experience by correlating items from a phenomenological questionnaire to objective ratings of subjects' behavior, as well as their responses to experimental tasks. They found that their phenomenological questionnaire was a more accurate indicator of the phenomena of the drug state than these other measures.

Following Barr et al.'s example, we constructed two questionnaires to measure the phenomena of self-hypnosis in an experiment where the subject defined both the suggestions and the responses to hypnosis. In advance of constructing our questionnaires, we agreed on four categories, which together would contain 11 state variables to be assessed from the questionnaires. These are listed in Table 4.2.

TABLE 4.2
A Priori Selection of 11 State Variables to Be Assessed from Questionnaires

A. Attention deployment
　　1. Attention, concentration, cognitive control, distractibility, and related information-processing functions
　　2. Ego Activity and Receptivity

B. Content
　　1. Imagery
　　2. Memory
　　3. Experiential aspects (thinking, emotions, and affect; perceptions; physiological sensations; awareness of time; self-perception)

C. Longitudinal variables
　　1. Initial reaction to self-hypnosis and adaptation to the state
　　2. Automatization of trance induction and self-suggestions
　　3. Trance depth
　　4. Reality construction

D. Interpersonal context
　　1. Interpersonal aspects and demand characteristics
　　2. Expectations of self and role perception

Based on the widely accepted view that hypnosis is an altered state of consciousness (Tart, 1969; Fromm, 1977), we hypothesized that the phenomena of self-hypnosis could be differentiated from waking-state phenomena and perhaps also from heterohypnosis along a variety of dimensions. Such an assumption is dependent, of course, upon one's theory of states of consciousness; a state of consciousness may be defined according to different theoretical positions. In other papers, members of our team have set forth two distinct theoretical positions, that of psychoanalytic ego psychology (Fromm, 1977, 1979; see also Chapter 9, this volume) and that of cognitive psychology (Brown, 1977). In ego-psychological terms, a state of consciousness may be defined by its reigning modes of Ego Activity, Ego Receptivity, or Ego Passivity (Rapaport, 1967a; Deikman, 1971; Fromm, 1977, 1979); by the balance of primary process versus secondary process (Fromm, 1978–1979); and by the quality of attention cathexis (Fromm, 1977), in cognitive terms, it may be defined as the quality of information processing—for example, the quality of attention, concentration, cognitive control, and cognition (Fischer, 1971; Tart, 1975; Brown, 1977). It may also be defined by the specific type of content that occurs—for example, the thoughts, images, memories, emotions, realistic perceptions or hallucinations, self-observations, bodily sensations, and the presence or absence of time distortion (Tart, 1975). Despite different ideological bases for these theoretical positions, we surmised that there might be genuine convergence around the issues of attention deployment on the one hand, and reported mental content on the other, as representative of the state of consciousness within self-hypnosis.

Despite theoretical differences, consensus was reached on the criteria for each of these categories. The raw pilot data from the journals and interviews were then sorted into the respective categories and used to generate a pool of several hundred questions about self-hypnosis.

QUESTIONNAIRES AS USED IN THE STUDY PROPER

Three versions of the questionnaire were developed. Two of them[1]—the Comparative Questionnaire (CQ) and the Longitudinal Questionnaire (LQ)—are discussed in this chapter. Both questionnaires contained roughly similar items from the categories named in Table 4.2 (as did the third questionnaire, which is discussed in the next chapter). However, each version contained a different set of instructions. The CQ consisted of 62 questions meant to discriminate between the relative frequency of occurrence of phenomena in self-hypnosis and heterohypnosis. In the instructions, subjects were asked to compare the first week of self-hypnosis practice with their five heterohypnosis experiences. The LQ contained 92 questions about the self-hypnotic experience, and asked the subjects to consider whether the phenomena in question changed or remained the same as subjects gained more experience with self-hypnosis, from their initial experiences to the final session of practice.

Each questionnaire was divided into 11 sections corresponding to the 11 a priori categories, but stated in a different order and with slightly changed names. The new names of the sections, and a representative question from each selection, appear in Appendix 4.1. At the end of every section, after the subject had completed the questions, he was told to which category the previous questions belonged. A last question asked the subject whether he had any additional experiences that might pertain to that category but were not covered in the questions. A blank space was left at the end of each section for this answer. In this manner, the subject was given some freedom to define his own response to the questionnaire. We wanted the experiment to manifest both a form of self-initiated suggestions and self-response to the questionnaire.

---

[1] Copies of the preliminary and final forms of the CQ and LQ, and details of the correlation matrices and factor analyses—as well as a more extensive version of this chapter—have been deposited with the National Auxiliary Publications Service (NAPS). Order Document No. 03821 from ASIS-NAPS, c/o Microfiche Publications, P.O. Box 3513, Grand Central Station, New York, NY 10163.

The two versions were written in slightly different formats, although both used a 5-point Likert scale. The CQ rating scale asked for relative degrees of difference ("much greater," "a little greater," "about the same," "a little less," "much less"). The LQ rating scale was worded in terms of relative frequency of occurrence ("increased greatly," "increased a little," "remained the same," "decreased a little," "decreased greatly"). Two negative ratings ("never experienced this" or "does not apply") were added for some questions. These questions provided information about other altered states of consciousness but not for self-hypnosis and heterohypnosis, and therefore were not made part of the statistical analyses.

The preliminary instructions to each questionnaire emphasized that subjects were not expected to have experienced all of the phenomena mentioned in the questionnaire. The wording of individual questions often began with "Some people experience. . . ." These devices were used to minimize the demand characteristics often inherent in questionnaire construction. The sequence of questions was scaled in randomly opposite directions in order to minimize response sets. With the CQ and LQ constructed, we were prepared to proceed with the investigation proper.

PROCEDURES IN THE EXPERIMENT PROPER

Subjects

In two pilot studies (see Chapter 3), it was found that highly hypnotizable subjects, but not poorly hypnotizable subjects, were able to discriminate between self-hypnotic and heterohypnotic subjective experiences. The highly hypnotizable subjects were also more capable of articulating subjective phenomena accompanying hypnosis. These findings are consistent with other research on altered states of consciousness, which distinguishes between high and low respondents to a given state (e.g., E. R. Hilgard's [1965] work on hypnotic susceptibility, and Maupin's [1965] work on initial meditative experience). Because of the highly hypnotizable subjects' greater ability to discriminate between the phenomena of self-hypnosis and heterohypnosis, the current study involved only highly hypnotizable subjects.

A total of 425 subjects were screened for hypnotizability using the HGSHS:A (Shor & Orne, 1962). Those subjects who attained a score of 9 (out of 12) on the HGSHS:A were tested individually with the SHSS:C (Weitzenhoffer & Hilgard, 1962). The subjects attaining a score of 9 or more (out of 12) on the SHSS:C were then given the Rorschach (Rorschach, 1954) in order to screen out those subjects with serious personality disorders. In addition, for the purposes of the experiment, subjects were also given the Minnesota Multiphasic Personality Inventory (MMPI; Dahlstrom, Welsh,

& Dahlstrom, 1972, 1975), the Personal Orientation Inventory (POI; Shostrom, 1972), the Personality Research Form (PRF; Jackson, 1974), and the Differential Personality Questionnaire (DPQ; Tellegen & Atkinson, 1974). The subjects who attained high scores on the HGSHS:A and SHSS:C and who did not evince serious psychopathology were selected for the study. All were volunteers.

At the outset of the study, the sample consisted of 58 subjects. A total of 33 subjects completed all aspects of the study. The other 25 subjects dropped out during the 4 weeks of self-hypnosis, or completed the self-hypnosis but failed to complete the questionnaires. As we had no grant, we could not pay our subjects. All were volunteers. If one considers that 1 hour of self-hypnosis practice per day for a full 4 weeks, including Saturdays and Sundays, is quite demanding of a volunteer's time, one can understand why only 33 subjects stayed with the project all the way. Some complained of the difficulty of finding the time to do self-hypnosis each day. Others complained that it was difficult to practice self-hypnosis on their own, with very little structure or assistance from the experimenters.

The sample consisted of individuals having some connection with the University of Chicago. Most subjects were undergraduate students, aged 18–21. Some were graduate students, between the ages of 21 and 30. Three subjects were professionals—a nurse, a psychologist, and a teacher; the oldest of these was 45 years of age.

Training

Because potential subjects differed widely in their attitudes and beliefs about hypnosis, an attempt was made to standardize the subjects' understanding of hypnosis. First, a Background Information Sheet, given to subjects as part of their screening, contained a number of detailed questions regarding previous readings about or actual experience with hypnosis and/or related states such as meditation, imagery, and psychedelic drugs. They were also asked whether they had been or were now in psychotherapy. Subjects who had more than passing prior experience with any of the altered states of consciousness were screened out. Thus, our subjects began with relatively little knowledge of hypnosis or related states.

These naive subjects were given identical training sessions with heterohypnosis to further standardize their understanding of hypnosis. During the screening, all subjects became familiar with the items on the HGSHS and the SHSS:C. In order to gain experience with other heterohypnosis tasks and phenomena, all subjects selected for the experiment were also given the Revised Stanford Profile Scale of Hypnotic Susceptibility, Form I (SPSHS:I; Weitzenhoffer & Hilgard, 1967). Taken as a unit, these three scales encompass the entire range of phenomena used in experimental studies of hypnosis: ideomotor phenomena, fantasy, and dreams; hypermnesias and regressions, negative and positive hallucinations, amnesias, and posthypnotic phenomena; cognitive and affective distortions; analgesias. In order to illustrate that subjects might also use such experiences in a self-hypnotic manner, they were then given Shor's (1970) Inventory of Self-Hypnosis, Form A (even though we doubt that it really represents self-hypnosis). In addition, subjects were taught to monitor their hypnotic depth with Tart's Extended North Carolina Scale (Tart, 1972, 1979). Through these training sessions, each subject became familiar with the domain of standardly defined laboratory hypnosis.

Setting

During the actual experiment, which consisted of 1-hour daily hypnotic sessions over 4 weeks, no hypnotist was present. Nevertheless, we knew from clinical experience and also from our pilot work that some subjects, once given experiences with heterohypnosis, are likely to imagine the hypnotist with them even during hypnotist-absent self-hypnosis. Hypnotic subjects often develop strong dependent transferences. In order to minimize the likelihood of such a transference fantasy or role behavior, we used a different experimenter for each pre-experimental and each experimental contact with the subject. This procedure was based on the observation that transference is not a significant effect in initial response to hypnosis, but increases in importance only with repeated induction by the same hypnotist (E. R. Hilgard, 1965).

The subjects were not allowed to practice their daily hour of self-hypnosis at home. For their daily self-hypnosis session, all subjects were required to come to identically furnished small studies containing only a desk, a couple of chairs, an empty bookcase, and a rug on the floor. There were no distracting interactions with other people.

Self-Suggestions and Self-Responses

At the outset of the experimental practice, each subject was given a written set of instructions for self-hypnosis. These instructions were worded so as to encourage subjects to engage over the course of the 4 weeks in *self-initiated suggestions* as opposed to experimenter-initiated suggestions. Subjects were told to engage in 1 hour of self-hypnosis in any way they wished. They were told that they might use their heterohypnosis training experiences as guidelines, but also that they might wish to create their own ways of inducing trance and experiencing trance. The exact instructions appear in Appendix 4.2.

Because we also wanted to see whether self-hypnosis practice increases heterohypnosis hypnotizability, midway into the experiment subjects were given a fourth heterohypnosis experience, with the SPSHS, Form II (SPSHS:II; Weitzenhoffer & Hilgard, 1967); they also received a fifth heterohypnosis experience upon completion of the experiment after 4 weeks, this time with the SPSHS:I.

The experiment was conducted over a 4-week period in order to discover how subjects created and developed their self-suggestions, relative to the suggestions of their training experience. In order to enable us to know what each subject was doing in his session, subjects were required to keep daily journals in which they had to narrate immediately after each session what had happened.

Each journal entry followed a standard format. (Appendix 4.2). For each session, subjects were to list the self-suggestions attempted both for induction and trance experience; to give at least one state report; and to describe their subjective impressions of the experience. To insure that subjects adhered to this format, subjects were contacted once a week by phone, and the journals were submitted to the experimenters for reviews on alternative weeks. A different experimenter was used for each contact with a given subject. Absolutely no suggestions were given during these contacts as to the types of descriptions subjects might report, although some subjects were occasionally asked to record their self-suggestions in greater detail. A list of the range of self-suggestions for each subject and across all subjects was compiled from these journal entries. (The journals, as noted earlier, are discussed in detail in Section B of Part II.)

At the end of 4 weeks, subjects were given the questionnaires, to be completed on successive days. The questionnaires were administered in random order. Altogether, each subject had experienced a total of 4 weeks of daily self-hypnosis sessions and a total of five heterohypnosis sessions— three pre-experimentally, one at the midpoint of the experiment, and one at the experiment's close.

DATA REDUCTION FOR
BOTH QUESTIONNAIRES

The CQ, designed to compare the relative frequency of occurrence of phenomena in heterohypnosis and self-hypnosis, consisted originally of 62 questions (from 2 to 13 per category). A post hoc reduction, eliminating questions that did not discriminate well between heterohypnosis and self-hypnosis, set aside 42 questions and retained 20 questions (32%) of the original list. Only two categories were not represented in the final list: Category VI, Awareness of Experiential Aspects, and Category XI, Ego Activity/Receptivity and Ego Splits. All other categories were represented by at least one question.

The LQ covered changes over time from the initial experience of self-hypnosis. It originally included 92 questions, of which 58 (63%) were discarded after the data analysis because they did not yield information on change. All categories were represented in the final list of 34 (37%) questions, with a minimum of a single question in Category VI, Awareness of Experiential Aspects, and a maximum of five questions in Category X, Expectations of Self. For samples of retained CQ and LQ questions, see Appendix 4.1.

In the data analysis, questions were discarded that either turned out to be answerable only by subjects who already had a great deal of knowledge about altered states of consciousness or were written too ambiguously. Here is an example:

> CQ, #22. How would you rate the amount of *selective attention* to a small range of the mental continuum in your first week of self-hypnosis in contrast to hypnosis with an experimenter?
> ☐ much more selective attention in self-hypnosis than hypnosis with an experimenter
> ☐ a little more selective attention . . .
> ☐ etc.

A small number of the retained questions had several parts (e.g., see Category VI, Awareness of Experiential Aspects: LQ #47, Appendix 4.1). Only branch parts of certain original questions were retained in the final reduced item pool. These branch questions were treated as separate items in the data analysis. In the CQ there were 120 possible items to be analyzed (instead of the 62 numbered questions). Of these, 84 questions or parts of questions were later discarded (70%), and 36 items were retained in the final analysis (instead of the 20 questions referred to above). The LQ eventually dealt with 60 items (instead of 34 questions).

THE STUDY COMPARING SELF-HYPNOSIS AND HETEROHYPNOSIS

One aspect of our research on self-hypnosis concerned the differences between subjects' perceptions of self-hypnosis and heterohypnosis. The subjects were asked to compare their experiences during the first week of self-hypnosis to their experiences with a hypnotist during the screening, interim, and final heterohypnosis sessions. Thus, five heterohypnosis sessions (HGSHS and

SHSS:C for screening; SPSHS:I pre-self-hypnosis; SPSHS:II after 2 weeks of self-hypnosis; SPSHS:I after 4 weeks of self-hypnosis) were compared to the seven self-hypnosis sessions of the first week of the experiment. The CQ, used to survey these differences, was delayed until completion of the experiment to prevent the questionnaire from altering the conditions of the remaining 3 weeks of the study.

Data Analysis

Responses to each question of the CQ were grouped into three categories. Each item was scrutinized for the number of subjects who reported the item as more characteristic of self-hypnosis, of heterohypnosis, or of neither. Only those items for which a minimum of 50% of subjects reported a difference between their two sets of hypnotic experiences were retained for further analysis and discussion. This preliminary analysis, as described above, excluded approximately 70% of the items; 36 items remained for further analysis.

The fact that nearly 70% of the items did not show any appreciable difference between these two hypnotic states suggests that their similarities outweigh their differences. There are many ways in which the two states are highly similar. For expository purposes, we have chosen to emphasize the differences rather than the similarities, despite the risk that in doing so we may overstate the differences in these two hypnotic states.

These 36 items reflecting the differences subjects reported between the two states could be divided into two large groups. One group of 28 questions consisted of those items reported as more characteristic of self-hypnosis; the remaining 8 items identified features thought by these subjects to be more characteristic of heterohypnosis. These two groups of questions are presented in Table 4.3, with the questions in each group separated into three broad categories, which were derived from our analysis of the data from the LQ. One category of questions dealt with the structural, state-related dimensions of the hypnotic experience. These dimensions were the use of attention and concentration, absorption in the experience (J. R. Hilgard, 1970), fading of the Generalized Reality Orientation (Shor, 1959), and trance depth. A second category of questions focused on the content of the sessions. Items dealing with sensations, thoughts, emotions, imagery, and memories were included in this category. The third category consisted of those items that reflected subjects' expectations about the nature of their forthcoming experiences. We refer to these items as contextual. (For easier reference, the questions in Table 4.3 are numbered consecutively; these numbers are not the numbers of the questions as they appeared in the version of the CQ used in this study.)

TABLE 4.3
Discriminating Features of Self-Hypnosis and Heterohypnosis

Type	Item content	% reporting greater frequency in self-hypnosis
	Predominant features of self-hypnosis	
Structure		
	1. Expansion of the attentional range	67
	2. Receptivity to internal events	64
	3. Fluctuations in trance depth	54
Content		
Imagery		
	4. Quantity of imagery	76
Qualities		
	5. Visual	82
	6. Thought associations	67
	7. Vivid, unconnected, and realistic visual imagery	64
	8. Vivid, connected, and realistic visual imagery	64
	9. Bodily sensations	58
	10. Kinesthetic	54
	11. Simple geometric shapes	52
Themes		
	12. Past events	67
	13. Personal problems or conflicts	64
	14. Fantasy	64
	15. Creative experiences	58
	16. Day's events, worries, etc.	54
	17. Fragmented, unconnected	52
	18. Intellectual problem solving	52
Thoughts		
	19. Abstract thinking	73
Memories		
	20. Distracted by personal memories	76
Emotional		
	21. Falling asleep	73
	22. Personal meaningfulness	54
Context		
	23. Actively performing self-suggestions	70
	24. Ease of following self-suggestions	64
	25. Instructed to deepen trance	54
	26. Letting oneself go	52
	27. Working on personal problems	52
	28. Doing self-revealing things	50
	Predominant features of heterohypnosis	
Structure		
	29. Able to concentrate—fixed attention	70
	30. Ease of concentration	67

(continued)

TABLE 4.3 (*Continued*)

Type	Item content	% reporting greater frequency in self-hypnosis
	Predominant features of heterohypnosis	
Structure (*Continued*)		
	31. Able to concentrate and avoid distraction	67
	32. Attention clear and easy to direct	58
Content		
Imagery		
	33. Seeing things not there (positive hallucinations)	61
Memories		
	34. Experiencing of memories of past events	54
Emotional		
	35. Felt self-conscious	61
Context		
	36. Following self-suggestions exactly	70

Structural Features

A consideration of the structural items revealed that two important structural items not appearing in Table 4.3—namely, absorption (i.e., the sense of being caught up in the phenomena or content of the session) and the perception of the fading of the Generalized Reality Orientation—did not show differences between the two states. It would appear that in both states there was a sense of immediate involvement with the events of trance and a complementary detachment from the surrounding external environment. These two factors seemed to set the stage, the structure, for the trance experience, whether self-induced or entered into with the aid of an experimenter/hypnotist. Without this shift from an awareness of the external world to the internal and a sense of engagement with the events taking place there, the subjects' experiences of trance were indistinguishable from those of everyday waking life.

Two other structural features, however—those items relating to the use of attention and concentration (#1, #2, and #29–#32) and at least one aspect of trance depth (#3)—manifested noteworthy differences. There were also differences in the quantity, type, and themes of imagery in the two states (#4–#18 and #33), as well as differences in thinking (#19), in the place of memories (#20 and #34), and in affective reactions to an experience in the two states (#21, #22, and #35). Finally, we were able to chart differences in expectations about experiences in the two states (#23–#28 and #36), which, as discussed below, played a role in the kinds of trance experiences revealed in these states.

During the first week of self-hypnosis, the attention of subjects was characterized as receptive and expansive when contrasted to their five heterohypnosis sessions (three of which preceded and two followed the first week of self-hypnosis). Roughly two-thirds of our subjects experienced self-hypnosis as a state in which the mind was free to wander, and in which they spent some significant portion of their time waiting and attending to whatever arose into consciousness. This development of attention was an effort to become aware of as much of the mental continuum as possible by being receptive to stimuli from within.

By way of contrast, the same proportion of subjects viewed their heterohypnosis experiences as characterized by a steady, focused attentional posture (#29–#32). They permitted few distractions, found it easy to direct their attention to relevant tasks or material, and saw the hypnotist as a facilitator of this process rather than as a hindrance.

These data revealed differences in the attentional modes that characterized the two sets of experiences. Heterohypnosis was reported as a state characterized by the direction of one's attention to specific mental events that were to remain focused in the attentional field, so that they might be concentrated on and observed. The subjects' use of attention in self-hypnosis was quite different. While specific mental events were brought to the foreground, here, too, they were ushered forth not through an active selection process, but rather through an effort to allow as much as possible to enter the field. Upon arrival, the fate of these events was different as well. They were not generally the objects of undivided attention, as were those that entered the field during heterohypnosis. Some of these events had, of course, to come under closer scrutiny during self-hypnosis. Nevertheless, there remained a difference with regard to the degree to which this occurred in the two experiences.

Trance depth was also different in the two states in one important aspect. The subjects reported that during the first few self-hypnosis sessions, fluctuations in trance depth were much more frequent than during their heterohypnosis sessions (#3).

Thus, differences could be discerned in the way in which attention was used and in fluctuations in trance depth, but no noteworthy differences were seen in the areas of Generalized Reality Orientation and absorption. Given such differences and similarities in structural characteristics, it is interesting to consider what patterns emerged with regard to the content of the two experiences. Here our analysis focused on the events of trance—the thoughts, images, memories, and sensations that were more characteristic of either experience. A consideration of such differences is useful, for it provides limited access to the subjective experience of the trance, a topic we consider in much greater depth in our analysis of the journals.

Content Features

The items relating to the content or events of trance showed several interesting differences. There was a greater quantity of imagery in self-hypnosis, a difference noted by three-quarters of the subjects (#4). This increase was apparent in all types of imagery. Vivid, realistic images were more frequent in self-hypnosis, both in connected, story-like sequences (#8) and in segmented, unconnected flashes (#7). Simple geometric shapes also appeared more frequently (#11). Complex, bizarre conglomerations, as are sometimes reported in hallucinogenic experiences, were not characteristic of either state; nor did amorphous, vague, or cartoon-like images distinguish between the two states. Also apparent from these data was the greater richness of the images experienced in self-hypnosis. Thought associations (#6), bodily and kinesthetic sensations (#9 and #10), and visual imagery (#5) were all frequent in self-hypnosis. Tactile sensations and hearing streams of words were equally frequent in the two states.

Probably in part because imagery played such a dominant role in these subjects' self-hypnosis experiences, each of the various themes around which imagery might have been centered—personal problems or conflicts (#13), fantasied trips or adventures (#14), creative experiences (#15), intellectual problem solving (#18), memory of past and recent events (#12 and #16)—was more frequent in self-hypnosis than in heterohypnosis, with the exception of the image of oneself being hypnotized or being in trance. Imagery that centered around personal problems or conflicts (whether from the recent or more distant past), fantasy, creative experiences, and intellectual problem solving were all more frequent in self-hypnosis.

One additional difference deserves mention here. Heterohypnosis sessions included guided experiences of age regressions and hypermnesias. Attempts to initiate such experiences during self-hypnosis were markedly less successful. In fact, the experiencing of personal memories during self-hypnosis was reported as a distraction by these subjects (#20). It prevented these subjects from actively following their self-suggestions (#23).

In summary, these reports lend themselves to a description of self-hypnosis as a state characterized by an expansion of the attentional range and a greater receptivity to internal events. Imagery played a greater role here than in heterohypnosis and tended to be qualitatively richer and oriented toward personally salient experiences and fantasy. It was seen as more personally meaningful, and—not surprisingly, as there was no outside observer in the room while the subjects engaged in self-hypnosis—the subjects reported less self-consciousness during self-hypnosis than during heterohypnosis.

Contextual Features

These differences in the structural and content features of the two hypnotic states seem quite understandable in light of the subjects' expectations about the two states listed in the context category. Heterohypnosis was seen as a state primarily characterized by the requirement that suggestions given by the experimenter/hypnotist be followed exactly (#36). Meeting this expectation would clearly be facilitated by the kind of attentional posture adapted by subjects in the present study, and could help to explain the lack of personal meaningfulness and the barrenness of imagery reported during heterohypnosis as compared to self-hypnosis.

In contrast, subjects understood self-hypnosis as a state characterized by letting oneself go (#26), working on personal problems (#27), and doing self-revealing things (#28). These expectations would be easier to meet with the kind of expansion of attentional range and receptivity to internal events that were displayed by subjects in the present experiment. Taken together, these structural and contextual features of self-hypnosis could be expected to promote a greater richness and wider diversity of content in self-hypnosis when compared to the heterohypnosis procedures used in the present study (the standardized HGSHS:A, SHSS:C, SPSHS:I, and SPSHS:II).

The subjects were also quite active in performing self-suggestions during self-hypnosis (#23) and found this comparatively easy to accomplish (#24). In addition, subjects actively attempted to achieve deeper trance states in self-hypnosis (#25).

Similarities between Self-Hypnosis and Heterohypnosis

Although our analysis of the two hypnotic states chosen for investigation was focused principally on differences, some interesting similarities emerged. These data are not reported in tabular form, but are discussed below.

In their initial encounters with self-hypnosis, the subjects were fairly equally divided with respect to the degree to which they were aware of their external surroundings in comparison to their heterohypnosis experiences. One-third of our sample felt they were more aware of their external surroundings in heterohypnosis, while somewhat less than one-half felt their awareness was greater in self-hypnosis. Approximately one-quarter of our subjects found no difference in their awareness in the two states. This pattern of results was roughly characteristic of the subjects' perception of their trance depth, absorption in the hypnotic experience, and ability to actively direct and selectively use their attention during their initial self-hypnosis experiences. It would seem that the subjects' initial experience of the phenomena of hypnotic trance when this was self-induced was very similar to their experience when the trance was induced with the aid of an experimenter/hypnotist. These elements of the generalized reality orientation, trance depth, and use of attentional mechanisms generally appear to be important features of *any* hypnotic experience and serve to highlight the role of attentional mechanisms in the characterization of hypnotic states.

Other items, while failing to achieve the cutoff criterion for a clear distinction between self-hypnosis and heterohypnosis, nevertheless revealed subtle differences between the two that largely confirmed the major differences noted above. Items that asked about various kinds or characteristics of trance events tended to be seen most often by subjects as more characteristic of self-hypnosis. These items included the awareness of various physiological sensations (e.g., posture, breathing, or fine muscle tremors); changes in the perception of time or one's own body; strong feelings associated with recalled memories or images; and the ability to recall forgotten or childhood events. Only an awareness of external distractions and the ability to relive childhood events and function in childlike ways were seen as more pronounced in heterohypnosis when compared to the subjects' first week of self-hypnosis experience.

THE LONGITUDINAL STUDY: CHANGES IN EXPERIENCE WITH REPEATED SELF-HYPNOSIS

Earlier, we have discussed the view of hypnosis that guided us in the design of our experiment and in our use of various strategies of data collection. Because of the focus on both self-initiated suggestions and self-initiated responses, we hypothesized that self-hypnosis phenomena would show changes over time, as the subjects became more experienced with and continued to explore these phenomena. It was further assumed not only that the subjects' experience would change across the 4 weeks of the experiment, but also that different aspects of the subjects' experience would covary in regular ways. It was expected that changes in certain aspects of the subjects' experience would be related to changes in other aspects. For example, it was surmised that the subjects would become increasingly accomplished at entering the hypnotic state, and that this ability would result in a change in the experiential quality of the events occurring during trance. It was also anticipated that changes in ability might just as easily be influenced by the phenomenological experiences of self-hypnosis itself. We had no experimental control over either the form of the suggestions subjects employed or the kinds of responses subjects attempted to achieve. Data gathered in this way would reveal nothing about why a particular change in subjects' phenomenological experience occurred, but it could indicate the existence of change and perhaps could reveal patterns of change if the ways in which various aspects of subjects' experience covaried with one another were studied.

The LQ has been described previously, along with the reduction in number of questions from 92 to 34. Because questions could be further divided, however, the pool adopted for further analysis consisted of 60 items to be further grouped.

As a result of an exploratory factor analysis of these 60 items—an analysis that could be only exploratory because there were only 33 cases—a total of 36 items was finally retained that could represent the familiar 11 categories. These are shown, with their tendencies to increase or decrease over time, in Table 4.4.

Further factor analyses were conducted, but they are too complex to present in a limited space.[2] Upon reflection, the final conceptualization in Table 4.5 appeared to represent the major findings regarding the factors of importance.

Four structural components thus emerged: Absorption, Attention, Trance Depth, and the fading of the Generalized Reality Orientation. These four structural dimensions seemed to be properties of the self-hypnotic state. They defined the experience within very broad parameters. They might be conceived of as superordinate structures of the phenomenological experience, underlying dimensions of the self-hypnosis experience.

Context

The particular details of trance—the content—may have been different for individual subjects, but it was found that the four aspects of Absorption, Attention, Trance Depth, and Generalized Reality Orientation always exerted some influence over the experience. We have conceived of these four features themselves as being interrelated. They exerted an influence not only on content dimensions, but also on one another. None of the four structural components was more important than the other three. Rather, these dimensions were interrelated and exerted complementary effects that reflected our subjects' relationship to the self-hypnosis experience as it changed over time. For example, Absorption was affected by how Attention was being used, but the reverse might also be true. As for how these components affected one another, we might consider the interrelationship of one's ability to focus attention on specific mental events, one's ability to enter trance, and one's awareness of external surroundings. The present data indicate that as subjects' attention was more specifically focused on things in trance, their ability to enter trance was enhanced. Moreover, their awareness of external surroundings faded

---

[2] Factor analyses have been deposited with NAPS. See footnote 1.

TABLE 4.4
Changes over Time on Selected Items of the LQ

Selected items	Questionnaire responses		
	Decrease	No change	Increase
I. Initial Reactions			
1. Naturalness of trance state	3%	9%	88%
2. Focusing attention	12%	9%	79%
3. Skepticism concerning experience	55%	30%	15%
II. Trance Induction and Suggestions			
A. 4. Time required to enter trance	81%	13%	6%
5. Ability to enter deep trance	3%	6%	91%
B. 6. Intuitive grasp of plan for sessions	3%	18%	79%
7. Time spent worrying about failure	73%	21%	6%
III. Trance Depth			
A. 8. Time to enter deep states lessening	13%	9%	78%
9. Ability to enter deep states	6%	24%	70%
B. 10. Awareness of external surroundings			
(generalized reality orientation)	79%	18%	3%
11. Absorption	6%	18%	76%
IV. Attention and Concentration			
12. Evenness of attention	12%	27%	61%
13. Drowsiness	33%	27%	39%
14. Selectively focusing attention	3%	24%	73%
15. Avoidance of inner distraction	9%	18%	73%
V. Imagery			
A. 16. Awareness of subtle detail in imagery	3%	30%	67%
17. Frequency of fragmented imagery	49%	27%	24%
B. 18. Amount of spontaneous imagery	21%	12%	67%
19. Quantity of imagery	15%	24%	61%
VI. Awareness of Experiential Aspects			
20. Awareness of detailed exploration			
of personal memories	9%	25%	66%
21. Awareness of change in experience			
of body	13%	23%	64%
VII. Quantity and Quality of Memories			
22. Time spent actively exploring			
personal memories	24%	30%	46%
23. Proportion of memories vividly	37%	27%	37%
recalled			
24. Time spent experiencing personal			
memories	27%	27%	46%
VIII. Reality of Trance			
A. 25. Different state than waking state	18%	30%	52%
26. Reality of images	3%	24%	73%
B. 27. Ease of eyes-open trance	3%	17%	79%

(continued)

TABLE 4.4 (*Continued*)

	Questionnaire responses		
Selected items	Decrease	No change	Increase
IX. Demand Characteristics			
28. Effort to remember and record experience	3%	15%	82%
29. Personal meaningfulness	76%	18%	6%
X. Expectations of Self			
A. 30. Self-consciousness	12%	24%	64%
31. Following self-suggestions	6%	18%	76%
32. Lack of role playing	6%	30%	64%
B. 33. Self-reliance	58%	9%	33%
34. Reliance on heterohypnosis	47%	12%	41%
XI. Ego Activity and Ego Receptivity			
35. Ego splits	30%	15%	55%
36. Waiting and listening	48%	18%	33%

further into the background. By the same token, as subjects' ability to enter trance developed, their absorption in the trance phenomena became greater, which effected an increase in the fading of the Generalized Reality Orientation.

Content dimensions were quite different. The content of an individual's daily self-hypnosis session was peculiar to that individual. Each subject decided what to try or experience. It was found, however, that certain phenomena were more often experienced or explored than others. Such areas as imagery, memories, age regression, feelings of skepticism, and the like may have been attended to in vastly different ways and in different proportions, by various subjects; however, the majority of subjects reported some experience of these phenomena and changes in their perception of them.

The thematic content in any self-hypnosis session, then, was peculiar to an individual's interests, needs, concerns, wishes, and so on. Yet the way these concerns were experienced phenomenologically was more closely associated with structural variables than with the individual's desires or the theme expressed. Thus, structural variables seem to have exerted a powerful influence on the nature of the individual's experience. They defined the intensity, depth of involvement, and so forth as a result of continued practice, as well as by their interaction in and of themselves. The same held true for the approach the subject chose (task motivation, self-help, etc.). The kinds of phenomena reported in any trance experience reflected each individual's choices, yet the quality of the experience was closely interwoven with the structural aspects of self-hypnosis.

We found, moreover, that content variables could be quite distinct from one another. Although the addition of structural variables gave more information about these content variables, it did not change their interrelationship. The complexity of changes in the self-hypnosis experience over time, however, could best be explained with the addition of the structural dimensions to the content data. The admixture of structure and content became visible.

This discussion has departed somewhat from the main objective of this part of the study, which was to deal with the changes over time. These changes over time are, as it turns out, quite well represented in Table 4.4, but they have been enriched by the further analysis.

The present findings are twofold: First, with continued practice over a moderately long period of time, changes in self-hypnosis phenomena occurred. Second, and more importantly, the analyses revealed self-hypnosis as a state

TABLE 4.5
Final Conceptualization of the LQ Dimensions

I. Structure
   A. *Attention*
      1. Focusing of attention
   B. *Generalized Reality Orientation*
      2. Awareness of external surroundings
   C. *Trance Depth*
      3. Time required to enter deep states
      4. Ability to enter deep states
   D. *Absorption*
      5. Absorption in the experience

II. Content
   A. *Memories*
      6. Detailed exploration of personal memories
      7. Time spent actively exploring personal memories
      8. Proportion of memories vividly recalled
      9. Amount of time spent experiencing personal memories
   B. *Imagery*
      10. Awareness of subtle detail in imagery
      11. Frequency of fragmented imagery
      12. Amount of spontaneous imagery
      13. Quantity of imagery
      14. Reality of images
   C. *Other Aspects of Self-Hypnosis*
      15. Skepticism concerning experience
      16. Time required to enter trance
      17. Ability to enter trance easily
      18. Grasp of plan of suggestions
      19. Time spent worrying about failure
      20. Awareness of changes in experience of body
      21. Self-consciousness
      22. Inner distractions avoided for long periods of time
      23. Lack of role playing

in which state-related (structural) features affected one another and the content (which was person-specific). During 4 weeks of use, it was noted how the intensity of phenomena changed; new aspects of the self-hypnosis experience emerged; and the interplay among practice, structural variables, and personal idiosyncrasies continued. The process was neither static nor unidirectional; it permeated each day's session as well as the entire 4 weeks' experience. Again, the LQ was not designed to ascertain causal relationships among self-hypnosis phenomena, nor did we conceptualize the structural components as having primary causal effects on each other or on the content.

The present work points to the existence of phenomenological changes over time in self-hypnosis. In fact, one of the hallmarks of self-hypnosis may be its changeability. The interplay between subject and state is constantly changing. We can only outline the broad dimensions via the superordinate state-related components, and then note their effect on more individually peculiar aspects of the experience.

The longitudinal study, in short, showed that in self-hypnosis each subject created his own experiences, aided and bound by four state-related features that emerged as interacting with one another and with content variables in self-hypnosis: the Generalized Reality Orientation, Absorption, Free-Floating Attention, and Trance Depth. The interactive process among the variables changed over time and revealed to the subject new facets of the self-hypnosis experience previously unknown to him.

PERSONALITY FACTORS

For the purposes of the present study, personality may be defined as a tendency of an individual to order experience in characteristic ways across situations. We were interested in exploring the extent to which subjects' experience of self-hypnosis could be understood vis-à-vis discernible personality patterns.

We are well aware that the sample of subjects who were eventually invited to participate in this study was biased by the selection criteria; indeed, as mentioned earlier, one of the prerequisites for participation in the study was a Rorschach record that appeared healthy by the criteria of clinical assessment. This screening was designed to eliminate subjects for whom self-hypnosis might have been too unsettling an experience.

As noted earlier, the subjects passing the final selection criterion of the Rorschach were administered a battery of the following standardized personality inventories: the PRF, the POI, the MMPI, and the DPQ. The MMPI (Dahlstrom et al., 1972, 1975) is designed essentially to measure psychopathological variables and is sufficiently well known not to warrant further description. Although primarily a clinical instrument, the MMPI has been standardized on thousands of normal individuals as well. The MMPI thus provided an index according to which any particularly pathological trends among subjects in the present sample could be discerned, and it further provided a baseline against which the present sample could be compared to thousands of others from various specified populations, including a large group of "normals."

The POI (Shostrom, 1972) was developed in an attempt to operationalize the concept of self-actualization (Maslow, 1968). The self-actualized individual is defined as one who is more fully functioning and who lives a more enriched life than does the average person. The POI essentially provided an index of psychological health according to which the present sample was viewed. Some of the major experiential polarities measured by the POI, such as time-competence–time-incompetence and inner-directedness–other-directedness, were felt to be potentially significant in understanding the nuances of the self-hypnotic experience.

The PRF (Jackson, 1974) is primarily focused on areas of normal functioning. It is based on the work of Murray (1938) at the Harvard Psychological Clinic and represents an operationalization of several psychosocial concepts. While empirically derived, the PRF scales are firmly grounded in psychoanalytic ego-psychological theory and are thus particularly relevant to the analysis of the phenomena of altered states of consciousness from the perspective proposed by Fromm (1977). The PRF proved to be by far the most useful of the instruments employed in the present study (empirically as well as theoretically), and is thus emphasized in the following discussion.

MMPI Scores

The MMPI scores of the self-hypnosis subjects were compared to the scores of a large population of Minnesota medical patients matched roughly for age (Swenson, Pearson, & Osborne, 1973). The self-hypnosis sample scored substantially lower than the medical patients on Scales 1 (*Hs*, Hypochondriasis), 4 (*Pd*, Psychopathic Deviate), 7 (*Pt*, Psychasthenia), and 8 (*Sc*, Schizophrenia), on all of which our subjects were below the mean of the standardization norms and the medical patients were well above the mean. The subjects tended as a group to be healthier than the normative sample. The experimental sample's scores on Scales 4, 7, and 8 suggested also that on the average subjects were less likely to be in conflict with their environment, were more emotionally stable, and reported fewer unusual thoughts and experiences than the comparison group.

POI Scores

Overall, the scores on the POI were more representative of the expected scores for normal individuals than of those for either self-actualizers or non-self-actualizers. Some scores on some variables (i.e., spontaneity and feeling reactivity), however, were strikingly similar to the scores of the self-actualizers. It might be hypothesized that these two variables are in fact valuable prerequisites for the exploration of one's own experience, especially in the self-hypnosis modality.

The one variable upon which subjects appeared particularly similar to non-self-actualizers was "view of the nature of man." It should be noted that Shostrom's (1972) data were collected in the early 1960s; the present data were collected in the mid-1970s, a historical period of substantial disillusionment for young people.

Variables Measured by the PRF

With one exception ("understanding"), the mean for the present sample of subjects on the PRF scales was within one standard deviation of the national average for each variable. When rank-ordered, Understanding and Sentience were at the high end of the continuum, while Social Recognition stood alone at the low end. It may be inferred from these data that the present sample was particularly curious, exploring, and inquisitive, as well as being sensitive, observant, aware, and alive to impressions.[3] On the other hand, these subjects were somewhat less approval-seeking and accommodating than the general population.

Factor analyses employing varimax rotation were performed on other personality scores as well, but multiple discrete factors were discernible only among PRF variables. Four PRF factors were found and retained for further analysis of the self-hypnosis data. These factors, the variables contained in each, and the amount of the total variance accounted for by each appear in Table 4.6.

While these factors did not all fall into clean conceptual categories, the variables contained within each did form conceptually meaningful sets. Factor 3, "Structuring," was the most clearly homogeneous factor. The subjects scoring high on this factor appeared to need to structure their experience in a systematic fashion, undisturbed by impulse. Factor 1, "Seeking," seemed to be comprised of a set of variables that might be particularly relevant to self-explorative work. The subjects who scored high on this factor appeared

---

[3] Fromm, who has been teaching at the University of Chicago since 1959, as a clinician and a teacher feels that the characteristics described above are the typical characteristics of the University of Chicago student in general. Except for three subjects, all subjects were University of Chicago students. Above and beyond these general prototypical traits of University of Chicago students, the explorative quality implicit in the understanding variable, and the sensitivity characteristic of the sentience variable, seem particularly relevant predispositions to successful experiencing of self-hypnosis phenomena.

TABLE 4.6
PRF Factors for Self-Hypnosis Sample (after Varimax Rotation)

Factor number/ code name	PRF variables included	Loading	% of variance accounted for
1. Seeking	Understanding	.82	31
	Sentience	.45	
	Endurance	.78	
	Social Desirability	.62	
2. Socially Vulnerable	Abasement	.89	19
	Aggression	−.68	
	Dependence	−.69	
	Nurturance	.61	
3. Structuring	Cognitive Structure	.77	15
	Impulsivity	−.67	
	Order	.61	
4. Socially Extroverted	Affiliation	.74	11
	Exhibitionism	.58	
	Play	.72	

to be inquisitive, sensitive, and steadfast. In addition, they were interested in "putting their best foot forward," a characteristic indicated by the high loading of the social desirability variable. Factors 2 and 4 seemed characterized by a stronger social orientation than the other factors. Due to the high loading of abasement and high negative loading of dependence, Factor 2 was labeled "Socially Vulnerable." Factor 4, with high loadings of affiliation, exhibitionism, and play, was given the label "Socially Extroverted."

Relationships between Personality Variables and Self-Hypnotic Experiences

Pearson product correlation coefficients were calculated between personality variables on the one hand, and the present study's measures of self-hypnotic phenomena on the other. The measures of self-hypnotic phenomena used were the two questionnaires previously described: the CQ, asking subjects to compare their self-hypnosis and heterohypnosis experiences, and the LQ, asking whether subjects experienced any changes in self-hypnosis phenomena over the course of the study.

Because the questionnaires had not been designed to be very suitable for the purposes of personality study, some consolidated scores were desirable, and the following four variables were constructed: (1) the sum of those experiences that increased in frequency during self-hypnosis ("sum increase"); (2) the sum of those experiences that decreased in frequency during self-

TABLE 4.7
Significant Correlations between PRF Factors and Summary of Self-Hypnosis and Heterohypnosis

PRF factor	Questionnaire variable	Correlation
2. Socially Vulnerable	Sum self-hypnosis	−.34*
2. Socially Vulnerable	Sum heterohypnosis	−.38*
3. Structuring	Sum increase	−.37*

* $p < .05$.

hypnosis ("sum decrease"); (3) the sum of those experiences considered more characteristic of self-hypnosis than heterohypnosis ("sum self-hypnosis"); and (4) the sum of those experiences considered more characteristic of hetero-hypnosis than self-hypnosis ("sum heterohypnosis").

Of the 16 correlations between these four variables and the four personality factor scores, three proved to be significant, each of them negative in sign, as shown in Table 4.7. What the first two of these correlations appeared to imply was that the qualities comprising the personality style of the socially vulnerable individual were not very likely to be found among those subjects who were successful in either heterohypnosis or self-hypnosis. The third correlation suggested that a personal style emphasizing order and cognitive structure, coupled with a low degree of impulsivity, was not conducive to a modification of hypnotic experience through repeated self-hypnosis.

There were also some significant correlations between PRF factors and discrete self-hypnosis variables, as shown in Table 4.8. Notice first that individuals who showed a need to structure their experience demonstrated a tendency toward greater trance depth in self-hypnosis than in heterohypnosis. It would seem that these subjects were able to use their own structuring

TABLE 4.8
Significant Correlations between PRF Factors and Self-Hypnosis Variables

PRF factor	Questionnaire variable	Correlation
1. Seeking	Aspects of trance (LQ)	.36*
	Absorption (LQ)	.39*
2. Socially Vulnerable	Generalized Reality Orientation (LQ)	−.39*
	Generalized Reality Orientation (CQ)	.40*
	Attention (CQ)	.34
3. Structuring	Depth (CQ)	.52**
4. Socially Extroverted	Generalized Reality Orientation (LQ)	.34*
	Absorption (LQ)	−.32*

* $p < .05$; ** $p < .01$.

ability and devices to move rapidly into the hypnotic experience best when they themselves were in control.

The subjects who were more typically socially vulnerable were more likely to experience free-floating attention and fading of the Generalized Reality Orientation in self-hypnosis than in heterohypnosis. Perhaps the solitary experience of self-hypnosis—as opposed to the interpersonal context of heterohypnosis—provided a more comfortable context within which these subjects could allow their attention to roam and permit themselves to become aware of their environment.

Seeking subjects tended to experience an increased sense of reality of the trance during self-hypnosis as time went on. Seeking also correlated positively with increased experience of absorption over time, while the Socially Extroverted factor correlated negatively with that same variable. It appeared, as may have been anticipated, that the ability to become increasingly absorbed in the self-hypnosis process was related to the tendencies comprising the Seeking factor—particularly understanding, sentience, and endurance—but was inversely related to the more externally oriented variable comprising the Socially Extroverted factor.

In summary, analysis of the personality data revealed that some meaningful—if at this point tentative—relationships existed between personality variables and experience involving self-hypnosis phenomena. While the present sample (of highly hypnotizable subjects) appeared generally within normal ranges vis-à-vis most of the indices of personality employed, a few characteristic variables seemed to describe particular features of this population that may be associated with the potential to experience hypnotic (and perhaps particularly self-hypnotic) phenomena. These included (1) spontaneity, (2) feeling reactivity (Shostrom, 1972), (3) understanding, and (4) sentience (Jackson, 1974).

Analysis of correlational data between personality factors and self-hypnosis phenomena suggested that certain personal styles may have influenced some apparent differences in subjects' experiences of self-hypnosis and heterohypnosis phenomena. While these data were rather sparse and by no means conclusive, they were illustrative of a way of exploring the relationship between personal style and experience that has rarely appeared in the hypnosis literature or the literature concerning other altered states of consciousness (for an exceptional example of such an approach, see Barr et al., 1972). Most previous studies dealing with the relationship between personality and hypnosis were concerned with issues of hypnotizability, the most extensive study being that of J. R. Hilgard (1970). The present study presupposed hypnotizability and asked what variables concerning personal style could account for some of the variance in qualitatively different experience. Despite the methodological handicaps discussed above, the present data revealed some significant results suggesting that self-hypnosis is not a unitary phenomenon, but varies to some extent according to personal style. Later chapters of this book examine personality factors in more detail.

DISCUSSION

The experiences we observed among our subjects, and the analyses of journals (see Section B of Part II) and questionnaires, are somewhat different from many of those experiences reported as self-hypnosis in the experimental literature. The key difference between the present and earlier studies is a difference between self-initiated suggestions with self-defined responses and experimenter-initiated suggestions with self-defined responses. Over the 4 weeks of daily practice, subjects created their own self-suggestions, rather than simply responding in their own ways to standardized tasks. Under these conditions, a specific feature of self-hypnosis emerged, along with a view of self-hypnosis that previously may have been obscured by experimentation using more standard designs and tighter controls.

The subjects did not expect their self-hypnosis experiences to differ from their heterohypnosis experiences in terms of the use of attention and concentration or the use of receptivity; subjects did expect that it would be easier to concentrate in heterohypnosis. An essential difference in subjects' expectations and understandings of self-hypnosis as far as fantasy is concerned may have been related to the nature of the instructions. The subjects saw heterohypnosis as a situation in which they were required to follow the hypnotist's instructions exactly. In direct contrast, self-hypnosis was perceived as an opportunity for creative self-exploration, in which subjects could initiate and carry out their own suggestions. This may have been due to the facts that the heterohypnotic experiences subjects were given were of quite a conventional kind (HGSHS:A, SHSS:C, SPSHS:I, and SPSHS:II), and that subjects were also told that in self-hypnosis they need not limit themselves to these sample experiences of hypnosis. In addition, in self-hypnosis subjects were very task-oriented (as Chapter 7 illustrates with examples from the journals); they developed methods to induce their own trance state and then gave themselves instructions to deepen the trance. Following this, they again initiated a number of self-suggestions and carried these out while in trance. The subjects discovered differences in the relative ease and difficulty with which they carried out their own suggestions. Often, before each session, subjects would actively plan out the tasks they wished to perform in trance. This self-initiated task orientation differed markedly from the same subjects' concern to follow a hypnotist's suggestions precisely during heterohypnosis.

The exact nature of the tasks subjects created depended largely on individual dispositions and interests. Although specific self-initiated suggestions were highly idiosyncratic, most subjects saw self-hypnosis both as a problem-solving activity and as a means of self-exploration. Problem solving might include reviewing one's daily worries and concerns, learning to develop better study habits, or conducting a form of self-therapy. Self-exploration involves a heightened sensitivity toward thinking and imaging processes; accordingly, subjects explored their internal world of thoughts, fantasies, and memories in order to learn more about who they were. These results lead us to assume that when subjects' self-hypnotic experiences are confined to self-defined responses, and subjects do not have the chance to give themselves their own suggestions, this view of self-hypnosis as creative self-exploration becomes obscured.

What Is Self-Hypnosis?

Are self-hypnosis and heterohypnosis the same altered state of consciousness, or does each have its unique properties? In order to answer these questions, we looked for state, content, and context variables that might provide a unique definition of self-hypnosis. According to Tart (1975), each altered state of consciousness has its own patterning of cognitive processes—such as thinking, attention, imaging, and memories. These findings show that common features as well as important differences exist between self-hypnosis and heterohypnosis.

STATE VARIABLES

Both self-hypnosis and heterohypnosis are states that involve a fading of the generalized reality orientation. Both are states in which a good subject feels deeply absorbed in his inner experience. Absorption and relinquishing of the Generalized Reality Orientation are the means by which a subject changes her orientation so as to become less preoccupied with distracting perceptions, thoughts, and feelings related to external reality. As a subject changes his orientation and becomes more absorbed in the focal internal experience, he enters trance, whether it be heterohypnosis or self-hypnosis. Nevertheless, there are certain features that differentiate self-hypnosis and heterohypnosis. In the structural area, they are depth of trance and attention/concentration.

Depth of trance fluctuated much more during self-hypnosis, particularly during the first week of self-hypnosis. We ascribe these fluctuations to the fact that in self-hypnosis our subjects had to create the structure of the state for themselves and thus—certainly in the first week—felt disoriented and/or unsure of themselves in self-hypnosis. In laboratory heterohypnosis, the hypnotist provides structure for the subject from the very beginning.

Another possible explanation lies in rhythmic changes in arousal level. Fluctuations in arousal level are common and well known in daily meditative experiences. These fluctuations are thought to be related to rhythmic changes in arousal level at certain times of the day as well as over different days. Daily self-hypnosis practice may also be affected by such rhythmic changes in arousal level, whereas in heterohypnosis the structuring of the experience by the hypnotist may obscure these effects. Our subjects were neither required to practice self-hypnosis at a specific time of the day, nor were they instructed to note regularly the time of the day in their journals. We can thus only point to this explanation as a conceivable hypothesis, worthy of future study.

Although both self-hypnosis and heterohypnosis require subjects to focus their attention in specific ways, there are subtle but perhaps important differences in the way subjects deploy attention. During self-hypnosis attention is both receptive and expansive. At times, subjects allow their minds to wander freely. They wait and listen for whatever thoughts, images, memories, sensations, and the like might spontaneously arise. At other times, subjects exert an effort to expand their attention, bringing into awareness events occurring in their stream of consciousness moment by moment. Although this receptive/expansive attention is more characteristic of self-hypnosis, subjects during self-hypnosis do not submit themselves entirely to receptive and expansive modes of attention. Occasionally, our subjects tended to concentrate in order to carry out certain self-defined tasks; many subjects complained that it was more difficult to concentrate during self-hypnosis.

By way of contrast, our subjects described heterohypnosis in terms of steady, focused attention and concentration in which few distractions were permitted. Receptive and expansive attention were used rarely during heterohypnosis (in the HGSHS:A, SHSS:C, SPSHS:I, and SPSHS:II—i.e., the four techniques used for heterohypnosis—neither is specifically suggested by the hypnotist).

CONTENT VARIABLES

The content of the phenomena experienced in laboratory-defined self-hypnosis with no experimenter present and with the subjects able to initiate their own suggestions showed some differences in quantity and quality from the content that emerged during the heterohypnotic part of the experiment. Imagery played a greater role in self-hypnosis than in heterohypnosis; it tended to be more vivid, more thematic, qualitatively richer, and more personally meaningful. These differences in content appear to be related to the differences in attention deployment in the two states, and to fluctuations in trance depth during self-hypnosis. The subjects who used a receptive and expansive attentional mode during self-hypnosis reported a significantly greater quantity of imagery. During times of the greatest fluctuation in trance depth, the imagery appeared fragmented and disconnected.

Personal memories and bodily sensations occurred spontaneously during self-hypnosis, but were seen as distracting from the self-initiated tasks and exploration of imagery. The subjects in heterohypnosis, on the other hand, were better able to use the hypnotist to guide them in their hypermnesias and in age regression; they reported a heightened awareness of personal memories. In heterohypnosis subjects could also experience successful positive and negative hallucinations, whereas subjects in self-hypnosis were less able to do so.

The *content* of the self-hypnosis sessions was idiosyncratic. Imagery, fantasy, and memories occurred in very different ways and proportions among various individuals. The data further imply that the content of self-initiated self-hypnosis experiences depends more on a person's interest, needs, concerns, wishes, and personality variables than on structural variables. Are some people better suited for self-hypnosis than others? One direction future research might take would be to look more closely at correlations between specific cognitive styles and patterns of self-initiated suggestions. The data suggest that "structuring" individuals are less likely to benefit from the pure type of self-initiated suggestions and self-directed responses used in the present study. What about subjects who walked out of the study? Did they drop out for situational reasons (lack of time, etc.), or because they were not the types of individuals likely to benefit from this form of self-hypnosis? We do not have the data to answer these questions conclusively.

CONTEXTUAL VARIABLES

The differences in the structure and content of self-hypnosis and heterohypnosis were correlated with differences in the context of these experiences. Again, subjects had different expectations of self-hypnosis and heterohypnosis. Since they expected self-hypnosis to be an opportunity for creative self-exploration, while in heterohypnosis subjects expected to follow the hypnotist's instructions exactly, it is not surprising that subjects used the daily self-hypnosis sessions to become more receptive to their own thoughts and fantasies, while in heterohypnosis subjects became self-conscious and concerned with the success or failure of their performance. Nor is it surprising that in heterohypnosis subjects reported less idiosyncratic imagery; with the concern for following the hypnotist's instructions, less time was available for self-exploration.

Important differences also arose due to the presence or absence of the hypnotist, the interpersonal variable. In self-hypnosis without a hypnotist, subjects spent a fair amount of time planning their trance sessions, constructing self-suggestions, and becoming aware of internal events in their stream of consciousness. In heterohypnosis, subjects, with the aid of the hypnotist, were able to fix their attention in more specific ways. Thus in self-hypnosis subjects' attention tended to wander, making them more receptive to internal events. In heterohypnosis, the hypnotist through constant suggestions helped the subjects concentrate more effectively. This may be the reason why subjects in heterohypnosis experienced more success with positive and negative hallucinations and with hypermnesias and age regressions. Transference phenomena (Fromm, 1968) are more likely to emerge in heterohypnosis, because of the presence of the hypnotist, and may lead to the subjects' reporting more regressive phenomena in heterohypnosis than in self-hypnosis.

The Development of Attentional Skills in Self-Hypnosis

Several researchers (Brown, 1977; Fromm, 1977, 1979; Tart, 1975) have reported a relationship between attention deployment and the specific content of altered states of consciousness. Tart (1975) believes that altering or manipulating attention in certain ways may be a critical variable in the specificity of altered states of consciousness. Brown (1977) reported that training of two very different types of attention during meditation (i.e., concentration and mindfulness) leads to different effects with respect to the kind of mental content experienced during meditation. In future research, subjects should perhaps be given different attentional tasks in order to study the respective effects on mental content experienced during hypnotic trance. The current design did not permit us to ascertain whether a causal relationship exists between the structural and the content variables.

Longitudinal Variables

When subjects practiced self-hypnosis daily for 4 weeks, they underwent a series of changes in their experience of self-hypnosis; they adapted to their own internal milieu. Initially, there was a short period of disorientation, anxiety, and self-doubt ("Can I do it alone?"); some subjects complained about the difficulty of inducing hypnosis in themselves; others became restless and bored. Nevertheless, within a few days subjects adapted to the experience. Once they adapted, several changes occurred. First, their means of inducing trance and giving themselves suggestions while in trance became automatized; they were able to enter trance more quickly and easily. Self-suggestions then were carried out with less planning and less self-coaxing. As trance experience became yet more automatized, subjects showed less preoccupation with success or failure when entering hypnosis. Instead, their awareness was free to explore their own internal milieu. The subjects reported a greater sensitivity to imagery, thoughts, and some bodily sensations. Affects were experienced more intensely; images were perceived more vividly. The events of their internal milieu became fascinating, as subjects now took the time to find out more about who they were and how their minds worked. Although the quality of these internal events may have changed over time (e.g., in terms of increasing vividness), subjects nevertheless reported great fluctuations in the depth of trance during the 4 weeks of the experiment. Many subjects reported that thoughts and images took on a reality of their own. With more experience, these internal events at times took on a quality of verisimilitude comparable to the way in which one experiences external reality itself. All of these changes might be viewed as a form of adaptation to the internal world, comparable to the way of adapting to external reality that the individual learns in the course of growing up.

One of the most important changes that occurred over time involves the training of attention. Our research shows that in daily self-hypnosis practice over a number of weeks, subjects learn to allow their attention to unfocus and to expand as their ego mode becomes more receptive. This process may have a direct effect on the patterning of the subject's state of consciousness as well as on the type of content that rises into awareness. Self-hypnotic and heterohypnotic subjects appear to train their attention in different ways. In heterohypnosis, the hypnotist's presence and constant suggestions may help the subject to become a better concentrator; because the hypnotist is present, the subject learns to concentrate his attention on the one important external stimulus, the voice of the hypnotist. In self-hypnosis without a hypnotist, subjects practice a more receptive and expansive mode of attention, and thereby become more aware of internal events such as imagery, thoughts, and affects.

In summary, we found four structural, state-related factors: Two appeared to be common denominators of heterohypnosis and self-hypnosis, and two seemed to differentiate between them. Absorption and relinquishing of the Generalized Reality Orientation are important common features of self-hypnosis as well as of heterohypnosis. They set the stage for all (deep) hypnotic experiences and are essential characteristics differentiating hypnotic states from waking states. Together, they form the axis, the sine qua non on which both self-hypnosis and heterohypnosis experiences rest, and in the absence of which neither deep heterohypnosis nor deep self-hypnosis phenomena occur. The two structural factors differentiating self-hypnosis from heterohypnosis are Attention/Concentration and fluctuations in Trance Depth. In contrast to the concentrative, steadily focused attention typifying heterohypnosis, in self-hypnosis attention is expansive. The mind is free to wander; the subject waits to see what contents will float into awareness. Trance depth, particularly in the first week of self-hypnosis, fluctuates more than in heterohypnosis.

With regard to what we have called content categories of the hypnotic experience, we found that imagery in self-hypnosis is even more frequent, rich, vivid, and personally meaningful than in heterohypnosis. Attempts to initiate age regressions and hypermnesias in self-hypnosis, however, are markedly less successful than such guided experiences in heterohypnosis.

The particular content of the self-hypnosis experience may be idiosyncratic, depending on each subject's needs, interests, and personality style, but the four structural factors (Absorption, Generalized Reality Orientation, Attention, and Trance Depth) always exert some influence on the content of the experience. They also exert complementary effects on each other. Although the thematic content in any session is peculiar to an individual's interests, needs, and wishes, the way these concerns are experienced phenomenologically is more closely associated with structural variables than with the individual's desires or the theme expressed. Structural variables exert a powerful force on the nature of the individual's experience. They define the intensity, depth of involvement, and so forth, as a result of continued practice as well as by their interactions. The same holds for the approach the subject chooses (task motivation, self-help, etc.). The *kind* of phenomena reported in any trance experience reflects each individual's choices; yet the *quality* of the experience is closely interwoven with the structural aspects of self-hypnosis.

In addition, we found definite changes in the phenomena of self-hypnosis as time progressed. In the beginning, subjects experienced anxiety, skepticism, and self-doubt. As they came to feel more at home with the self-hypnotic state and adapted to it, the state felt more natural and comfortable; the ability to enter it quickly and easily increased, as did absorption, the fading of the Generalized Reality Orientation, and the ability to go to greater self-hypnotic depth with confidence.

The data generated by the present study should be viewed cautiously. A number of factors may have had a good deal of influence on the pattern of results, making generalization difficult. First, the study was undertaken with subjects who were highly hypnotizable; subjects with low or medium degrees of hypnotic susceptibility, as measured by standardized rating scales, were systematically excluded. Second, those subjects chosen to participate were explicitly encouraged to expand their self-hypnosis experience as broadly as possible—indeed, to go beyond whatever they learned in their hetero-hypnotic sessions. Thus, these data were derived from a study designed to maximize the potential differences between heterohypnosis and self-hypnosis. Yet, in spite of the attempt to maximize those differences, more than two-thirds of the items assessed by the CQ failed to distinguish between the two states.

A further set of difficulties can be discerned in the design of the study. The subjects were asked to compare their first seven self-hypnosis sessions with five heterohypnosis sessions. Three of the heterohypnosis sessions preceded the self-hypnosis sessions and two followed them. The comparisons between the two took place retrospectively, with a good deal of additional intervening self-hypnosis experience prior to the comparison.

If these differences are set aside, however, it appears that self-hypnosis at least can alter one's orientation so that internal events are attended to in new ways. Our subjects appeared to make an active effort to expand their attentional range—an effort that may have been derived in part from their expectations that in self-hypnosis one does things somewhat differently from the way one does them in heterohypnosis.

These data reveal that the effects of expectations about an experience, concomitant with the adoption of an attentional strategy consonant with such expectations, have the capacity to modify highly hypnotizable subjects' trance experiences in several uniform ways. Moreover, there appear to be specific parameters of the self-hypnotic states that are worthy of future experimental investigation.

SUGGESTIONS FOR FUTURE RESEARCH

Some of the qualitative material reported in this research (and originally published in 1981) appears to be similar to what meditators report. Brown, Forte, Rich, and Epstein (1982–1983) have replicated the experiment described in this chapter with groups of subjects who practiced self-hypnosis, mindfulness meditation, and waking imaging related to a previous nocturnal dream, repeatedly over extended periods of time. They used a questionnaire containing only the reduced item pool of our CQ and LQ, which they called the Profile of Trance, Imaging, and Meditation Experience (TIME).

Brown et al.'s subjects' reports on self-hypnosis, on the whole, confirm the reports given by our subjects. In both studies, subjects reported that self-hypnosis is a cognitive state that utilizes certain thought processes in the service of self-suggestion and in accessing the stream of consciousness. Further research comparing the phenomena of self-hypnosis with those of other types of meditation could be undertaken.

Another area future researchers need to investigate is alert self-hypnosis—such as that of the jogger who through rhythmic activity can let pain and exhaustion fade into the background of his awareness. One could also compare a group of subjects who practice self-hypnosis in the absence of a hypnotist (as the present subjects did) with a group of subjects who practice self-hypnosis in the presence of the hypnotist and at his urging. In these cases, the hypnotist does nothing but tell subjects repeatedly to "go deeper, go deeper," as Tart (1972, 1979) did with one subject who went into an extremely deep hypnotic state, and reported near-mystical experiences. E. R. Hilgard[4] has often, in informal demonstrations, used the same technique of encouraging a subject to go deeper by himself.

Perhaps rhythmic fluctuations in arousal level at certain times of the day, week, or month (the last of these especially with regard to women's

---

[4] Personal communication, February 13, 1980.

menstrual cycles) influence the daily practice of self-hypnosis, particularly as far as depth and content variables are concerned. This hypothesis deserves investigation.

The need for further research in the areas of (1) cognitive styles and patterns of self-initiated suggestions; (2) influences exerted by different attentional tasks on the content arising in the mind of the person practicing self-hypnosis; and (3) personality type and benefit to be derived from self-hypnosis has already been mentioned.

APPENDIX 4.1. REPRESENTATIVE QUESTIONS FROM THE COMPARATIVE QUESTIONNAIRE (CQ) AND THE LONGITUDINAL QUESTIONNAIRE (LQ)

I. *INITIAL REACTIONS*

CQ #2. Compared to your experience with an experimenter, *your ability to concentrate* (i.e., hold your attention fixed) during your first few experiences with self-hypnosis was:

- ☐ much greater in self-hypnosis than in your hypnosis experiences with an experimenter
- ☐ a little greater in self-hypnosis than in your hypnosis experiences with an experimenter
- ☐ about the same in self-hypnosis as in your hypnosis experiences with an experimenter
- ☐ a little less in self-hypnosis than in your hypnosis experiences with an experimenter
- ☐ much less in self-hypnosis than in your hypnosis experiences with an experimenter

II. *TRANCE INDUCTION AND SUGGESTIONS*

LQ #10. As you gained more experience with self-hypnosis, the length of time that it took you to induce trance:

- ☐ increased a great deal
- ☐ etc.

III. *TRANCE DEPTH*

LQ #18. As you gained more experience in self-hypnosis, your ability to enter deep trance states became:

- ☐ much greater than at first
- ☐ etc.

IV. *ATTENTION AND CONCENTRATION*

CQ #19. The ability to concentrate (i.e., hold your attention steady without too much distraction) was:

- ☐ much greater in the first week of self-hypnosis than in hypnosis with an experimenter
- ☐ etc.

V. *IMAGERY*

CQ #28. Compared to your experiences with an experimenter, the quantity of imagery you experienced in your first week of self-hypnosis was:

☐ much less
☐ etc.

VI. *AWARENESS OF EXPERIENTIAL ASPECTS*

LQ #47. In particular as you gained more experience with self-hypnosis, your awareness of *each* of the following particular mental events became: (Rate each with the appropriate code number: 1–5, 1 = much greater . . . 5 = much less.)

☐ a. awareness of particularly strong feelings, either pleasant or unpleasant
☐ b. periods of detailed exploration of personal memories
☐ c. periods of detailed exploration into thought trains, thought interconnections, plays of words, intellectual insights, etc.
☐ d. being aware of awareness itself
☐ e. wondering about the connection of mind and body
☐ f. wondering where, how, or why thoughts arise and cease
☐ g. marked perceptual changes upon opening the eyes (e.g., unusual clarity or distortion)
☐ h. changes in the way you experience your body during hypnosis
☐ i. changes in the way you experience your sense of self during hypnosis
☐ j. changes in the experience of time during hypnosis
☐ k. other mental events

(Only branch questions b and h were kept after the data reduction)

VII. *MEMORIES AND RE-EXPERIENCING OF PAST EVENTS*

CQ #32. In comparison to hypnosis with an experimenter, the amount of experiencing of memories of past events in self-hypnosis was:

☐ much greater in your first week of self-hypnosis than in your experiences with an experimenter
☐ etc.

VIII. *REALITY OF TRANCE*

CQ #40. You found that seeing, hearing, feeling, and smelling things that are *not* really there in front of you when you open your eyes in trance was:

☐ much easier in your experiences with an experimenter than in your first week of self-hypnosis
☐ etc.

IXa. *INTERPERSONAL ASPECTS*

CQ #44. Some people find a hypnotic experience more *personally meaningful* when a hypnotist is present as part of the experience; others find it more personally meaningful when they have the experience alone. The *meaningfulness* of your hypnotic experience was:

☐ much greater in hypnosis with an experimenter than in your first week of self-hypnosis
☐ etc.

IXb. *DEMAND CHARACTERISTICS*

LQ #71. The fact that you were expected to write about your experience in the journal immediately after each session may have influenced your self-hypnosis *sessions* in a number of ways during your four weeks of self-hypnosis. Use the numbers 1–5 to estimate how each item below changed, comparing the *fourth-week* experience to your first week of self-hypnosis.

- [ ] you were generally aware of the fact that you were going to write up the experience, and this affected your self-hypnosis session
- [ ] you were generally aware of the fact that you were going to write up the experience, but this had little or no effect on the self-hypnosis session
- [ ] you tended to shorten the session in order to have more time for detailed write-up of the few experiences you had
- [ ] you tended to lengthen the session in order to have more material to write up
- [ ] you tended to do things which would seem rich in content to the experimenter
- [ ] you tended to avoid or curtail things that came up which would be too revealing of yourself to the experimenter
- [ ] you made an extra effort to remember things as you went along in order to be able to write about them afterward

X. *EXPECTATIONS OF SELF*

LQ #79. As you gained more experience in self-hypnosis, the frequency with which you followed your self-suggestions *exactly* became:

- [ ] much greater
- [ ] etc.

XI. *EGO ACTIVITY AND EGO RECEPTIVITY*

LQ #85. As the four weeks of your self-hypnosis progressed, part of you created the suggestions while another part acted as a speaker in directing the suggestions:

- [ ] much more frequently
- [ ] etc.

APPENDIX 4.2. PROCEDURAL INSTRUCTIONS

You are now going to being your four weeks of self-hypnosis. During your two pre-experimental standardized hypnotic experiences with the experimenters, you have become familiar with a good number of hypnotic procedures. You may use these as an example of what you can do in your hour of self-hypnosis each day. However, do not feel that you need to limit yourself to these. You may wish to think up suggestions for some other experiences, and then experiment with them. You may also wish at times just to remain in trance but not do anything specific.

We want you to experience self-hypnosis for about 60 minutes every day for four weeks by yourself, and to keep a daily journal on your experiences in self-hypnosis. Please make entries in your journal every day, right after finishing the self-hypnosis. In the journal we want you to note:

- The date.
- The time of day.
- The duration of the trance.
- Specific self-suggestions attempted and whether they were successful or not.
- Amount of time you remained in trance without doing anything specific; record anything that may have occurred during these times.
- The depth of your trance by means of a number according to the instructions of the North Carolina Scale each day at the beginning of your experience (i.e., after the induction), sometime during the middle of your trance, and before termination of trance. Record these three numbers in your journal after awakening.

Most important:

- Critical reflection on *each* aspect of the experience and also a *general* reflection on the entire experience that day.
- Finally, the most significant experience that day.

Your thoughts and reflections about the experience are of great value to us, and we would appreciate your describing them in detail.

You will be given a notebook in which to write. Once a week an experimenter will contact you by phone, and once a week an experimenter will make arrangements to meet with you.

CHAPTER 5

Aspects of Self-Hypnosis Proper

In Chapter 4, we have discussed the structural dimensions of the hypnotic experience that differentiate self-hypnosis from heterohypnosis and from the waking state (and probably from other altered states of consciousness as well), by means of the results of the Comparative Questionnaire (CQ). We have also described the phenomena and the process of getting accustomed to self-hypnosis over a period of time, through the results of our Longitudinal Questionnaire (LQ). In this chapter we discuss the results of a third questionnaire, the Self-Hypnosis Proper Questionnaire (SHPQ), by means of which we investigated the phenomena and characteristics of self-hypnosis proper. That is, we used the SHPQ to evaluate self-hypnosis (1) without regard for the effects of time and practice, (2) without comparison to any of the aspects of heterohypnosis, and (3) regardless of the particular time at which the phenomena occurred during the 4 weeks of the experiment.

METHOD

Subjects and Procedure

The selection of subjects has been described in detail in Chapter 4 and is summarized only briefly here. A total of 425 volunteer subjects were screened for hypnotic susceptibility and freedom from psychotic trends. Of these, 58 normal and deeply hypnotizable subjects started on the experiment. For various reasons roughly half of them dropped out, but 33 subjects finished the month-long experiment and completed the questionnaires given at the end. These 33 subjects form our pool.

The experimental procedure has likewise been described in detail in Chapter 4. Subjects practiced self-hypnosis for 1 hour daily over the course of 4 weeks. At the outset, each subject was given a written set of instructions for self-hypnosis (see Appendix 4.2). These informed subjects that they might use their experiences with heterohypnosis during the course of experimental screening as guidelines, but also encouraged them to engage in self-initiated suggestions and to experiment with their own ways of inducing and experiencing trance. In addition, subjects were asked to keep daily journals in which they would chronicle their self-hypnosis experiences.

The Questionnaire

The SHPQ was the third of the three questionnaires each subject completed at the end of his 4 weeks of self-hypnosis. (The results for the other two, the CQ and the LQ, have been described in Chapter 4.) The SHPQ tapped the same 11 structural and content categories as the LQ and the CQ; however, the questions on the SHPQ were designed to obtain information about the state of self-hypnosis without reference to time and to heterohypnosis. Some representative questions appear in Appendix 5.1. The SHPQ contained 54 questions. Many of these questions utilized the same 5-point Likert scale ratings as the CQ and LQ but were asked with reference to the *absolute* amount of time engaged in a particular state, rather than a relative amount of time. The 5-point scale ranged from "never occurred" (or "less than 25% of the time") to "always occurred" (or "more than 75% of the time") with points in between (e.g., 25%, 50%, 75%). Other questions were checklists of specific events that may have occurred, and left it to the subject to indicate the percentage of time involved. As with the CQ and LQ, each of the 11 sections ended with an unstructured portion designed to elicit experiences not covered by the structured questions (see Appendix 5.1). The wording of all inquiries was constructed to minimize demand characteristics.

RESULTS AND DISCUSSION

Initial Goals

The initial goal most often mentioned by subjects was the desire to explore the particular phenomenon of self-hypnosis. Part of this may have overlapped with the next most mentioned category (mentioned by two-thirds of our subjects)—that of the desire to become more aware of the workings of one's mind and body. Over half of the subjects mentioned their wish to use self-hypnosis as a means of self-improvement, although about a third wanted to use it to solve personal problems.

Structural Categories

As indicated in the preceding chapter, the General Reality Orientation faded into the background of awareness in self-hypnosis as well as in heterohypnosis. On the second structural dimension, that of Absorption, almost all of our subjects reported that they felt intensely absorbed during most of the time they were in trance.

USE OF ATTENTION AND ACTIVATION LEVELS

Attention in self-hypnosis has many complex facets. For almost all subjects, attention alternated between ego-active and ego-receptive states. Throughout the 4 weeks of the experiment, there were periods in which people actively directed their attention to certain mental events and other periods in which they allowed their attention to be receptive (i.e., they waited and listened to what would come up). The distributions of time between the active and receptive modes were as follows: 38% felt that 75% of the typical self-hypnosis hour was spent actively directing their attention, while 31% felt they were primarily receptive in their use of attention. The remaining subjects felt that they alternated equally between the active and receptive modes.

Looking broadly over the total time frame of the experiment, 72% of our subjects found themselves "selectively focusing on specific mental events"; most of these 72% alternated between doing this actively and just letting it happen. Another 22% used their time to expand their attentional range so that few mental events escaped attention. Again, most of these 22% alternated between an active and a passive approach to this expansive style. A scant 6% found that the self-hypnotic state was generally not very different from the waking state in terms of their attention. In terms of the amount of time spent in expansive versus selective attention in the typical self-hypnosis hour, two-thirds of the subjects used selective attention most of the time, and almost all used selective attention over half of the time.

The great majority of our subjects (77%) experienced sensations, thoughts, and images one at a time rather than experiencing many simultaneously. Only 10% of the subjects felt that their attention encompassed several mental events simultaneously more often than they focused on a single one. This indicates that a focused, singular kind of attention dominates the self-hypnotic experience, although the degree to which it dominates may be considerably less than in the waking state. We do know from another phase of this study that this singular and focused type of attention occurs less often in self-hypnosis than in heterohypnosis (see Chapter 4).

In terms of activation levels, our subjects rarely experienced in self-hypnosis the racy excitement that is so typical of psychedelic states, and there was very little drowsiness. A majority, 60%, felt that their minds had an "even alertness" for most of the time. This may or may not mean that it is like the waking state; however, almost three-fourths of our subjects felt that for the majority of the time spent in self-hypnosis, the mind is activated in a way different from the way in which it is activated in the waking state.

Content and Context Categories

IMAGERY

Imagery, as in the other questionnaires, again turned out to be the most important content category. When comparing thoughts and images in the self-hypnotic state to those in the waking state, our subjects found that their self-hypnotic thoughts and imagery were very clear. We probed our subjects to find out the different kinds of imagery they experienced. Very rarely did imagery occur in the form of tactile or other bodily sensations. Kinesthetic imagery was also rare, and practically no streams of words—a special form of auditory imagery—appeared. Visual imagery, on the other hand, was by far the most frequent type of imagery, followed by thought association (simple free association).

When our subjects were asked to rate the vividness or faintness of their imagery on a Likert-type scale, the vast majority (84%) found their imagery to be vivid, with 55% finding it very vivid.

There are many different ways in which visual imagery might be experienced, so we asked our subjects about this. Most felt that unconnected images were rare, and that bizarre image conglomerations were very rare. Often, when one closes one's eyes in the waking state and looks at the back of the eyelids, simple shapes and swirls appear, but these too were rare in self-hypnosis. The rarest form, practically nonexistent among our subjects, were faint, veiled, fragmented images. Only very occasionally did images oscillate between being faint and being vivid, and never did they seem to look like cartoons. What our subjects did "see" in varying amounts were vivid, realistic scenes, connected as in a story.

When we asked about this last aspect in more detail, most of our subjects stated again that they experienced imagery in self-hypnosis in coherent, thematic, or story-like sequences. They did not perceive it as fragmentary imagery, nor did they alternate between coherent and fragmentary images.

Our subjects were also asked to compare the ways in which imagery overall, not just visual imagery, was experienced qualitatively (i.e., as being "ordinary," "dreamlike," "bizarre," "thought-like," or mixed with many memories). A full three-fourths of our subjects had dreamlike images 40% of the time or less. These dreamlike images, however, seemed to be connected rather than fragmentary. Almost three-fourths of our population also experienced imagery as ordinary (just as one experiences it in the waking state) for about half of the time during their 4-week-long experiment with self-hypnosis. Bizarre (psychedelic-like) imagery, thought-like imagery, and imagery mixed with many memories were all very rare.

In self-hypnosis, imagery nearly always arises from inside; that is, it arises through Ego Receptivity to stimuli from within rather than from without. Of course, this finding is mitigated by the facts that (1) our subjects practiced self-hypnosis in a barren experimental situation, one where there were no or very few stimuli from the outside; and (2) no hypnotist or experimenter was in the room with a subject.

By far the most frequent themes of imagery had to do with fantasies of trips or of adventure, followed closely by a preoccupation with personal problems. Themes occurring less often were creative experiences, intellectual problem solving, and concentration on the day's events. The least frequent theme or image was seeing oneself as being in trance.

TIME DISTORTION

Practically *all* of our subjects experienced time distortion in self-hypnosis. As noted above, we had told them that they should practice self-hypnosis for 1 hour daily; thus, the demand characteristic was to remain in trance for 1 hour. Fifty-three percent of the subjects stated that they had some difficulty measuring time. For 31%, time in trance seemed to move faster than clock time, and for another 31% it seemed to move slower.

AGE REGRESSION AND HYPERMNESIA

Only 25% of our subjects ever or rarely spent time in self-hypnosis recalling material that did not have deep personal meaning for them. Overall, the material recalled in self-hypnosis tended to have a deep personal meaning for our subjects. Almost all of the subjects set out at one time or another to willfully explore personal memories; very few experienced either age regression or hypermnesia spontaneously. For the majority (69%), these personal memories or re-experienced childhood events were described as extremely vivid in detail and quite powerful.

As regards the content of these hypermnesias and age regressions, our subjects reported that most of the time they found them to be pleasant rather than conflict-ridden. However, over half of our subjects found that these were memories that they had experienced previously (i.e., relatively few memories revealed repressed content).

One might expect the occurrence of true age regression in self-hypnosis to be a relatively rare phenomenon. However, almost half (40%) of our subjects felt that the majority of their memories were vividly relived rather than clearly remembered. This fact is tempered somewhat by the fact that, as stated earlier, these subjects were selected for their hypnotizability. In addition, two-thirds of the subjects felt that for a good amount of time the particular images or thoughts during the trance were just as real as their sense of reality while awake, although this was not as much in evidence for the overall trance state.

PRESENCE OF OUTSIDE HYPNOTIST

Most of our subjects never imagined that an outside hypnotist was present who was actively involved during the experimental period. In fact, during the last 2 weeks only one subject fantasized that one was there. Even more rare was the imagining of the presence of an outside hypnotist who simply acted as an observer. Apparently our subjects felt quite free to experiment (since we encouraged them to do so and since this was a highly imaginative group, this is not at all surprising). Over four-fifths of them felt that the majority of the time they gave themselves suggestions that were not similar to those of the experimenter.

EGO ACTIVITY AND EGO RECEPTIVITY

Earlier in this chapter we discussed the uses of attention in hypnosis. In addition to questions about the deployment of attention, our subjects were asked how they felt generally during self-hypnosis. Were they actively giving themselves suggestions, directing their activity, or were they simply waiting and watching to see what emerged?

The questions on Ego Activity and Receptivity indicate that both occurred relatively often, although Ego Receptivity was reported to occur more frequently. All but a couple of our subjects actively gave themselves suggestions at some time during their trance. Almost two-thirds in fact felt they were active in deciding what they would do for much of the time they were in trance, although only half manifested this by designating a part of them to act as a "speaker." Some of this activity was directed toward solving problems, while a lesser amount went toward directing the flow of imagery. However, all but two of the subjects waited for stretches of time during the trance and "let things happen by themselves." These states were for many characterized by a feeling of passivity at least some of the time. In terms of their experiences while waiting and listening in a receptive mode, most subjects felt that the occurrence of images and thoughts was frequent and quite prominent, while surges of emotion, streams of words, and suggestions occurred much less frequently.

CONCLUSIONS

There are two general conclusions to be drawn from this study. First, since the subjects were selected for their high hypnotizability and self-selected for a high level of interest and persistence, and since the procedure was largely exploratory, the findings need further substantiation through research on larger samples testing specific hypotheses generated by this study. In addition, some of the questions in the SHPQ were too general, and more precise questions may help clarify the ambiguity of current responses.

Second, the ways in which aspects of self-hypnosis differ from those of our waking experience is not entirely clear. Our previous research (see Chapter 4) has demonstrated that attention is less focused in self-hypnosis than in heterohypnosis. However, from the current study, we know that attention for the most part is selectively focused in self-hypnosis: Many of our subjects alternated between actively focusing their attention and just letting it focus by itself. That is, our subjects seemed to vacillate between making active efforts to try to direct attention and at times receptively allowing material to drift into the focus of attention. Although attention in self-hypnosis is spent in selectively focusing on mental events, it may not be the same quality of focused attention that occurs in the waking state or in heterohypnosis (i.e., it vacillates).

Imagery in self-hypnosis, particularly visual imagery, is another area that needs further differentiation from imagery while awake. Visual imagery, sometimes felt to be dreamlike and sometimes felt to be like imagery in the waking state, was experienced in clear and vivid scenes, connected as in a story. These scenes involved fantasies of trips or adventure or dealt with personal problems. Most images, along with sensations and thoughts, were experienced as separate and discrete (i.e., one at a time rather than simultaneously). Thus, on the surface, imagery in self-hypnosis would not seem to be that different from imagery in the waking state. However, in terms of our subjects' experience of this state of consciousness, most felt that the activation of the mind was different from that in the waking state. Also, according to our subjects' descriptions in the diaries of their experiences in self-hypnosis (see Section B of Part II), they perceived not only the imagery but the entire experience as qualitatively different. Thus, it becomes imperative to more sharply distinguish self-hypnotic imagery in particular and self-hypnotic phenomena in general from those of our waking experience. It will be important to do research in which subjects compare their experiences in self-hypnosis, in heterohypnosis, and while awake—especially with regard to their imagery and modes of attention. To include the waking state would give us a reliable standard of comparison for both self-hypnosis and heterohypnosis, so that the unique characteristics of the three would be thrown more clearly into relief.

APPENDIX 5.1 REPRESENTATIVE QUESTIONS FROM
THE SELF-HYPNOSIS PROPER QUESTIONNAIRE (SHPQ)

(Roman numeral sections correspond to those in Appendix 4.1.)

II. *TRANCE INDUCTION (ABSORPTION)*

SHPQ #1. During self-hypnosis, you felt intensely absorbed in your trance experiences:

☐ more than 75% of the time

☐ between 50% and 75% of the time

☐ between 25% and 50% of the time

☐ less than 25% of the time

☐ never felt at all absorbed in your self-suggestions

IV. *SELECTIVE VS. EXPANSIVE ATTENTION*

SHPQ #6. If you were to describe a typical self-hypnosis hour, how would you rate the amount of *selective attention* to a small range of mental events in contrast to the amount of *expansion in attentional range* to include as many mental events as possible?

☐ a. nearly always selective; hardly ever expansive

☐ b. 75% selective; 25% expansive

☐ c. 50% selective; 50% expansive

☐ d. 25% selective; 75% expansive

☐ e. hardly ever selective; nearly always expansive

☐ f. you typically used your attention in some other way. Describe below:

V. *IMAGERY*

SHPQ #13. Below is a list of ways in which imagery may be experienced qualitatively. Check those ways which describe your experience in self-hypnosis; and to the right of those ways you checked, estimate the percentage of time your imagery was experienced in this way.

Occurred?   %

☐ resembled ordinary imagery as one can experience it in the waking state   ⎯⎯

☐ resembled the imagery experienced in dreams while asleep   ⎯⎯

☐ looked bizarre, complex, more like psychedelic imagery   ⎯⎯

☐ was more thought-like   ⎯⎯

☐ was mixed with many memories of past events   ⎯⎯

VI. *EXPERIENTIAL ASPECTS (TIME)*

SHPQ #17. Did your experience of time while in trance during self-hypnosis differ from your experience of time in the waking state? (Check those that apply.)

☐ trance time seemed to go faster than clock time

☐ trance time seemed to go slower than clock time

☐ it was difficult to measure how long you had been in trance

☐ you did not experience any difference between trance time and clock time

XI. *EGO ACTIVITY/RECEPTIVITY*

SHPQ #48. Long periods when you just waited for something to happen occurred in self-hypnosis (check one):

☐ more than 75% of the time

☐ between 50% and 75% of the time

☐ between 25% and 50% of the time

☐ less than 25% of the time

☐ never

CHAPTER 6

Structural and Content Characteristics of Self-Hypnosis

Self-hypnosis, like heterohypnosis (Fromm, 1977, 1978–1979, 1979), is an altered state of consciousness in which imagery plays an enormous role. As a result of our research, we differentiate between *structural* and *content* categories of phenomena that characterize self-hypnosis. Most of them are common to self-hypnosis and heterohypnosis, though some to varying degrees.

STRUCTURAL CHARACTERISTICS

The structural factors that comprise the essence of self-hypnosis are as follows:

1. The fading of the General Reality Orientation
2. Absorption in the experience
3. Expansive, free-floating Attention; that is, an ability to let the mind wander freely
4. Ego Receptivity; that is, the ability to relax and to allow preconscious and unconscious material to float into awareness
5. Rather large fluctuations in Trance Depth, particularly in the beginning of learning to employ self-hypnosis

The first two (the fading of the General Reality Orientation, and Absorption) set the stage for hypnosis per se—heterohypnosis as well as self-hypnosis. They are essential characteristics of both.

Certain parts of this chapter were presented in August 1982 by Erika Fromm as a paper at the Ninth International Congress of Hypnosis and Psychosomatic Medicine in Glasgow, Scotland, and published in 1985 by Fromm under the title "The Essential Aspects of Self-Hypnosis" in D. Waxman, P. C. Misra, M. Gibson, & M. A. Basker (Eds.), *Modern Trends in Hypnosis* (pp. 209–214). New York: Plenum Press. Reprinted by permission of the volume editors and the publisher.

However, two other structural characteristics differentiate self-hypnosis from heterohypnosis: expansive, free-floating Attention, and Ego Receptivity to stimuli coming from *within*. They are state-specific for self-hypnosis; by contrast, concentrative attention, and receptivity to stimuli coming from a single outside source (the hypnotist on whom the subject or patient steadily focuses her attention), are state-specific for heterohypnosis.

Self-hypnosis requires adaptation to the altered state. In the beginning of self-hypnosis there is a great deal of anxiety and self-doubt, particularly in the first few days. As the subjects become more familiar with the state, they feel more comfortable in it. They spend less time worrying about failures in self-suggestions or failures to reach a deep hypnotic trance state; their ability to enter trance easily and quickly increases, as does the fading of the General Reality Orientation, the absorption in the experience, and the trance depth.

Absorption, the sense of being caught up in the content of the session or in the phenomena experienced, has been recognized as being an important characteristic of heterohypnosis (J. R. Hilgard, 1970; Tellegen & Atkinson, 1974). It is equally important in self-hypnosis. The same holds for Shor's (1962) GRO factor, the fading of the General Reality Orientation. These two factors set the stage for *any* hypnotic experience and seem to be interdependent (see Chapter 4). Without the shift from the awareness of the world around us to a stronger sense of and absorption in the inner world, hypnotic trance, whether self-induced or induced by another, simply does not occur. Hypnotic trance essentially requires a shift away from the awareness of the external world to a greater sense of engagement with the events of one's inner world.

However, structurally, heterohypnosis and self-hypnosis are not entirely identical. Our 33 volunteer subjects—all highly hypnotizable in hetero-hypnosis—reported differences in the use of attention and concentration, differences in Ego Receptivity, and differences in depth of trance between heterohypnosis and self-hypnosis. More than two-thirds of our subjects felt that whereas in heterohypnosis they were very receptive to thoughts and ideas coming from the hypnotist (i.e., from *one* outside source), in self-hypnosis their Ego Receptivity turned to stimuli from within. In addition, they reported that in heterohypnosis their attention was concentrated (on the hypnotist), focused, and steady. In self-hypnosis *at times* it was concentrated on suggestions they gave to themselves; at other times in the same hour it would be relaxed and expansive. They would then do what William James (1902/1935) has described for other altered states as watching the stream of consciousness flow by.

After the first week of practice with self-hypnosis, more of the time was spent in states of focused attention than during the first week, when subjects explored the phenomena of self-hypnosis by "letting themselves go." In the beginning of practicing self-hypnosis, most subjects will allow their minds to roam and wander, and let as much material as possible enter their attentional field. Once our subjects had become accustomed to the altered state of self-hypnosis, their attention began to focus more often. It became more selective and concentrative. Thus in the beginning stages of self-hypnosis practice, the stance of attention is very different from that in heterohypnosis, where it is focused and concentrated. But as time goes on, it vacillates between expansion and concentration. Altogether, however, a significantly greater amount of time is spent in expanded, free-floating attention in self-hypnosis than in heterohypnosis.

In our comparison of heterohypnosis and self-hypnosis, we used standardized laboratory scales for heterohypnosis. Had we, as a comparison, run a heterohypnosis session such as one might do in hypnoanalysis, perhaps we might have found that in heterohypnosis, too, there can be a good deal of expansive attention, such as when the hypnoanalyst asks the patient to free-associate (i.e., to say whatever happens to come up in his mind).

Trance depth also undergoes greater fluctuation in self-hypnosis than in heterohypnosis. Our subjects reported that, particularly in the first week of self-hypnosis, they experienced fluctuations in trance depth much more frequently than in heterohypnosis. They also had greater trouble in the first week with getting into trance than they had when there was an outside hypnotist to help them. This first-week difficulty was probably due to skepticism. Many subjects doubted that they would be able to go into self-hypnosis, and it took about a week of practice before they could trust their own ability to induce trance.

CONTENT CHARACTERISTICS

Among the content categories, heightened, vivid imagery in self-hypnosis stands out above all from other content categories, such as memories spontaneously experienced or intentionally explored, working on one's problems, age regression, and feelings of skepticism as to whether one would be able to reach a "deep enough" hypnotic state.

The imagery characteristic of self-hypnosis is very vivid and realistic, occurring both in story-like sequences and in segmented, unconnected flashes. Subjects are struck by the quantity and richness of the imagery experienced in self-hypnosis. It is much more vivid than the imagery induced in heterohypnosis in the laboratory without therapeutic intent. The imagery in self-hypnosis tends to be oriented toward personally important experiences and fantasies; it is personally meaningful. Geometric shapes also are often seen. But no complex, bizarre conglomerations, as one might find in hallucinogenic experiences, arose in any of our subjects.

While there was a good deal of self-doubt about being able to achieve deep stages of trance in self-hypnosis, particularly in the first week of practice, subjects reported much less self-consciousness during self-hypnosis than during heterohypnosis. Self-consciousness occurs when one is embarrassed or doubts oneself in the presence of somebody else. Our subjects were alone in a room. No one was with them, and thus there was less self-consciousness.

DISCUSSION

As stated before, our subjects practiced self-hypnosis for a month daily. As time went on, they became better acquainted with the self-hypnotic state, felt more "at home" with it, spent less time worrying about occasional failures in self-suggestions, and no longer needed to give themselves detailed self-suggestions. In order to go into a self-hypnotic trance, often our "highly successful" and "successful" subjects after a week or two needed to do no more than sit in a chair and close their eyes. The self-hypnotic trance state became more comfortable and more natural. The ease of entering trance increased, the time required to do so decreased, and focusing attention when one wanted to do so became easier. Reality awareness (General Reality Orientation) faded more and more, and feelings of absorption increased, as did the ability to enter deeper states of trance quickly. But we did find that not all subjects who are deeply hypnotizable by someone else can hypnotize themselves deeply. One of the main criteria in our process of selecting subjects had been that they be deeply hypnotizable in heterohypnosis. However, 3 of our 33 subjects, throughout the whole month of practice, could induce only very light states of self-hypnosis. Another 27 achieved medium and sometimes deep states, and only 3 went into very deep stages of trance practically every day.

Depending on the subjects' particular needs and problems, the content of the self-hypnotic trance may be different for individual subjects. But the five structural components—absorption, expansive attention, trance depth, fading of the General Reality Orientation, and Ego Receptivity—are exerting some form of influence on the content dimensions, as well as on one another. They are interdependent. For instance, as one becomes more and more ego-receptive to stimuli coming from one's preconscious and unconscious, more and more absorbed in the inner experience, the General Reality Orientation fades increasingly into the background and one goes into deeper trance states. Similarly, when attention is more focused in trance, one's ability to go deeper is enhanced and one's awareness of the outside world fades further into the background. But we could also say that as the subject's ability to enter trance quickly and efficiently develops, his absorption in the trance phenomena becomes greater, which in turn is related to the fading of awareness of the external surroundings.

Thus, absorption is affected by the way in which Ego Receptivity and attention are being *used*, but the reverse is also true. If Ego Receptivity and expansive or concentrative attention are turned toward the inside, absorption occurs. In self-hypnosis, absorption, Ego Receptivity, and attention are turned toward the inside. In heterohypnosis, they are fixated on what the hypnotist suggests.

We do not conceptualize the structural components as having primary causal effects on one another or on the contents of the self-hypnotic experience. But we do conceive of them as interdependent structures superordinate to the content of the experience in self-hypnosis.

The content of the phenomena reported in any self-hypnosis experience reflects the individual's choices. The quality and the strength of the experiences are closely interwoven with the structural aspects of self-hypnosis. These structural variables exert a great influence on the nature of the experience. On the basis of their interaction and as the result of continued practice, they define—within broad parameters—the intensity, the depth of involvement, and the beauty of the experience.

Analyses of the Diaries:
Cognitive Processes
and Personality Correlates

CHAPTER 7

The Analysis of the Self-Hypnosis Journals: Introduction

Self-hypnosis is a very subjective, personal, inner experience. How did subjects participating in these studies make use of their newly learned self-hypnosis skill? Since subjects were required to keep a journal following each daily self-hypnosis session, the subjective reports of subjects were used as idiographic data for a more complete description and understanding of the phenomena of self-hypnosis.

All entries in journals were made immediately following each session. The record of each session included this information:

- The date
- The time of day
- Duration of trance
- Specific self-suggestions attempted and whether they were successful or not
- Amount of time subjects remained in trance without doing anything specific, and whatever may have occurred during those times
- Depth of trance as specified in Tart's (1972, 1979) instructions for the Extended North Carolina Scale (ENCS) right after induction, during the middle of the trance, and before termination of trance
- Critical reflection on each aspect of the experience, and general reflection on the entire experience
- The most significant self-hypnosis experience of that day

An earlier version of this chapter was published as a portion of a paper titled "The Phenomena and Characteristics of Self-Hypnosis" by Erika Fromm, Daniel P. Brown, Stephen W. Hurt, Joab Z. Oberlander, Andrew M. Boxer, and Gary Pfeifer in the July 1981 issue of the *International Journal of Clinical and Experimental Hypnosis, 29*, 189–246. Copyrighted by The Society for Clinical and Experimental Hypnosis, July 1981. Reprinted by permission of the coauthors and the journal editor.

Journals were turned over to experimenters after the 1-month experiment was terminated. Six subjects frequently forgot to make entries into their journals; therefore their journals were not used in this qualitative analysis, which was based on the daily journal entries of the other 27 subjects.

These written reports of subjects were taken as introspective testimony to aid in the elucidation of individual differences and variations not readily apparent in the more objective, statistical treatment of other data collected (see Section A of Part II). Each journal was coded according to criteria developed from the pilot studies (see Chapter 3):

- Ease of induction
- Kinds of self-suggestions used and styles of carrying out suggestions
- Depth of trance
- Personal meaningfulness of the self-hypnosis experience
- Changes in primary- and secondary-process thinking
- Changes in attention and concentration
- Changes in memory
- Changes in Ego Activity, Passivity, and Receptivity
- Changes in awareness of mental processes
- Initial versus final reactions to self-hypnosis
- Task orientation of the subject—that is, how the subject approached self-hypnosis (was she goal-directed or more oriented to exploration?)

The four salient and stable characteristics that emerged from the quantitative analyses as structural aspects of self-hypnosis (Absorption, Generalized Reality Orientation, Attention, and Trance Depth) were readily discernible in the journals and formed the background against which the multitude of experiences were reported by subjects.

SUCCESS WITH SELF-HYPNOSIS

While there was a great deal of variation in the styles and experiences of self-hypnosis reported by subjects, they may be roughly grouped into three categories that reflect the overall success and enjoyment of their month-long experiment with self-hypnosis, as they perceived and wrote about it.

The first group, containing only 2 subjects of the group of 27 who made daily journal entries, had many difficulties entering and achieving what they felt was an acceptable trance. This small number of individuals defined their self-hypnosis experiences as mostly unsuccessful, even though they had proven themselves highly capable of heterohypnosis on the standard scales. On Day 1 John wrote,

"Very agonizing experience. Did not feel like I could get into a trance at all. Body felt tired, aching (maybe not enough sleep). Tried to do the 150-breath induction. Kept losing count and drifting away, which made me more and more frustrated. . . . There are many things I want to try, but I feel as though I am incapable of even a light trance. If I can concentrate enough, I think I will overcome this negativity and frustration."

At the end of his experience, a month later, John wrote,

"This last week was so bad I didn't enter anything into the journal. I either fell asleep or became so tensed up and frustrated that nothing happened. I think that having come to the last week without getting to the state I wanted has been the source of extreme frustration and tension. . . . I want to get into a deep state—period. I have things to try, both for intellectual curiosity and practical ends."

The particular case of John may underscore the importance of personality factors and self-imposed demands in this experiment and in self-hypnosis in general, since all subjects who participated had tested at high levels on the heterohypnotic susceptibility scales. Whether his expectations were just unrealistic, or whether he was trying too relentlessly, is difficult to discern from what he wrote in his journal. Although John's frustration may tell us more about his personality than his experiences with self-hypnosis, both subjects in this "unsuccessful" group struggled with trying to achieve a "deep," or what they considered to be a satisfactory, state of self-hypnosis.

The second group of individuals' experiences fell into what we have called the "successful" group. The 22 subjects in this group—the great majority of the sample who completed the study and kept regular journals—all adopted individual styles of induction that suited their tastes and needs, and proceeded to experiment with self-hypnosis. Some found their experiences more satisfying and meaningful than others did, but overall they found their experiment with self-hypnosis interesting and successful over the 4 weeks of practice.

On Day 3 Ronald reported,

"I began with the same induction procedure I have been using—staring at a target—relaxation—elevator imagery—counting breaths. The only difference I noticed today was that the trance inducement occurred much more spontaneously and I was more absorbed in the process (i.e., I felt less those nagging little voices that tell me all the other things I should be doing). I was capable of entering a much more absorbing inner focus. The problem seems to be one of loosening the mind from the preoccupation with those mental frameworks which are associated with the accomplishment of reality-oriented daily tasks. If it had not been for the experiences this self-hypnosis session brought to my awareness (my acid-induced experiences [4 years earlier]), I would probably have remained much more exclusively aware of conventional reality and a lot less convinced about inner possibilities of another sort of 'reality.' "

The remaining three subjects had highly successful, unusual, and re-markable self-hypnosis sessions. The journals of these individuals were quite innovative and creative. Some subjects even illustrated their journals with elaborate drawings made during their self-hypnosis experiences. Susan, perhaps our most self-hypnotizable subject, wrote on Day 1,

> "I went into hypnosis fairly easily and let myself sink. I did the arm-rigidity suggestion to start out with. Then I let myself go deeper and into a trance. Then I began to regress first to 14 years and then down to second grade. I became 10 years old and at the time when my first cat died. I started to cry and then sob as I did when it actually died. I held onto it and rocked it in my arms and cried. I had to bury it so I found a beautiful spot under an acacia tree. I dug a hole and put Sasha into it."

At times, when subjects gave themselves no specific suggestions, they experienced some drowsiness. Shor (1979) has discussed drowsiness as an important variable of hypnosis, although unrelated to hypnotic depth. It is important to note, however, that drowsiness may have served different functions for different subjects. For John, who had little success with self-hypnosis and never really got off the ground, drowsiness and frequent sleep may have served as a defense against self-hypnosis of which he was perhaps unconsciously afraid, although he desired it consciously (e.g., "Nothing to report but sleep. Frustrating . . ."). Susan, on the other hand, often experienced drowsiness and rarely fell asleep, although once she wrote,

> "I was in this trance and woke up the next morning somewhat disoriented since I hadn't finished my hypnosis last night and hadn't written anything down. I realized, of course, I had fallen asleep; I wasn't really very tired either."

VOLITIONAL CONTROL OVER INDUCTION AND DEEPENING

As reflected in these journal entries, induction became an automatized pro-cedure for most subjects, and they often developed idiosyncratic cues that quickly brought them into trance. For the two subjects in the unsuccessful group, induction continued to be difficult throughout the month-long period. The 25 subjects in the other two groups, by the halfway mark, were able to flow with the self-hypnosis experience relatively easily. Being able to control their self-hypnosis experience, however, was an issue of concern to all subjects—both in terms of trance induction and, once in trance, with directing their self-hypnosis experience for that particular day. As John (the subject quoted earlier) indicated, the more he struggled to control and achieve self-hypnosis, the more failure he experienced. Julie, however, a representative of the large middle group, presented a different perspective. On Day 6 she wrote,

> "I've been finding it easier and easier to get into trance. I barely have to use devices (staring at a paper clip or my thumbnail); just 'wanting to' puts me in a light trance. I have to work harder to get from, say, the 20s or 30s to the 50s–70s [she changed the ENCS to go to 100]. Sometimes I get in a deeper trance, but I'm not sure why."

Julie spoke for those of our successful and highly successful subjects who were able to enter hypnosis more easily with practice, but some of whom often experienced spontaneous fluctuations in trance depth.

It seems appropriate to think of a control issue in terms of nonconscious involvement (see Shor, 1979). In adapting and accustoming themselves to experiencing self-hypnosis, subjects had to learn to think of two levels of volitional control. One level was within the boundaries of their own conscious directives; the second was beyond their conscious control. This often proved perplexing to subjects, as Madeleine wrote on Day 10 of self-hypnosis:

> "Experiences become so real that control seems to be out of my hands. And it is a different sort of control loss from simply daydreaming or sleeping, because I can come out of it whenever I want to. It is as if I become so entranced by the places my mind goes that I want to stay there."

COGNITIVE CHANGES

Quantitative data (see Chapter 4, Table 4.4) indicated that 79% of subjects experienced a decrease in the Generalized Reality Orientation over time. This was commonly expressed in the journals of subjects by their recognition of the reality of their experiences. Malcolm aptly expressed this (Day 24):

> "Today's entire experience will be hard to relate, since all of it was experienced as one big daydream. Each experience seemed very real, as if I was experiencing them then and now."

After ending their self-hypnosis sessions, subjects reflected upon the logical inconsistencies of their experiences. During self-hypnosis it appeared as if there was little or no self-reflection. Louise wrote (Day 14),

"I continue to be impressed by the intensity of feeling these images evoke, and how, at least in trance, their meaning seems so clear. Once awake, some of it feels rather silly and immature."

This is similar to the so-called "profound" thoughts reported by individuals in other altered states of consciousness, such as a marijuana-induced state.

Slightly over three-quarters of our subjects (76%) were able to become increasingly absorbed in their self-hypnosis experiences during the course of the month. This manifested itself in subjects' journals through the variety of activities, images, and ideas that they experienced and wrote about. On Day 12 Marilyn wrote,

"I did 150 breaths. I notice a timelessness when I am at this point. Kind of like no past, no future, only the present. I also feel very singular and alone. Like I am it? I will try to be clearer. It sometimes is as if nobody else exists, although I'm not actively thinking that. I just feel so isolated and secure. I went into my dream. I was on a green hill somewhere in Europe. It was a fine day. I was looking at an ancient castle. I was walking toward it. It was huge and very impressive."

These three-quarters of our successful and highly successful subjects experienced alternations in attentional processes. They would often try to selectively focus their own attention to a particular end—having a dream, an ideomotor task, a posthypnotic suggestion. Or subjects would simply let things happen and give themselves no specific suggestions. At the beginning of her self-hypnosis experience, Sarah described this (Day 2):

"Spent at least half the time not doing anything—that is, not consciously controlling anything. But thoughts would slip into my head—daydreams pulling me along. There is a great deal of difference between when I try to dream . . . (when I actually tell myself that I will have a dream), and when this type of uncontrolled daydreaming occurs (which is very much like having a real dream). . . . What is the difference? The thoughts of my past . . . were extremely vivid, but more like snapshots than movies, remembering one single instance. And when I tried to explore the instant longer by moving [making it into a movie?], it was very difficult to do so."

Previous research conducted in our laboratory has shown that perceptual and cognitive processes are infused with more primary process in hypnosis than in the waking state (Fromm, Oberlander, & Gruenewald, 1970). In the present study, 64% of our subjects experienced greater receptivity in self-hypnosis than in heterohypnosis, and it appeared from the journals that subjects were more receptive to *internal* states. Peter noted in his journal on Day 16 of self-hypnosis,

"Today I again tried to have a dream but it didn't work. Instead I got a number of disconnected images, friends, family, scenery. Also, I heard simultaneously the first movement of Bach's 'Second English Suite,' which my father plays; and the song from *Sgt. Pepper*—'I'm Fixing a Hole Where the Rain Gets In.' This last seemed particularly appropriate: I couldn't 'stop my mind from wandering.' Also, I couldn't hear only one piece of music. I could get one to predominate, but couldn't halt the other one. After about 20 minutes I gave up and stopped."

The subjects were sometimes receptive and other times, after they had become accustomed to self-hypnosis, actively chose to be receptive. As Mitchell wrote on Day 13,

"I decided to let my mind wander. It came to focus on a beautiful Oriental rug, composed of the colors blue, red, and white. I proceeded to ask myself what was so important about this rug. This is when the dream began to happen. I found that I lay down on the rug and rolled myself up in it. I did not remain rolled up in it too long before a beautiful girl with the most extraordinary long brown hair arrived upon the scene. She unrolled the carpet and took me by the hand. She led me to a flight of stairs until I became exhausted. I fell asleep and that was the end. It was amazing how vivid this experience was to me."

Like Mitchell's, the journals of 75% of subjects were filled with abundantly rich descriptions of imagery.

Many subjects reported experiencing, partially successfully, what they called "age regressions." We suspect that some of these incidents were hypermnesias rather than actual age regressions, as Justin himself distinguished:

"I spent the remaining time [today] on suggesting a regression to childhood experiences and a dream. I wanted to regress to climbing a tree in the backyard at the time I was about 7–8 years old. Again, this was only partially successful. I had moderately clear images of the experience but I was only an observer— there was little, if any, 'first-person' experience. I then explored other locations in my childhood environment to see if I could encounter an experience or memory that would allow me to regress totally and actively participate, but this was not successful."

Some subjects reported associations from the past based on experiences in self-hypnosis, as Marilyn did on Day 22:

"I dreamt I went into our cuckoo clock. All of the wooden characters formed a path or a lane. I walked down this lane (all of the characters were life-size and beautifully painted) into a park. Everything in the park was made of candy or ice cream and beautifully decorated. I think that this is from an Oswald Rabbit comic book I read as a child. . . . Everything was lovely and I was the only real person there."

Others tried to recall and regress to more recent events as Charles did (Day 19):

"I suggested to myself that I go back in time 10 weeks to spring quarter break. I saw myself with my friend from the university. I could see the sun shining and a wide expanse of country from the inside of the boxcar in which we were riding. I could see cotton in the fields before the train slowed. We came through a very small town and I could see a group of children about ages 10–14. They didn't see me and were trying to throw rocks into the open boxcar. I almost got hit."

INTERPERSONAL CONTEXT

A special effort was made, throughout the self-hypnosis project, to minimize transference. For this reason, no subject was ever seen by any given experimenter more than two times. One subjects' response to our efforts to minimize transference is clearly illustrated in Rita's "hypnotic dream," which she wrote about on Day 3 of her self-hypnosis:

"First of all, bubbles—large soap bubbles reflecting the rainbow on their surfaces appeared. Some floated independently, but most were joined together. I found myself floating more, and as I floated lower and lower I went into a deeper and deeper trance. Soon I noticed other people in bubbles. The first I met was a unicorn.[1] Vain, haughty, but incredibly beautiful, the unicorn could not pierce her [its?] bubble. It spoke to me, saying, 'You do not need my help.' I could not reply, for that bubble drifted away with the unicorn admiring itself or perhaps the world in general. Next was my friend Dana. She was rolling in her bubble trying to get out. . . . Dr. Fromm was in another bubble, but far away, with many bubbles between us. Her bubble, to my surprise (in the dream, that is), was larger, and she wasn't struggling to get out. I met some other people and just talked—friendly people, interesting. . . ."

TWO FORMS OF SELF-OBSERVATION

In self-hypnosis, self-observation can be based on seeing what one can *do* with regard to distorting reality, as well as on watching the imagery that

---

[1] This is a reference to one of the experimenters, who at that time wore his long hair knotted into a bun above his forehead.

arises in one's mind. McConkey, Sheehan, and White (1979) have pointed out these two facets in the items of the Creative Imagination Scale (CIS) of Wilson and Barber (1978). On the CIS the subject is asked to "think along" with the hypnotist—which we conceive of as doing some self-hypnosis while heterohypnosis is being induced.

The subjects' diaries abounded with reports of fantasy and imagery. They also contained instances of self-observation, while attempting to distort reality in self-hypnosis. Two examples follow. Donald conducted his self-hypnosis experiences in a highly experimental and structured manner. On Day 11 he wrote,

> "Suggestions [today]: that I would smell a lemon without visualizing it first; that I would feel my legs and feet moving as if walking without visualizing anything; that I would smell freshly cut grass . . . and that I would taste a specific candy bar without visualizing it. Suggestions were successful."

George's journal reads largely as a series of challenges and motor items that he tried and usually was successful experiencing, while with fantasy items he rarely succeeded. For example, he wrote on Day 11,

> "Lightness in legs, rising in air. Sensation of being in a boat. Dream, unsuccessful."

George never made any real personal use of self-hypnosis, and his experiences in self-hypnosis were always exploratory of what he could do, never emotionally profound.

MOTIVATION FOR THE SELF-HYPNOTIC EXPERIENCE

There is a good deal of variation in the personal meaningfulness that self-hypnosis held for subjects. We believe this is related to what we have termed "task orientation." Some subjects approached self-hypnosis as explorers embarking on an exciting journey. They tried to experience different things, from imagery and age regression to negative hallucinations. Other subjects were oriented to specific goals, giving themselves a set of self-suggestions that they had previously structured. Many tried to make some functional use of self-hypnosis, be it for studying better, for stopping smoking, or for more profound problems (such as one woman who was in the midst of working through the untimely death of her husband; see Chapter 14 for more details). Joel was our prototypical explorer. At the beginning of his journal he wrote,

"Before I begin my first self-hypnosis session, I want to clarify why I'm doing it and what I hope to get out of it. The focus of my self-hypnosis shall be extending and deepening my dialogue with the unconscious. Through inducing deep trance states and experimenting with suggestions I hope to facilitate a more fruitful exchange between my normal waking state and inner realms generally outside my range of experience. I believe that much . . . (images, energy, inspiration) is to be gained by cultivating a receptivity to the unknown within."

By Day 24, Joel's journal allowed us to glean the impact of his experience with self-hypnosis:

"I thought I'd take a little time to reflect on the impact of my self-hypnosis experiences on my life. First, the vividness (i.e., the clarity, autonomy, and affective power) of my inner geography has been stunning to me. By its salience it has claimed a "reality" in my life I wouldn't have thought possible. In a way this is great, it's fantastic. It provides a sense of mystery and adventure—creates a fascinating world to explore. Yet it is disturbing, too, and wreaks havoc in a sense with my ordered, disciplined life."

As subjects became more familiar with self-hypnosis, many of them began to work on problems of a personal nature. Sarah gave herself suggestions that she eat less. On Day 15 she wrote,

"Not only have I decreased my food intake appreciably, but I have also virtually stopped smoking, and I have become more aware of myself in relation to other people around me."

Two days later she began to explore her overeating in more depth:

"I began by asking why it is that I feel I must eat so much—where the compulsion to eat arose. The image that came to my mind was first a fuzzy one of being in a cradle—then I saw myself as a little girl stealing cookies from the cookie jar in defiance of my mother. By stealing food I could rebel against her authority, but at the same time I was punishing myself by being overweight. . . . I began suggesting a way out of this—being that I have totally grown out of my mother's judicial range."

Malcolm expressed a great deal of anger at his parents by fantasizing their death:

"Tonight's experience was quite strange, but a very deep and successful one. It mainly worked as a method of venting my anger toward my parents, with whom I had a serious fight right before. All of the suggestions occurred in my mind spontaneously. The first suggestion was that I scream. I did not actually scream, but saw myself screaming and heard this scream quite vividly. I was in a room with my two parents and two brothers. The first thing I noticed was a chain lying on the floor."

Malcolm wrote that in his fantasy he killed his parents and then further noted,

"The most disturbing factor about this dream was that none of it seemed unpleasant to me as I was having it. It was all very pleasant, in fact. The . . . entire experience today was a very intense emotional experience. I felt the most relaxed I have ever felt in a long time."

While the factor analyses (again, see Chapter 4, Table 4.4) indicated that the personal meaningfulness of self-hypnosis decreased over time for 76% of our subjects, the journals revealed that individuals had both "peak" experiences and times when the same subjects were bored, grew tired, or experienced some frustration in not succeeding with the particular suggestions they initiated. There were both ups and downs across the 4 weeks for most individuals in the middle group, but not for those subjects in the high- and low-success groups.

Self-hypnosis was a skill or a tool that was used in a multitude of ways. Having to practice every day in a specific environment and to report on those experiences was a constraint, the effects of which cannot fully be determined. One subject wrote,

"I intend to continue to practice [self-hypnosis] but my sessions will be of shorter duration."

On their final day, most subjects reported a good deal of satisfaction at having participated in the study. Sandra wrote,

"I have enjoyed it [self-hypnosis] and feel I have learned a lot—I will continue with it, I hope, for a long time. It has been very much a learning experience."

It might be useful to know whether and which subjects continued after some years to use self-hypnosis and to what particular ends.

It is interesting to note what Susan, our most imaginative and self-hypnotizable subject, revealed in her last journal entry:

"I did my hypnosis on the bus coming back to Hyde Park along Lake Shore Drive [she was, of course, not supposed to practice self-hypnosis in any place other than in the designated study]. It was very interesting. The people and the inside of the bus were like an illustration. Each person became somebody to me. I felt apart from the scene, just watching. I watched the bus driver, who seemed like a character in a short story. When I got off the bus I walked very slowly. And time slowed down with me. I suggested that my legs be very heavy and difficult to move. They became so. Then I suggested they be light, and I floated home. It was very pleasant. I believe I've walked around in trances before without realizing it. The world becomes a new place. Never dull."

But even Susan, who was at the top of the distribution of all subjects in terms of hypnotizability and imagination, did not always consistently report unusual and deep self-hypnotic experiences.

Some of our subjects undoubtedly reread the accounts of their self-hypnosis experiences written during the month-long experiment; this unique intersection of past and present, via the subjects' own works, likely had some effect on the ways in which they ordered and reordered their experiences and changes in themselves, in personally meaningful ways.

In summary, considering all of the subjects' self-reports, it can certainly be concluded that even among these highly hypnotizable individuals, at least within self-hypnosis, there was a great deal of individual variation of ability. Although the structural characteristics we have outlined are important boundaries within which self-hypnosis is organized, there are definite limits to what these characteristics tell us about the experiences of any given individual practicing self-hypnosis. The reports in subjects' journals did indicate that within any particular individual, the phenomena of self-hypnosis have the possibility of an infinite number of forms and meanings. Each subject's journal constitutes a personal text; in the next chapter, we hermeneutically examine three of these texts in greater detail.

CHAPTER 8

Representations of Self-Hypnosis in Personal Narratives

This chapter also is based on the analysis of the journal narratives. The 33 journals, as noted in Chapter 7, were divided into three groups based on the subjects' overall success in self-hypnosis (as perceived by the subjects themselves): (1) One group of 3 subjects had extraordinarily successful self-hypnosis sessions; (2) 27 subjects felt their sessions were successful; and (3) the remaining 3 subjects defined their self-hypnosis experiences as unsuccessful.[1] Three journals have been selected, one from each group. The most noteworthy parts of these journals are presented and discussed here.

The diaries of the three highly successful subjects were extremely interesting, imaginative, and colorful. Those of the three unsuccessful subjects were boring because they are totally without fantasy.

SCORING CATEGORIES

Scoring categories had been developed from the quantitative results of the self-hypnosis questionnaires (see Chapter 4). Many of these were also used in the analyses of the diaries. But in analyzing the diaries we were also open to the possibility of finding new categories. Indeed, several new categories emerged: insight, strong affect, dissociation, and amnesia.

---

[1] Actually, 6 of our 33 subjects did not make regular entries in their journals. The 27 remaining subjects included the 3 who were highly successful, 22 who were successful, and 2 who were unsuccessful.

An earlier version of this chapter was published under the same title in 1985 by Erika Fromm, Andrew M. Boxer, and Daniel P. Brown, in D. Waxman, P. C. Misra, M. Gibson, and M. A. Basker (Eds.), *Modern Trends in Hypnosis* (pp. 215–222). New York: Plenum Press. Reprinted by permission of the coauthors, the volume editors, and the publisher.

As we had done before, we established three types of categories: structure, content, and context. This chapter is concerned only with structure and content.

The structural categories included the following:

Concentrative Attention
Expansive Attention
Ego Activity
Ego Receptivity
Ego Inactivity
Trance Depth
Vacillation of Trance Depth
Fading of the General Reality Orientation
Absorption

The content categories we established on the basis of the analysis of the diaries were as follows:

Imagery
Age Regression
Personal Memories
Dreams (usually induced by self-suggestion)
Strong Affect
Working on Problems
Suggestion of Motor Phenomena
Suggestion of Sensory Phenomena

To our surprise, diary entries that could be scored as indicating fading of the General Reality Orientation, or Absorption, were very rare. In the questionnaires that were given at the end of 4 weeks of self-hypnosis, we asked our subjects specific questions about these areas. Their answers showed that General Reality Orientation and Absorption were very important structural factors. But only a few subjects spontaneously mentioned in their diaries that they were so absorbed in the experiment that the General Reality Orientation seemed to fade into the background. We felt that to become spontaneously aware of these two categories requires a good deal of psychological sophistication, more than our naive subjects had. In their diaries they tended to report what they had *done* each day (giving themselves suggestions, working on their own problems, etc.) or the content of what they had experienced, such as vivid Imagery, Strong Affect, or an Age Regression. Most of them reported Absorption and the fading of the General Reality Orientation only when specifically asked about them after the month-long experiment was over.

Let us now sample three diaries, and note the differences we have observed among our very successful, our successful, and our unsuccessful subjects. We start with a subject from our largest group (27 out of a total of 33 subjects), the successful subjects; we then proceed to the very successful group, and conclude with the unsuccessful group.

A SUCCESSFUL SUBJECT'S NARRATIVE

Michael, a successful subject, developed a great deal of imagery, particularly between the 7th and 23rd days. He also made a task for himself to dream a dream every day—that is, to *suggest* to himself that he dream a dream.

Already on the second day Michael experienced vacillations between Ego Activity and Ego Receptivity, as well as between Concentrative Attention and Expansive Attention.

> "I closed my eyes and continued to observe the colors and patterns on my eyelids. I was able to suggest seeing various colors, especially blue and magenta. I also observed several patterns and shapes moving and changing against the color background. Oddly, the more I tried to focus my attention on these patterns, the fewer and less interesting the patterns became. I continued to watch the patterns but without paying strict attention to them. In general, most of the shapes were abstract or geometric, but occasionally I would recognize a person's face or body or some other object. These images continued to appear, as if they were being generated effortlessly by my mind. I found this stream of images and patterns intriguing and satisfying."

On Day 4, Michael became frustrated because the harder he tried to concentrate on the suggestions that he gave to himself, the less he succeeded in deepening the trance. He still wanted to control the experience.

On Day 7, he added Imagery to Ego Activity to deepen the trance, quickly followed by Ego Receptivity. He let it happen rather than trying to force it, and thus became much more successful in his endeavor to deepen the trance.

On Day 8 he allowed even more Ego Receptivity, which led to Imagery; he also used less Ego Activity and control.

> "In this session I decided to take a less structured approach to any deepening suggestions. After induction I concentrated solely on my breathing—I tried to see it as an involuntary and effortless process, and I tried to concentrate on the movement of air through the nose and lungs. This was very relaxing, and before long my concentration was diverted by many types of spontaneous images."

On Day 9 he again allowed more Ego Receptivity and Expansive Attention, which led to a wealth of Imagery and a beautiful dream, the latent content of which exemplifies self-hypnosis as a regression in the service of the ego:

> "I spent rather longer than usual in trying to go deeper, but it seemed that trying even in this abstract way was not very effective for producing a deep trance. As soon as I stopped concentrating on my breathing, imagery began to occur spontaneously. There was such a quantity of imagery that I felt I didn't have time to evaluate or explore it—I could relax and observe. It was as if my imagination was overflowing with miscellaneous ideas.
>
> "My dream for this period was somewhat disjointed and discontinuous. First I am with a group of people—they seem to be my friends, although I don't recognize any of them. We are on our way to a sports arena to watch some kind of professional game. We arrive and buy our tickets and walk into the arena through a long series of dingy corridors. When we get inside there are only a few people present, although the arena is huge. While I am talking to my friends, I suddenly notice the playing field has changed to grass and the 'inside' of the arena is actually 'outside.' Further, everyone is now dancing on the grass—I think this is very puzzling. But I don't mention it to anyone. My next image is that I am dancing myself—swinging a girl around very fast, like I used to do playing as a child."

But he continued to struggle between the tendency to want to control all of his experiences and the rising knowledge that he should let go. Because he could not really relinquish control, he was unable to learn that letting go (i.e., Ego Receptivity and Expansive Attention) would lead deeper and faster into the profound stages of trance he wanted to achieve than would Ego Activity and Concentrative Attention.

Michael was a successful, talented subject. But unlike Susan, the *highly* successful subject we discuss next, he also was a person to whom control meant a great deal. This prevented him from being *very* successful in self-hypnosis.

A VERY SUCCESSFUL SUBJECT'S NARRATIVE

Contrast Michael's report with the narrative of Susan, one of our excellent (very successful) subjects who was not a bit concerned about "letting go." This subject, in reality, was an 18-year-old girl, but her imagination encompassed a wide range of ages. Here is an excerpt from Day 3:

> "Again I spent more time in a quiet trance with occasional thoughts running through. I regressed to a baby, first newborn, then 8 months, and then 1 year

old, then 2, and then 9, and back to 18. As newborn I hardly moved. I just lay there and looked around the room. Everything looked new and big. At 8 months I moved and sucked my hand and made sounds. At 1 I rocked and repeated 'mommy' and 'daddy' and made odd sounds. By the time I was 9 I was bargaining with the popsicle man to give me a popsicle and some dry ice. I then went back up to 18. I was a cat for a few minutes and did a lot of purring. The most interesting part tonight was being a baby. Not being able to talk or sit up, just gurgle."

Effortlessly, she went into all kinds of interesting experiences and imagery, but kept enough control (again effortlessly) to get herself out of uncomfortable hypnotic situations and into more enjoyable ones, as in the following example (Day 6):

"First of all today, I suggested I was a prisoner in my room. I was going to be in it alone for a year. I went around, pacing, touching the walls and doors nervously. I became quite upset. I sat down and dreamed I was in a dungeon with bread and water being thrown in to me.

"Then I was no longer a prisoner in my room or in a dungeon. I was in a harem. Just lying around lazily doing nothing except draw, bathe, munch, and talk, and sitting in total luxury. Then it appeared that some of my friends were in it. Then I was in a tent in the desert by myself. The dry cool wind was blowing over my body. I was a dancer; I was tired but cool after a hot day. Then I became wounded, a dying person on a battlefield with dead and dying bodies around me. It was so very awful and hideous that I quickly changed before I fully took on the suggestion. At this point a deck of cards was shuffled right before me. An old woman was telling my fortune. I didn't want to hear it, however, so I picked up the cards. Also today my back hurt; so I suggested this pain wasn't there, and it felt better.

"The highlights today were being in a harem and lying in the tent just because I found it pleasurable. However, being in prison made me very upset and I almost cried. It was terrible to think of being completely alone in the room for a year. I also disliked being a dying person today on a battlefield and I'm glad I didn't get into it (although I think I should have)."

Most of Susan's experiences were delightful and interesting to her. They also give the reader the strong impression that the subject always experienced Deep Absorption and fading of the General Reality Orientation. But she rarely mentioned these two factors in her diary.

This 18-year-old girl, in her typical adolescent identity struggle (Erikson, 1959/1980), used the self-hypnotic experience to put herself into many niches and life roles in order to find one that would fit her.

Here are some more examples showing Susan's rich imagery. On Day 16 she reflected:

"Today I went into trance for 10 minutes and decided to become an old woman. I had some crocheting next to me that I was doing, and so I started it. I was talking to a grandchild—telling a story. I was very old. I moved creakily and slowly. Every chain I made crocheting was an effort. I was telling a story about my brother and a woman. I told it carefully, and each word was said so slowly that I'd forget what the entire sentence was. I got tired telling the story and crocheting, so I told my grandchild to let me rest. I went back into a restful trance. I really like becoming different characters. I go into a trance and either decide what character I want to be ahead of time, or just let whatever happens happen. I count to 5 or so, and then suddenly I'm that person. I get more and more into the role as time goes on. When I have no character in mind I count and then just start talking. Soon I realize what person I am, and it seems natural. I can then just slide into new roles, each as real as the last. My feelings become those of the new person. I laugh, think, cry, gossip over my new character's concerns. I suddenly know all sorts of different people involved in her life. It's really interesting, and I enjoy doing it."

AN UNSUCCESSFUL SUBJECT'S NARRATIVE

Of our two unsuccessful subjects, one, Joe, was too cerebral. He constantly observed himself, analyzing what he was doing or not able to do, and tried to find a computer-like system that would enable him to be both ego-active (giving himself instructions) and able to let go and be ego-receptive. The other, Bryan, did nothing else but give himself suggestions, most of them the same that he had received in heterohypnosis, and often noting for each one in his diary whether it was successful or unsuccessful. By a "plus" he indicated that he was successful; by a "minus" he indicated that with this particular task he had been unsuccessful. Here are some typical excerpts from Bryan's diary. Day 4:

"+ left hand light—floating
− whole body floating
− dream
+ memory of kindergarten shopping trip
+ mental chess game
+ taste of corned beef sandwich
"Ability to concentrate definitely heightened chess game; sufficient although not astounding. Still unable to experience dream. Felt distracted by minor noises in room (some noisy plumbing, mostly)."

Day 14:

> "At the end of the 2nd week, these sessions seem to be getting less, rather than more interesting; and I am having more and more trouble using up an hour."

Day 23:

> "I fell asleep after about 30 minutes of trance during which I gave myself no specific suggestions. I still can't quite tell the difference between trance and this light, normal sleep."

Poor self-hypnotic subjects like Bryan lack the ability for Imagery, Ego Receptivity, Expansive Attention, and creative experiences in self-hypnosis. It may be possible to teach them self-hypnosis for the control of pain by teaching them to divert their Concentrative Attention to pleasant thoughts or memories. But we doubt that they can use self-hypnosis creatively for working on emotional problems, even for diminishing anxiety. We believe that successful and very successful self-hypnotic subjects can work on their problems by means of their ability to listen and look at that which comes up from within (Ego Receptivity), their capability for Expansive Attention, and their facile imaginations and little need to defend against Strong Affect.

SUMMARY

The richness of imagery and the much greater variety of structural and content categories used in self-hypnotic experience differentiated the diaries of our successful and highly successful subjects from those of our poorer ones. Thus, it would seem wise for us to give subjects at least an imagery test before deciding to teach them self-hypnosis for anything else but relaxation and perhaps pain control.

Meanwhile, we did a great deal more research on the fascinating self-hypnosis diaries we collected, and this research is presented in the chapters that follow.

CHAPTER 9

The Modes of the Ego in Self-Hypnosis

Three modes of ego functioning have been postulated in the psychoanalytic literature to date: Ego Activity, Ego Passivity (Rapaport, 1967b; Stolar & Fromm, 1974), and Ego Receptivity (Deikman, 1971). In attempts to understand the essence of hypnosis, these modes have been investigated further by Fromm (1972a, 1977, 1979) and Fromm and her collaborators (Fromm & Gardner, 1979; Fromm & Hurt, 1980). Additional research on ego modes has been carried out with regard to the self-hypnotic experience in hypnotist-absent self-hypnosis (Fromm, Brown, Hurt, Oberlander, Boxer, & Pfeifer, 1981; see Chapter 4 of this book).

We thought that people would be very likely to reveal a high degree of Ego Activity when they had to induce hypnosis in themselves daily for an extended period of time and no hypnotist was present to hypnotize them. Furthermore, we expected that subjects would be able to open themselves up to stimuli from within themselves that arose spontaneously in self-hypnosis; in other words, they would tend to reveal a high degree of Ego Receptivity in self-hypnosis—much higher than in the waking state, where Ego Activity predominates.

Thus the principal focus of the current study was on demonstrating the presence and prevalence of the ego modes, particularly Ego Activity and Ego Receptivity, in self-hypnosis. Once this was clarified, we also investigated how these modes relate to other self-hypnotic phenomena. Finally, we focused on personality characteristics that, in self-hypnosis, may be conducive to experiencing one ego mode more than others.

An earlier version of this chapter was published under the same title in 1987–1988 by Erika Fromm, Sarah R. Skinner, Lisa S. Lombard, and Stephen P. Kahn in *Imagination, Cognition and Personality*, 7(4), 335–349. Copyright 1988 by Baywood Publishing Company, Inc. Reprinted by permission of the coauthors, the journal editor, and the publisher.

DEFINITIONS OF THE EGO MODES

"Ego Activity" has been defined as decision making; goal-directed activity; sequential logical reasoning; relative autonomy of the ego from the demands of the id, the superego, and the environment; and the erection and maintenance of defenses (Rapaport, 1967b; Fromm, 1972a; Stolar & Fromm, 1974). Ego Activity in self-hypnosis comprises directed mental activity (i.e., decisions, thoughts, or specific suggestions made by the subject to himself). Ego Activity and behavioral activity are not synonymous. For instance, the person who sits in a chair for an hour and thinks but does not move a limb is ego-active, but not behaviorally active. And, conversely, one who runs amok is behaviorally active but not ego-active (Fromm, 1972a).

"Ego Receptivity," in contrast to Ego Activity, has been defined (Deikman, 1971; Fromm, 1976, 1977, 1979) as a mode in which deliberate control of internal experience, critical judgment, and goal-directed thinking is temporarily relinquished, and an individual allows unconscious and preconscious material to emerge freely. It is what William James (1902/1935) has described as watching the stream of consciousness flow by. Fromm (1977, 1979) has noted that in heterohypnosis Ego Receptivity is encountered primarily as increased openness to stimuli coming from the hypnotist—in other words, suggestibility.

A third mode, "Ego Passivity," has been defined as an ego-dystonic state of helplessness in the face of internal drive demands or environmental constraints (Rapaport, 1967b; Fromm, 1972a) or superego prohibitions (Stolar & Fromm, 1974). Rapaport (1967b) viewed Ego Passivity as a *temporary* inability to make autonomous decisions (in a healthy individual), or as a pathological regression (in psychotic patients). It is a state in which the person feels helpless or overwhelmed. In self-hypnosis, Ego Passivity is present when the subject feels overwhelmed by imagery or thoughts arising from conflict within himself. In the present study severe Ego Passivity was not expected to occur to any significant degree, because individuals with serious personality disorders had been screened out prior to the start of the experiment. However, we were aware of the possibility that at times in self-hypnosis subjects would not be able to make autonomous decisions if they were temporarily overwhelmed by a feeling or an image, but we expected that this would be transitory.

A fourth mode of ego functioning, which has not been discussed in the ego-psychological or hypnosis literature to date, is ego inactivity. We have defined "Ego Inactivity" as the apparent absence of any functioning. That is, in self-hypnosis, we expected that it would be represented by a period of time wherein self-suggestions were not initiated or executed; images, thoughts, or feelings did not spontaneously emerge; and the ego was not overwhelmed by internal or external demand.

Hypotheses

The specific hypotheses that we made and that we investigate in this chapter are as follows:

1. (a) Ego Activity and Ego Receptivity are likely to be present in self-hypnosis, with Ego Receptivity predominating over Ego Activity. (b) Ego Passivity and Ego Inactivity *may* be present.

2. Ego Receptivity is positively related and Ego Activity is negatively related to the following self-hypnotic phenomena: (a) hypnotic susceptibility; (b) trance depth; (c) vivid, realistic imagery and primary-process imagery; and (d) the capacity to become deeply absorbed.

3. Ego Receptivity is related to personality characteristics associated with an openness to internal, self-initiated experiences. Ego Activity, on the other hand, is related to personality characteristics associated with independent initiative and the ability to structure and monitor internal experiences in self-hypnosis, in the absence of external sources of support.

METHOD

Measure and Procedures

The sample consisted of 30 (of the original 33)[1] volunteers from the study on self-hypnosis (see Chapter 4 of this book), the data for which were collected in the mid-1970s. Most of the volunteers were University of Chicago undergraduate students, aged 18 to 21 years. Some were graduate students, and three were professionals, the oldest participant being 45 years of age. Seventeen subjects were male; 13 were female. Only highly hypnotizable subjects were selected to participate in the study: those who attained a score of 9 or above out of a possible score of 12 points on the Harvard Group Scale of Hypnotic Susceptibility (HGSHS; Shor & Orne, 1962) and a score within the same range on the Stanford Hypnotic Susceptibility Scale, Form C (SHSS:C; Weitzenhoffer & Hilgard, 1962). Prior to participating in the month-long experiment, all applicants were given the Minnesota Multiphasic Personality Inventory (MMPI; Hathaway & McKinley, 1967; Dahlstrom, Welsh, & Dahlstrom, 1972, 1975) and the Rorschach (Rorschach, 1949, 1954) as screening tests, to exclude individuals with psychopathology from the sample. In addition, all subjects chosen for the study were given the Revised Stanford Profile Scales of Hypnotic Susceptibility, Form I (SPSHS:I; Weitzenhoffer & Hilgard, 1967) to give them some familiarity with the range of phenomena

---

[1] Three subjects had some data missing and were therefore excluded from the analysis.

that can occur in heterohypnosis. Because we also had an interest in finding out whether heterohypnotizability would improve with continuing practicing of self-hypnosis, Form II of the SPSHS (SPSHS:II) was administered midway through the experiment (after 2 weeks), and the SPSHS:I once again at the completion of the experimental run. Another procedure consisted of an assessment of the subjects' personality characteristics. For this purpose, the Personality Research Form (PRF; Jackson, 1974), the Personal Orientation Inventory (POI; Shostrum, 1972), and the Differential Personality Questionnaire (DPQ; Tellegen & Atkinson, 1974) were administered prior to the subjects' initial self-hypnotic experience.

Subjects practiced self-hypnosis alone in a small room for 1 hour daily for 1 month. At the outset, they were instructed to make daily journal entries after each session describing the content of their self-hypnotic experience (see Chapter 4). From these instructions and from uniform training sessions in heterohypnosis "to standardize their understanding of hypnosis" (see Chapter 4), the subjects knew how to induce and deepen trance, and they were permitted freedom to explore their internal experiences in trance. The diary entries included self-suggestions, recordings of trance depth via the Extended North Carolina Scale (ENCS; Tart, 1972, 1979), and the subjects' impressions of their experiences with self-hypnosis. The journals yielded the raw data from which scores of all four modes of ego functioning, as well as other variables pertaining to the self-hypnotic experience, were culled.

Variables

EGO MODES

Each daily hypnotic session was scored for the presence of the four ego modes on a 5-point scale ranging from 0 to 4, with a score of 0 indicating the absence of a particular mode, 1 indicating its presence for 1–25% of each session, and so on up to 4 indicating its presence for 75–100% of the session spent in that mode. The modes were mutually exclusive and exhaustive, but *not* independent. If one mode was given a score of 2 (or between 25% and 50% of the total trance experience per day), the scores of the other three modes on that day when added could not total more than 50% of the trance experience. Interrater reliability of 81% was achieved by two independent raters for Ego Activity, 84% for Ego Receptivity, 87% for Ego Inactivity, and 90% for Ego Passivity. Discrepancies in the raters' independent codings were submitted to an arbitrator, and a consensual judgment was obtained. The scores for the modes were averaged across days to yield a mean score for each mode per subject. In this manner the average Ego Activity, Ego Receptivity, Ego Passivity, and Ego Inactivity scores for each subject were obtained.

IMAGERY

Hypnotic imagery was a variable analyzed in the present study for a possible relationship to the ego modes. Imagery was scored in two ways: as reality-oriented imagery or as imagery that had a primary-process quality. "Reality-oriented" imagery was defined as inner fantasy, often with a sensory or affective component, that seemed real to the subject. It was scored as present if the image was logical, intense, and rich in detail. Imagery with a "primary-process" quality was defined as imagery of a fantastic nature (which might also be vivid). It was characterized by the eruption of primitive drive derivatives, prelogical thinking, loose or fluid associations, condensation, a disregard of reality, and peculiarities of perceptual or linguistic organization and expression (Fromm, Oberlander, & Gruenewald, 1970). A primary-process score was recorded if any or all of the above-described phenomena were assessed as present in a subject's account of a session.

After two independent raters reached 85% interrater reliability, one rater scored these two aspects of imagery as separate measures on a 3-point scale, ranging from a score of 0 (the absence of the particular aspect of imagery) to a score of 2 (a high degree present). Each subject's daily score for reality-oriented imagery and for primary-process imagery was averaged across the 4 weeks to yield two mean scores for each subject for the experimental period.

ABSORPTION/FASCINATION

Absorption was also analyzed for a possible relationship with the ego modes in the self-hypnotic state. "Absorption" in self-hypnosis was defined as a subject's engrossment in an image, memory, thought, feeling, or some other event that occurred during trance. An example of the attitude of fascination or deep attentional involvement with an image would be the following:

> "I still can't believe how real it was. I could hear every note as if the record were really being played. I got absorbed in the music as I was able to completely 'let go' of any thought that there was really no record."

Absorption was scored as either present or absent. Comments such as "I *am* fascinated by the things experienced when I *was* in trance" were not scored, as they did not pertain to fascination or absorption *during* the trance, but represented comments *about* it. Also excluded were certain words such as "interesting" or "beautiful" without evidence that supported the presence of absorption. Such expressions may have been reflective solely of a subject's writing style and not of the feeling of being absorbed in a particular trance experience. After interrater reliability of 81% was obtained by two independent raters, one rater scored all the journals for absorption.

RESULTS

Incidence of the Ego Modes

Table 9.1 shows the average total scores for Ego Activity, Ego Receptivity, Ego Inactivity, and Ego Passivity. Ego Activity was the most frequently occurring ego mode. That is, on the average, 26–50% of the subjects' ego functioning in self-hypnosis was Ego Activity. Suggestions, thoughts, and decisions made in trance accounted for the high incidence of Ego Activity.

Table 9.1 also shows that, on the average, close to 25% of the trance experience was spent in the ego-receptive mode. Only about 1% of the subjects' time in trance was spent in Ego Inactivity and Ego Passivity.

Ego Activity scores were normally distributed, and fell within a range of 1.192 to 3.929. The scores for Ego Receptivity were also normally distributed, falling in a range of 0.107 to 3.5. Due to the relative infrequency of Ego Inactivity and Ego Passivity, and to the resulting lack of a normal distribution for each, neither were included in any of the correlations that follow.

As might be expected, Ego Activity correlated negatively with Ego Receptivity ($r = -.75$, $p = .0001$). Ego Activity and Ego Receptivity were not perfectly correlated, because Ego Inactivity and Ego Passivity also accounted for a minor portion of the self-hypnotic experience. When the frequency distributions for each sex were compared, it was evident that the females tended to be more ego-receptive ($F = 6.58$, $p < .01$) and the males more ego-active ($F = 6.29$, $p < .02$) during self-hypnosis. Although the amount of Ego Receptivity and Ego Activity differed for males and females, this was the only time a sex difference appeared in the analysis of ego modes. That is, neither the direction nor the magnitude of correlation between the ego modes and other variables was significantly different for males and females.

TABLE 9.1
Four Modes of Ego Functioning in
Self-Hypnosis ($n = 30$)

	Mean	SD
Ego Activity	2.4427	0.8043
Ego Receptivity	1.6747	0.9644
Ego Inactivity	0.5360	0.5405
Ego Passivity[a]		

[a]The incidence of Ego Passivity was so infrequent across subjects that it was virtually nonexistent.

Correlations with the Scales of Hypnotic Susceptibility and Trance Depth

Spearman correlations were calculated between Ego Activity and the SPSHS:I (two administrations) and SPSHS:II, as well as between Ego Receptivity and these same scales. Likewise, correlations were calculated between each of these two modes and the ENCS (Tart, 1972, 1979). The results (see Table 9.2) revealed that subjects assessed pre-experimentally as being most deeply hypnotizable in heterohypnosis (SPSHS:I, first administration) tended to be highly ego-receptive in self-hypnosis. A negative correlation was found between Ego Activity and these same scales: Those subjects who were assessed as most highly hypnotizable in heterohypnosis tended not to be ego-active in self-hypnosis.

Self-hypnotic depth, as measured with the ENCS, tended to be highly related to Ego Receptivity in self-hypnosis. On the other hand, those subjects who attained great depth scores tended not to be ego-active in self-hypnosis.

Correlations with Imagery and Absorption

Table 9.3 shows Spearman correlations calculated separately between ego activity and ego receptivity and (1) reality-oriented imagery, (2) primary-process imagery, and (3) absorption. Results indicate that subjects who revealed a high degree of both aspects of imagery in self-hypnosis tended to be highly ego-receptive and tended to manifest very little ego activity. Subjects who became deeply absorbed in hypnosis tended to exhibit higher levels of Ego Receptivity and diminished Ego Activity. Both of the imagery subcategories were negatively correlated with Ego Activity, but only the correlation between

TABLE 9.2
Spearman Correlations of Ego Activity and Ego Receptivity with Scales of Hypnotic Susceptibility and Trance Depth

	Ego Activity ($n = 30$)	Ego Receptivity[a] ($n = 30$)
Susceptibility scales		
SPSHS:I (first administration)	−.4043*	.5644**
SPSHS:II	−.161	.4125*
SPSHS:I (second administration)	−.163	.4481*
Scale of trance depth		
ENCS	−.313	.6218***

[a] Ego Receptivity and Ego Activity were highly negatively correlated, so it was expected that correlations with other variables would reflect this.

* $p < .05$; ** $p < .005$; *** $p < .0005$.

TABLE 9.3
Spearman Correlations of Ego Activity and Ego Receptivity with
Absorption and the Two Aspects of Imagery

	Ego Activity (n = 30)	Ego Receptivity[a] (n = 30)
Reality-oriented imagery	−.313	.6534†
Primary-process imagery	−.5520**	.8638†
Absorption (rater's judgment)	−.4424*	.5312***

[a] Ego Receptivity and Ego Activity were highly negatively correlated, so it was expected that correlations with other variables would reflect this.

* $p < .01$; ** $p < .001$; *** $p < .005$; † $p = .0001$.

primary-process imagery and Ego Activity attained statistical significance ($p < .001$).

Correlations with Personality Variables

The 10 subscales of the POI were created to reflect different aspects of self-actualization (Shostrom, 1972). We conducted a factor analysis of the POI to arrive at a single category representative of the self-actualizing personality. We called this factor the Actualized Personality Factor, and found it was the first to emerge in a principal components analysis, with a varimax rotation. It accounted for 52% of the variance in the POI.

Table 9.4 shows the significant correlations between the two ego modes and (1) personality variables from the PRF (Jackson, 1974) and (2) the Actualized

TABLE 9.4
Spearman Correlations of Ego Activity and Ego Receptivity with Personality
Variables from the PRF and the Actualized Personality Factor from the POI

	Ego Activity (n = 30)	Ego Receptivity[a] (n = 30)
Personality variables from the PRF		
Autonomy	−.3406	.4451
Cognitive Structure	.3988**	−.3817*
Harmavoidance	.4295**	−.5143***
Order	.5073***	−.254*
Succorance	.4723**	−.6934‡
Understanding	−.3729*	.069
POI Actualized Personality Factor	−.5523†	.5200***

[a] Ego Receptivity and Ego Activity were highly negatively correlated, so it was expected that correlations with other variables would reflect this.

* $p < .05$; ** $p < .01$; *** $p < .005$; † $p < .001$; ‡ $p = .0001$.

Personality Factor, derived from the POI. Of the six PRF variables that correlated significantly with Ego Activity, four also were significantly correlated with Ego Receptivity, but in the opposite direction.

The PRF Autonomy variable correlated negatively with Ego Activity and positively with Ego Receptivity. Autonomy measures the need to be free from external restrictions, chiefly those imposed by interpersonal relationships. High Autonomy scores indicate a person who is likely to be independent, self-reliant, and nonconforming. Autonomous individuals, who set goals from an internal standard of their own, tended not to be ego-active in self-hypnosis. Instead, they were likely to be receptive to internal stimuli—thoughts, feelings, and imagery—while in self-hypnosis.

The second PRF variable that correlated significantly with both ego modes was Cognitive Structure. It correlated positively with Ego Activity and negatively with Ego Receptivity. Cognitive Structure measures the need for definite and accurate information prior to decision making, the need to have all questions answered fully, and the need to maintain certainty in life in general. The correlation between Ego Activity and Cognitive Structure indicated that subjects with a strong need for certainty, exactness, and structure in their daily lives tended to assert themselves actively in structuring their self-hypnotic experience. They revealed little ability to open themselves up to any free flow of impressions, images, or feelings that might surface in trance.

The Harmavoidance variable also correlated positively with Ego Activity and negatively with Ego Receptivity. In general, the harmavoidant person avoids risks of any kind, preferring instead to maximize her own personal safety. Subjects with high Harmavoidance scores revealed a high degree of Ego Activity in self-hypnosis: They structured their experience with suggestions and goal-directed activities.

The fourth PRF variable that was significantly correlated with both ego modes was Succorance. Succorance correlated positively with Ego Activity and negatively with Ego Receptivity. Succorance measures a person's need to seek reassurance and direction from others. High Succorance scores are characteristic of individuals who feel helpless or insecure without such external support. The correlation between Ego Activity and Succorance suggested that subjects with a strong need for external support were likely to be ego-active but not very ego-receptive to their own internal stimuli within trance.

Two other PRF variables, Order and Understanding, were significantly correlated only with Ego Activity. Order correlated positively with Ego Activity. Order, as one might expect, measures a person's need for order and organization. Subjects who scored high on the Order variable tended to be systematic, consistent, deliberate, and methodical in their behavior. The correlation between Ego Activity and Order indicated that subjects with a strong need for order were also highly ego-active in self-hypnosis. They needed to organize their self-hypnotic experience, preferring to make many self-suggestions and engage in active decision making.

The sixth PRF variable, Understanding, correlated negatively with Ego Activity. This variable measures a person's orientation toward logical thought and study of diverse fields of knowledge. Such a person is intellectually inclined, curious, and reflective. Subjects with high Understanding scores tended to reveal little Ego Activity in self-hypnosis.

The POI factor measuring "self-actualization" was found to correlate significantly with both ego modes—negatively with Ego Activity and positively with Ego Receptivity. That is, subjects who had few of the traits of the Actualized Personality factor to a high degree tended to assert themselves ego-actively in trance, while subjects who obtained a high score on this factor tended to let themselves go in self-hypnosis and remained open to their internal experiences.

DISCUSSION

The Ego Modes

The results of this study provide strong support for part (a) of our first hypothesis—namely, that Ego Activity and Ego Receptivity are both present in self-hypnosis. Sex differences were found, with males tending to be more ego-active and females being more ego-receptive during self-hypnosis. This is parallel to our finding that women are more capable of experiencing primary-process imagery in self-hypnosis than men (Lombard, Fromm, & Kahn, 1990; see Chapter 10). However, the results do not support the hypothesis that Ego Receptivity predominates over Ego Activity in self-hypnosis. The reasons became clear upon closer scrutiny of our operationalization of Ego Activity and upon taking into consideration the fact that our subjects were not told how to structure the self-hypnotic experience.

Ego Activity has been defined as making decisions, as organizing and evaluating, and as actively attempting mastery or defense (Hart, 1961; Rapaport, 1967b; Fromm, 1972a, 1979). This was the definition of Ego Activity that we employed for scoring our subjects' journals. In hypnotist-absent self-hypnosis, subjects must organize and direct their own experience—functions that would, in hypnotist-present situations, fall to the hypnotist. In self-hypnosis our subjects used ego activity to structure their experience by giving self-suggestions, making decisions, and solving the problems of how to go deeply into trance. As we (intentionally) had not instructed our subjects in techniques of deepening and maintaining self-hypnotic trance or in what they would do or experience in it, the greater-than-expected incidence of

Ego Activity *may* have been caused by the subjects' need to organize their self-hypnosis sessions.

In a few instances, subjects defended themselves against too much affect by *deciding* (i.e., by employing Ego Activity) to change the topic of their imagery to a more neutral content, or even to terminate the particular trance session.

The remaining two ego modes, Ego Passivity and Ego Inactivity, occurred infrequently if at all. Because all of our subjects were basically normal and not suffering from emotional difficulties of any severity, we expected that Ego Passivity (i.e., feeling overwhelmed) would be rare, and it was. We also expected that many subjects would report that "nothing happened" for extended periods, but few subjects did report ego inactivity, and that only rarely. Perhaps—in order to keep its structures from withering (Holt, 1965)—the ego needs to provide its own stimulation in self-hypnosis when stimulation coming from the outside is minimal, and can let Ego Inactivity happen only for very short times or infrequently. As both Ego Passivity and Ego Inactivity were omitted from further analysis, because they so seldom occurred, the subjects' Ego Activity and Ego Receptivity scores became even more inter-dependent.

The Ego Modes and Self-Hypnotic Phenomena

Perhaps the clearest set of findings established a strong link between the ego modes and phenomena indicative of a powerful hypnotic experience. Hypnotic susceptibility, trance depth, absorption, and reality-oriented imagery all were strongly related to Ego Receptivity. It thus appears that, as hypothesized, Ego Receptivity is at the very heart of self-hypnosis (perhaps even more central than it is to heterohypnosis).

The concept of Ego Receptivity and its relationship to aspects of hypnosis are not new to the literature. This mode is very similar to what Patricia Bowers (1978, p. 184; 1982–1983, p. 3) calls "effortless experiencing," which she has defined as "non-volitional, effortless associations" involved in a task response. She showed that effortless experiencing is an important aspect of heterohypnosis, accounting for most of the variance in the relationship between hypnotic susceptibility and creativity. Bowers worked with heterohypnosis. Our results demonstrate relationships between Ego Receptivity and other aspects of hypnosis in self-hypnosis. Our subjects engaged in self-hypnosis while alone; no hypnotist was present. The stimuli that arose did not come from an outside person, but from the subjects' own imagery. The high correlation between Ego Receptivity on the one hand, and imagery and absorption on the other, shows that in self-hypnosis the ego opens itself and becomes receptive to stimuli coming from *within*.

Furthermore, it appears that some forms and relative amounts of Ego Activity interfere with the self-hypnotic process, where the ability to open oneself to internal experience is clearly essential. The predominant forms of Ego Activity we found (self-suggestions, decision making, and problem solving) provide a scaffolding for the self-hypnosis experience. However, for some subjects, these forms of Ego Activity represent the primary approach to self-hypnosis. When Ego Activity overshadows Ego Receptivity—rather than when it occurs just to provide structure for self-hypnosis—the phenomena of self-hypnosis become constricted. The negative correlations between Ego Activity and hypnotic susceptibility, as well as imagery and absorption, reflect this.

Of particular interest is the relationship between Ego Receptivity and primary-process imagery, which represented the strongest correlation found among the variables. When the ego is receptive, defenses are relaxed, allowing into consciousness the emergence of more fluid associations and of images of a fantastic nature. Kunzendorf (1985–1986) draws a similar conclusion regarding (hetero)hypnosis. He suggests that it is an "'unmonitored' state, in which repressed images are allowed to achieve more vivid representation" (p. 35). It would seem that Ego Receptivity is an essential precondition for the occurrence of primary-process imagery. However, the reverse is not true. In our subjects, Ego Receptivity did occur at times without the presence of primary process. We thus conclude that Ego Receptivity is a necessary but not a sufficient condition for primary-process imagery to come into awareness.

The Ego Modes and Personality

In the literature on heterohypnosis, few relationships between personality variables and hypnotizability have been demonstrated. Notable exceptions are J. R. Hilgard's (1979) and Tellegen and Atkinson's (1974) work. However, it seemed to us that there is a relationship between personality style and certain aspects of hypnosis. In an earlier phase of this study (see Chapter 4), we found some significant correlations between the self-report of the content and structure of self-hypnosis on the one hand and personality traits on the other. Subjects who were inquisitive, sensitive, and steadfast tended to become more immersed in the self-hypnotic experience over time. Those who were externally oriented, as well as those who tended to need structure, found that their self-hypnotic experience did not deepen or become more varied during the experiment.

Since these results suggested that personality style is related to some aspects of self-hypnosis, we were able to hypothesize a relationship between Ego Receptivity (i.e., openness to internal, self-initiated experiences) in self-hypnosis. Indeed, individuals who were independent, were willing to take risks, required little external support and succorance, and did not need a high degree of order in their lives were likely to be highly ego-receptive during self-hypnosis. This allowed them to experience the phenomena of self-hypnosis more fully than was possible for those subjects who in self-hypnosis functioned largely on the basis of Ego Activity. Rønnestad (1989), in a recent study on hypnosis and autonomy, arrived at a similar result.

CONCLUSIONS

All but two of our hypotheses were confirmed. Ego Activity and Ego Receptivity are both present in self-hypnosis; however, Ego Receptivity does not occur with greater frequency than Ego Activity. We also had hypothesized the presence of Ego Inactivity and Ego Passivity in self-hypnosis, but they were practically nonexistent in our sample.

In the well-adjusted personality, Ego Receptivity is at the very heart of self-hypnosis.[2] It is a necessary precondition for deep and powerful self-hypnotic experiences, and is strongly positively related both to vivid reality-oriented and to primary-process imagery, as well as to absorption, hetero-hypnotic susceptibility, and self-hypnotic trance depth. The outstanding personality characteristics of people who demonstrate high Ego Receptivity in self-hypnosis are that they have a need to be independent and self-reliant, and are at ease with themselves, trusting their own unconscious.

On the other hand, individuals who have a need for order, certainty, and exact structure in their lives, and who need reassurance and direction from others, are likely to be so ego-active in self-hypnosis and to give themselves so many self-suggestions that they deprive themselves of some of the more pleasurable aspects of hypnosis. In particular, those more controlled and orderly individuals do not allow imagery to emerge naturally, and therefore do not become absorbed in the process or go into deeper stages of self-hypnotic trance. However, they may be highly susceptible to heterohypnosis, in which they get instructions and support from the hypnotist.

Ego Receptivity to stimuli arising from within is a very powerful construct, one central to self-hypnosis. Not only does it occur with some frequency in self-hypnosis, but it is also strongly related to variables indicative of relatively deep self-hypnotic trance (see Chapter 11). Individuals who are more open to their internal experiences and who require less external structure are more likely to be ego-receptive in self-hypnosis.

---

[2] In the borderline and the psychotic, we believe that self-hypnosis may result in Ego Passivity, and unleash the feeling of being overwhelmed by unacceptable, ego-dystonic, unconscious wishes and affect. It was in order to prevent this danger that we screened our subjects for severe psychopathology.

CHAPTER 10

The Role of Imagery in Self-Hypnosis: Its Relationship to Personality Characteristics and Gender

This chapter contains an analysis of (1) the kinds of imagery that occur in self-hypnosis; (2) imagery changes when self-hypnosis is practiced daily over 4 weeks; (3) imagery as related to the sex of the subjects; and (4) the question of whether imagery is related to certain personality characteristics of subjects.

Imagery in the waking state and in heterohypnosis has been widely studied. It is considered a significant feature of heterohypnosis (Binet & Feré, 1886/1888; J. R. Hilgard, 1970) and is related to hypnotizability (P. G. Bowers, 1978). A nonlinear relationship between hypnotic susceptibility and imagery has also been reported (Sutcliffe, Perry, & Sheehan, 1970; Perry, 1973). Our earlier work (Fromm, Brown, Hurt, Oberlander, Boxer, & Pfeifer, 1981; see Chapter 4) indicated that imagery is a prominent aspect of self-hypnosis as well. In the present study we explored imagery in self-hypnosis in greater detail, and used a phenomenological approach.

Imagery has also been studied in relation to gender. Results of research on imaginative processes in heterohypnosis and in the waking state suggest that gender influences imagery production. Women seem to have a higher capacity for imagery production than men. For example, females tend to produce more idiosyncratic, fantasy-like responses on the Rorschach than males (Pine & Holt, 1960). Fromm, Oberlander, and Gruenewald (1970) showed on the Rorschach that all subjects in heterohypnosis produce more imagery than in the waking state, but that women produce more than men.

An earlier version of this chapter was published under the same title by Lisa S. Lombard, Stephen Kahn, and Erika Fromm in the January 1990 issue of the *International Journal of Clinical and Experimental Hypnosis, 38*, 25–38. Copyrighted by The Society for Clinical and Experimental Hypnosis, January 1990. Reprinted by permission of the first author and the journal editor.

In the current study we investigated self-hypnotic imagery separately for males and females to determine whether gender influences imagery in self-hypnosis as it does in heterohypnosis.

Several attempts to render the relationship between personality characteristics and *hetero*hypnotic phenomena exist in the literature. Primary suggestibility and the need for psychological change have been positively correlated with hypnotizability (Ås & Lauer, 1962; Ås, 1963). Tellegen and Atkinson (1974) found that an openness to absorbing and self-altering experiences is related to hypnotic susceptibility. Shor's (1960, 1970) work and J. R. Hilgard's (1965, 1970, 1974, 1979) analyses of detailed semistructured interview data indicate that the highly hypnotizable person is capable of deep involvement in imaginative, "feeling" areas of experience (e.g., reading a novel, listening to music, having an aesthetic experience of nature, or being absorbed in a physical or mental adventure). Studies of hypnotizability and personality characteristics (assessed by paper-and-pencil tests) have not shown replicable patterns of association (Furneaux & Gibson, 1961; E. R. Hilgard & Lauer, 1962; Bentler, 1963; E. R. Hilgard & Bentler, 1963; Barber & Calverley, 1964; E. R. Hilgard, 1965; E. R. Hilgard, Lauer, & Melei, 1965). In all of these studies, heterohypnosis was employed. As we (see Chapter 4) have shown, self-hypnotic phenomena such as absorption, depth, and the fading of the General Reality Orientation are related to personality characteristics. In the current study we explored the relationship between *self*-hypnotic imagery and selected personality characteristics.

The relationship between personality characteristics and imagery production has also been pursued in relation to gender. Gender has been found to play an important role in the relationship between personality characteristics and imagery in several contexts, such as daydreaming (Singer & Antrobus, 1972) and heterohypnosis (K. S. Bowers & Bowers, 1972). Forisha (1978, 1983) suggests that personality characteristics associated with gender development and socialization (i.e., field dependence) are relevant to imagery production. We therefore decided also to explore the relationship between self-hypnotic imagery and personality characteristics for males and females, as well as for the entire sample.

METHOD

Subjects

Thirty of the original 33[1] volunteer subjects, screened for high hypnotizability (via various standard heterohypnotic scales) and emotional health (via the

---

[1] Three subjects had some data missing and were therefore excluded from the analysis.

Rorschach and the Minnesota Multiphasic Personality Inventory [MMPI]), participated in a self-hypnosis experiment in 1975 and 1976. (See Chapter 4 for a detailed account of the selection procedure.) These subjects (17 males and 13 females) provided the data for the current analysis of self-hypnotic imagery; the sample of 30 is described in Chapter 9.

Experimental Procedure

Subjects practiced self-hypnosis while alone in a room, 1 hour per day, for 4 weeks. At the beginning of the experiment subjects were given brief written instructions that permitted them to induce and deepen their self-hypnotic experiences in ways they might discover by themselves, as well as by using methods they had learned during their three pre-experimental heterohypnotic sessions. Subjects were required to keep a daily record of their self-hypnotic experiences upon awakening from each session. They were instructed to carefully describe their self-suggestions and subjective experiences, and to give three estimates of their trance depth of that day (using a form of the Extended North Carolina Scale; Tart, 1972, 1979). At the conclusion of the 4-week experiment, the diaries were returned to be typed by a secretary. These diaries served as the raw data source for measures of imagery in this study.

Personality Measures

The Personality Research Form, Form AA (PRF; Jackson, 1974), an omnibus personality inventory measuring 22 traits, and Shostrom's (1972) Personal Orientation Inventory (POI), were administered prior to the 4-week experimental period.

Rating Procedures for Imagery

The reality-oriented quality of the imagery in the diaries was rated on a 3-point scale ranging from "absent" to "very vivid." It was scored according to the subject's own report of how "real" the imagery seemed to be, how detailed the image was, whether only one or several sensory modalities were used in the production of the image, and how prevalent detailed imagery was for the day being scored (these are similar to Horowitz's [1970] criteria). Subjects' reports of their daily self-hypnotic experiences were rated as follows: A score of 0 indicated the absence of imagery; a score of 1 indicated the presence of moderately vivid reality-oriented imagery; and a score of 2 indicated a preponderance of highly reality-oriented imagery. Thus subjects accumulated approximately 28 scores (the average number of days subjects participated in the study was 28), each of which represented the reality-oriented quality of the reported imagery per day. Each subject's daily score was then averaged across days to yield a single reality-oriented imagery score per subject for the entire experiment. Examples of reality-oriented imagery include imagining explicit directions on a street map, visualizing a lemon (including the smell and taste), or clearly picturing a friend's face. Here is an illustration of one subject's highly reality-oriented imagery:

> "[I] imagined I went to a row of lilac bushes near an iron fence and was picking a few and smelled them—successful. . . . This spring there was an entire row of them behind the school near an iron fence. I saw myself near this fence picking them, and then I actually smelled a few of them."

A similar scoring method, also ranging from 0 to 2, was used to assess the primary-process quality of the imagery for each session. Primary process is characterized by intrusions of primitive drive derivatives, condensation, fragmentation, a loosening of associations, autistic logic, logical contradictions, and disregard of reality (Freud, 1900/1953; Fromm et al., 1970). The judgments of primary-process functioning were based on the presence of any or all of the above (i.e., the prelogical, fantastic, or idiosyncratic aspects of the imagery). This method of scoring levels of primary-process functioning was based on Holt's (1970) concept of scoring primary-process responses on the Rorschach. Total absence of primary-process imagery was given a score of 0. Culturally derived images (e.g., the Wizard of Oz, Icarus), which were not peculiar to a subject, received scores of 1 on the primary-process scale; original, idiosyncratic, fantastic imagery produced by subjects received a score of 2. An example of the latter was as follows:

> "I imagined I was leaning out of a window and a silvery man was flying towards me, reaching out for my hands so I could fly. It was beautiful, dark with two silver figures flying. He was the moon . . . the sun came and we slid on sunshine. Then I sat on a rain cloud and blew up some wind and rain."

To establish interrater reliability for the scoring of self-hypnotic imagery, five subjects' diary entries were coded for each of the approximately 28 days they participated in the study. Agreement was reached between the two raters for 85% of the days. Once this level of interrater reliability was established, one rater coded all of the subjects' diaries for the reality-oriented and primary-process qualities of imagery.

Imagery was not scored exclusively as either reality-oriented or primary-process. For example, one subject imagined

". . . going into a stone castle. Everyone stops and looks up, then welcomes me gladly. The queen has returned, they cry. . . . A minister of state approaches me, but my face turns into a witch and scares him away. I turn into a scraggly rooster, then a crane, a stork."

This set of images was judged for both its reality-oriented and primary-process qualities. The two qualities of imagery were frequently intertwined.

A measure of verbal expressivity was developed to examine the relationship between subjects' writing styles and reality-oriented and primary-process imagery. For each subject, the average number of words was calculated by (1) averaging the number of words on three randomly selected full typed pages of text, (2) multiplying this number by the total number of pages in the diary, and (3) dividing this number by the number of days the subject participated in the study.

RESULTS

Personality Characteristics of the Sample

The aggregate personality configuration of the subjects depicted by the personality tests reflects, in part, the social context from which the sample was drawn—most subjects were college students at the end of the Vietnam War. (The PRF was standardized on a similar population.) Subjects obtained their highest average score on the PRF variable "understanding" and their lowest average score on the PRF variable "Social Recognition." The means were 61.10 with a standard deviation of 10.06, and 42.13 with a standard deviation of 9.88, respectively. These results from the PRF suggest that the most outstanding personality characteristics of the sample were their theoretical orientation, intellectual curiosity, and lack of concern for the opinions of others.

Results from the Masculinity/Femininity (*MF*) scale of the MMPI suggest that another striking personality characteristic of the entire sample was the subjects' tendency to describe themselves in stereotypically feminine ways. Male subjects obtained an average score of 71.0 with a standard deviation of 7.98 on this scale. This elevated score on the MMPI *MF* scale (although not uncommon for a college population) represents sex-role flexibility. Male subjects strongly rejected stereotypically masculine qualities in favor of qualities typically considered feminine (sensitivity, idealism, aesthetic awareness, and nonaggressiveness). Alternately, the mean score female subjects obtained on the same scale (39.31 with a standard deviation of 7.51) was more than one standard deviation below the expected score. They too described themselves as slightly more feminine than expected.

Imagery

DESCRIPTIVE STATISTICS

Table 10.1 shows the means and standard deviations of the imagery scores for male and female subjects. All but one subject reported at least 1 day of "moderately reality-oriented" imagery. 80% of the subjects reported some imagery on at least half of the days they participated in the study. It is our impression that this represents a relatively large amount of self-hypnotic imagery. Our preliminary coding of other self-hypnotic phenomena indicates that subjects reported the fading of the General Reality Orientation (Shor, 1959), absorption/fascination, and dreams far less often (e.g., no subjects experienced absorption more than 50% of the days).

RELATIONSHIP BETWEEN TYPES OF IMAGERY

The two aspects of self-hypnotic imagery measured in this study were related. Spearman correlations showed that reality-oriented imagery and primary-process imagery were highly correlated ($r = .692$, $p = .0001$). As noted earlier, the two types of imagery were not coded as mutually exclusive. However, despite their close association, they were qualitatively different. That is, the subjects' primary-process imagery was characterized by its fantastic quality, while reality-oriented imagery was characterized by sharp, brilliant, and realistic-looking detail.

CHANGES OVER TIME

The production of reality-oriented imagery did not vary significantly with time. There were no systematic trends, either up or down, to indicate a change in imagery production over time. Subjects' average reality-oriented imagery score for the first half of the experiment was 1.11 with a standard deviation of 0.51, and for the second half of the experiment it was 1.12 with

TABLE 10.1
Reality-Oriented and Primary-Process Imagery Scores

	All ($n = 30$)	Males ($n = 17$)	Females ($n = 13$)
Reality-oriented			
Mean	1.10	0.92	1.35
SD	0.54	0.59	0.37
Primary-process			
Mean	0.46	0.28	0.70
SD	0.41	0.30	0.41

a standard deviation of 0.63. Similarly, the subjects' average primary-process score for the first half of the experiment was 0.45 with a standard deviation of 0.45; for the second half of the experiment it was 0.49 with a standard deviation of 0.42. The data were examined closely for evidence of systematic patterns of change within each of those 2-week periods (first half and last half). No pattern or trends across individuals emerged.

GENDER DIFFERENCES

Standard two-tailed independent t tests were performed to study the effects of gender on imagery production. Significant sex differences emerged in the amount of reality-oriented and primary-process imagery produced. Results show that on the average, the female subjects experienced more reality-oriented imagery than the male subjects ($t = 2.42$, $p < .03$). Also, the female subjects on the average produced significantly more primary-process imagery than the male subjects did ($t = 3.11$, $p = .005$). Clearly, the amount and degree of reality-oriented and primary-process imagery produced during self-hypnosis varied significantly with gender.

RELATIONSHIP TO VERBAL EXPRESSION

As a way to control for the influence of verbal production on our measures of self-hypnotic imagery, we developed a measure of verbal expressivity. Results indicate that female subjects were more verbally expressive than male subjects (standard two-tailed independent t score $= 2.11$, $p < .05$). To determine whether higher verbal expressivity was associated with increased imagery production, correlations between verbal expression, reality-oriented imagery, and primary-process imagery were calculated. For the entire sample, a moderate relationship between reality-oriented imagery and verbal expression and between primary-process imagery and verbal expression emerged (Spearman $r = .45$, $p < .05$, and Spearman $r = .40$, $p < .05$, respectively). However, when the data were analyzed separately for males and females, only the relationships between verbal expressivity and reality-oriented and primary-process imagery for male subjects reached significance (Spearman $r = .52$, $p < .05$; Spearman $r = .49$, $p < .05$). Verbal expression was unrelated to the female subjects' reality-oriented imagery ($r = .29$, $p < .34$) or primary-process imagery ($r = .03$, $p < .92$).

Upon finding that self-hypnotic imagery was related to verbal expressivity for the male subjects, we standardized imagery scores (by dividing the average daily imagery score by the average daily number of words in the diary) to minimize the effect of verbal production. The relationship between gender and self-hypnotic imagery production (controlled for the effects of verbal expression) was then re-examined using a standard two-tailed independent *t* test. A significant sex difference in the amount of primary-process imagery experienced by males and females was still obtained. Female subjects produced more primary-process imagery than male subjects (unpaired *t* score = 2.31, $p < .03$). However, a significant difference between reality-oriented imagery for male and female subjects was not evident when verbal expressivity was considered.

RELATIONSHIP TO PERSONALITY

The relationship between self-hypnotic imagery production and personality characteristics for the female subjects was explored by calculating Spearman correlations between PRF variables and self-hypnotic imagery scores that had been corrected for verbal expressivity. All PRF personality variables were normally distributed for each sex. Conceptually, we grouped several PRF variables into two categories: "Impulse Expression" and "Outgoingness." Empirically, the PRF variables that formed these constructs were highly intercorrelated.

The first composite variable is modeled on the factor Jackson (1974) also extracted from the PRF and called "Impulse Expression and Control." Five component variables—Impulsivity, Cognitive Structure, Harmavoidance, Change, and Order—intercorrelated significantly, implying a cohesive construct. The strongest relationships within this construct were between the PRF variable of Cognitive Structure on the one hand and the variables of Impulsivity and Order on the other (Spearman $r = -.58$, $p < .001$; Spearman $r = .57$, $p < .001$, respectively). Therefore standardized scores from these five scales were added together. Impulse Expression assesses an individual's ability to tolerate and express his impulse life. The means and standard deviations for this composite variable and the individual scales comprising it are displayed in Table 10.2. Although females tended to score higher than males on this factor, standard independent *t* tests showed that these scores were not significantly different.

The second composite factor that correlated with primary-process imagery is called "Outgoingness." It is comprised of three highly intercorrelated PRF variables that were standardized and added together: Dominance, Exhibition, and Harmavoidance. The most powerful relationship within this construct was between Exhibition and Dominance (Spearman $r = .58$, $p < .001$). Outgoingness describes an individual who is forceful, is dramatic, and enjoys risk-taking adventures (see Table 10.2). Standard independent *t* test results show that male and female subjects' scores on Outgoingness were not significantly different.

Table 10.3 displays the correlations of Impulse Expression and Outgoingness with reality-oriented and primary-process imagery. In the present study, Impulse Expression was positively correlated with primary-process

TABLE 10.2
Personality Scores from the PRF and Combined Personality Factor Scores

	Males (n = 17)		Females (n = 13)		All (n = 30)	
	Mean	SD	Mean	SD	Mean	SD
Impulse Expression	−0.83[a]	3.82	1.15[a]	2.82	0.0005[a]	3.52
Impulsivity	54.67	9.88	56.46	7.83	55.42	8.98
Cognitive Structure	48.17	11.08	46.92	3.75	47.65	8.70
Harmavoidance	52.11	10.03	41.15	8.75	47.52	10.86
Change	50.67	7.07	51.08	7.26	50.84	7.03
Order	48.33	8.76	43.62	7.18	46.35	8.35
Outgoingness	−0.40[a]	2.46	0.55[a]	2.10	0.0005[a]	2.32
Dominance	51.44	12.28	51.54	6.70	51.48	10.17
Exhibition	52.28	10.95	51.54	11.04	51.97	10.81
Harmavoidance	52.11	10.03	41.15	8.75	47.52	10.86

[a] These are standard scores.

imagery for the female subjects (see Table 10.3). That is, female subjects who were able to express their impulses, but not to be overwhelmed by them, were more likely to experience prelogical, fantastic imagery than those who maintained strict control over their impulses.

Results also show that primary-process imagery was significantly positively correlated with Outgoingness for the entire sample; this relationship was particularly robust for the female subjects (see Table 10.3). Subjects who

TABLE 10.3
Spearman Correlations between Imagery (Corrected for Verbal Expressivity) and Personality Factors and Their Component Variables

	Reality-oriented			Primary-process		
	Males (n = 17)	Females (n = 13)	All (n = 30)	Males (n = 17)	Females (n = 13)	All (n = 30)
Impulse Expression	−.01	.49	.07	−.18	.76***	.34
Impulsivity	−.04	−.01	.09	.18	.25	.24
Cognitive Structure[a]	.17	−.18	−.06	.06	−.59**	−.21
Harmavoidance[a]	−.02	−.54*	−.20	−.14	−.59**	−.50**
Change	.02	.33	−.10	−.56**	.33	−.06
Order[a]	−.11	−.35	.03	.03	−.70**	−.29
Outgoingness	−.09	.39	−.03	.20	.61**	.43*
Dominance	.00	.28	−.14	.17	.58**	.23
Exhibition	.01	.13	−.14	.13	.37	.26
Harmavoidance[a]	.02	.54*	−.20	−.14	−.59**	.68***

[a] In deriving the total scores for Impulse Expression and Outgoingness, the direction of these variables was reversed before they were added to the equation. This accounts for the negative direction of the correlations between these variables and reality-oriented and primary-process imagery.

$* \ p \leq .05; \ ** \ p \leq .01; \ *** \ p \leq .001.$

were persuasive, were adventurous, and had dramatic flair were more likely to produce primary-process imagery than those who were reserved.

DISCUSSION

Results support our earlier observation (see Chapter 4) that imagery is a prominent aspect of self-hypnosis; the presence of imagery was a dramatic common denominator among subjects' self-hypnotic experiences. It may be considered a marker of self-hypnosis itself. Indeed, another research study done by our group on the same data pool has shown that imagery in self-hypnosis positively correlated with the depth of trance (Kahn, Fromm, Lombard, & Sossi, 1989; see Chapter 11). Further research, such as measuring baseline frequencies of other self-hypnotic phenomena, is necessary to measure the significance of self-hypnotic imagery in relation to other self-hypnotic phenomena. Comparisons between the frequencies of self-hypnotic imagery and heterohypnotic imagery could also be examined.

Results also support our conceptualization that self-hypnotic imagery is a multidimensional phenomenon and must be investigated as such. Although the significant correlation between reality-oriented imagery and primary-process imagery suggests that they are intertwined, they remain qualitatively distinct constructs. A unidimensional measurement of imagery would not have captured the richness of self-hypnotic imagery. In the current study, both the reality-oriented quality and the fantastic quality of self-hypnotic imagery were key features.

The production of self-hypnotic imagery remained virtually constant throughout the experiment. Subjects' average primary-process imagery scores varied slightly, but not systematically enough to suggest a practice effect. The stability of imagery production may be attributed, in part, to the intentionally limited instructions given to the subjects: They were given the freedom to explore a variety of aspects of self-hypnosis. They were *not* asked to try to improve their imagery skills. A more structured research study could be designed to explore whether the production of self-hypnotic imagery can be improved over time.

Our systematic coding of the diaries indicates that self-hypnotic imagery did not increase over the course of the experiment. However, subjects did report on their Longitudinal Questionnaire responses (see Chapter 4) that the intensity of their self-hypnotic experiences increased over time. Future researchers should be aware of the discrepancy between these two forms of data collection and measurement.

Within this small sample of subjects, there emerged some sex differences in imagery produced during self-hypnosis. Although male and female subjects where highly hypnotizable and manifested many similar personality characteristics—they were intellectually curious, were aesthetically oriented, and showed a tendency toward stereotypically feminine personality characteristics—their production of imagery differed significantly. Male subjects produced significantly less vivid and primary-process imagery than the female subjects did. Results from other studies have shown a similar sex difference in nonhypnotic or heterohypnotic imagery produced by males and females. Van Dyne and Stava (1981) found that female subjects experienced more vivid heterohypnotic imagery than male subjects did. Crawford (1982) found that women had more vivid waking-state imagery than males. Pine and Holt (1960), Fromm et al. (1970), K. S. Bowers (1971), and Coe, St. Jean, and Burger (1980) also obtained results in which the vividness or amount of imagery produced was greater for female subjects than for male subjects. Our results show, then, that imagery production varies for males and females in self-hypnosis, just as it does in other contexts.

Another significant set of findings is that certain personality characteristics were associated with self-hypnotic imagery for the female but not for the male subjects. For female subjects, the PRF composite Variable Impulse Expression was positively correlated with primary-process imagery (even when verbal expression was considered). Outgoingness, the other composite variable, was positively correlated with primary-process imagery (with verbal expressivity considered) for all subjects, but especially for the female subjects. This suggests that the ability to express impulses rather than rigidly controling them, and a dramatic, forceful, risk-taking stance, are positively associated with primary-process imagery in self-hypnosis. The relative absence of a relationship between personality characteristics and self-hypnotic imagery for the male subjects may indicate that these personality characteristics have less of an influence on imaginative processes in males.

Several authors have suggested that the integration of masculine and feminine personality characteristics may facilitate imaginative processes (Forisha, 1978; Kihlstrom, Diaz, McClellan, Ruskine, Pistole, & Shor, 1980). Among female subjects, the expression of impulses and an outgoing, forthright, and adventurous nature correlated with the production of self-hypnotic imagery. Our results also point toward the importance of sex-role flexibility as a route to imagery production.

In conclusion, we found that the production of reality-oriented and primary-process imagery in self-hypnosis was greater for the female subjects than for the male subjects. This finding is consistent with results from studies of heterohypnotic and waking-state imagery, and thus adds strength to the general conclusion that there are sex differences in imagery production. To better understand this difference in imagery production, we studied the relationship between Impulse Expression and Outgoingness on the one hand and self-hypnotic imagery on the other. For the female subjects, these personality characteristics were significantly related to imagery production.

However, they did not relate significantly to imagery production for the male subjects. This suggests that the ability to express impulses and a dramatic, forthright quality are not relevant for imagery production in male subjects, but are relevant for female subjects. It remains for future researchers to identify whether other personality characteristics are associated with self-hypnotic imagery production for males.

CHAPTER 11

The Relation of Self-Reports of Hypnotic Depth in Self-Hypnosis to Hypnotizability and Imagery Production

Self-report scales of hypnotic depth have been used successfully in measuring the depth of heterohypnosis, when the hypnotist asks the subject for depth reports (Tart, 1978, 1979; Laurence & Nadon, 1986). However, in hypnotist-absent self-hypnosis, the subject must ask himself for depth reports. The self-hypnotic situation may be qualitatively different from the heterohypnotic situation in terms of self-reported depth scales. Thus, the research question posed here—that is, whether self-report scales of depth are valid indicators of self-hypnotic depth—is not a trivial one. The question centers on whether, in hypnotist-absent self-hypnosis, subjects can deliberately ask themselves for spontaneous judgments that are reliable indicators of self-hypnotic depth. The present chapter attempts to answer this question by comparing reports of self-hypnotic depth (defined as the maximum depth reported during the self-hypnotic session) to two phenomena that we hypothesize to be related to depth: hypnotic susceptibility and imagery production.

Hypnotic depth is not synonymous with hypnotic susceptibility, though the two are related. Tart defines hypnotic depth as a "momentary state of [the subject] along some dimension of 'profundity' of the hypnotic state" (1970, p. 206). During a hypnotic session, the depth can vary anywhere between zero and the maximum attainable for a given subject (Friedlander & Sarbin, 1938; Tart, 1970). Susceptibility can be conceived of as a trait; it can be operationally defined as the "depth achieved under standard conditions

An earlier version of this chapter was published under the same title by Stephen Kahn, Erika Fromm, Lisa S. Lombard, and Michael S. Sossi in the October 1989 issue of the *International Journal of Clinical and Experimental Hypnosis*, 37, 290–304. Copyrighted by The Society for Clinical and Experimental Hypnosis, October 1989. Reprinted by permission of the coauthors and the journal editor.

of induction" (E. R. Hilgard, 1965, p. 67). The "standard conditions" referred to by Hilgard are those under which standardized scales of hypnotic susceptibility are administered. Presumably, if hypnotic depth were a simple, unidimensional phenomenon, depth reports taken in conjunction with the administration of susceptibility scales should correlate almost perfectly with scores on those scales.

However, hypnotic depth is not a simple, unidimensional phenomenon. Tart (1970, p. 105) characterizes hypnotic depth as "complex" and "poorly understood." Studies by Radtke and Spanos (1981, 1982) suggest that unidimensional depth scales are actually composed of complex combinations of other dimensions, among which is "absorption."

A theoretical model of the multidimensional nature of hypnotic depth was constructed by Shor (1962, 1979). Shor theorized that depth is actually composed of three dimensions: trance, nonconscious involvement, and archaic involvement. To determine whether a self-report scale of hypnotic depth would be a valid indicator of depth, one would have to examine how well the scale measured the other dimensions of depth. Previously, only a few studies (Field, 1965; Tart, 1970, 1972, 1979) involving comparisons of self-report measures of hypnotic depth with other measures have examined some of the components that make up hypnotic depth reports (see Laurence & Nadon's [1986] review). No one has examined the interactions of those components, nor has anyone examined these in self-hypnosis. In the study described in this chapter, we examined susceptibility and imagery production as indicators of hypnotic depth in self-hypnosis.

A number of heterohypnotic studies have demonstrated a relationship among the various dimensions of depth. Self-reported depth has been associated with susceptibility (LeCron, 1953; Hatfield, 1961; E. R. Hilgard & Tart, 1966; O'Connell, 1964; Palmer & Field, 1968; Perry & Laurence, 1980) and with other hypnotic phenomena (Tart, 1963; Shor, Orne, & O'Connell, 1966).

Only a few studies have explored the relation between self-reported depth and imagery production. The Brief Stanford Scale was found to be associated with vividness of hypnotic dreams (E. R. Hilgard & Tart, 1966). Palmer and Field (1968) also found a relationship between self-reports of depth and Ganzfeld imagery scored for vividness and detail of visual imagery.

The relationship between imagery and hypnotic susceptibility has also been examined, though findings are far from consistent. Early studies include those by Arnold (1946), McBain (1954), and Richardson (1969, 1972). These studies have been criticized by Sheehan (1979) on the grounds that the measures of imagery were deficient. A standard measure of imagery, The Betts Imagery Questionnaire (Betts, 1909) was linked to hypnotizability in several studies (Diamond & Taft, 1975; J. R. Hilgard, 1979; Shor et al., 1966; Spanos, Valois, Ham, & Ham, 1973; Wagman & Stewart, 1974). Perry

(1973), however, found no evidence of a relationship between susceptibility and imagery. Other studies have found relationships between various measures of imagery and susceptibility (Coe, St. Jean, & Burger, 1980; Palmer & Field, 1968; Tart, 1966). There seem to be gender differences in this relationship as well. Sutcliffe, Perry, and Sheehan (1970) found the relationship obtained for men, while J. R. Hilgard (1979) found the effect for females. A general discussion and summary of these areas of research can be found in Fromm and Shor (1979).

The current study explored the multidimensional nature of self-hypnotic depth. Self-hypnotic depth was compared to both heterohypnotic susceptibility and to self-hypnotic imagery production. Both susceptibility and imagery production were examined as individual and as joint predictors of self-hypnotic depth. The relationship between susceptibility and imagery was also examined.

METHOD

Subjects

In an earlier phase of this study (see Chapter 4 for full details), 58 subjects were selected for high hypnotizability (using various standard heterohypnotic scales; see below) and an absence of serious psychopathology (using the Rorschach and the Minnesota Multiphasic Personality Inventory [MMPI]) from an original group of 425 volunteers. Of these 58 subjects, a total of 26[1] volunteers formed the pool of subjects for the current study. The distributions of the variables to be examined in this study were found to be badly skewed. Four subjects who were identified as the outliers responsible for skewing the distribution were removed from the sample. Two were rejected based on the distribution of the Revised Stanford Profile Scales of Hypnotic Susceptibility, Form I (SPSHS:I; Weitzenhoffer & Hilgard, 1967) scores, and two based on the distribution of the Extended North Carolina Scale (ENCS; Tart, 1972, 1979) scores (see "Procedures," below). Consequently, the sample for this study consisted of 22 subjects, 10 females and 12 males. Nearly all were undergraduate or graduate students at the University of Chicago, 18 to 26 years of age. The oldest was 45. The mean age of the sample was 25.18 with a standard deviation of 9.04.

A number of personality characteristics differentiated this sample from the population at large. For these individuals, a strong theoretical orientation, a high level of curiosity, and a disregard for the opinions of others were clearly in evidence (as measured by the PRF). The only scale on the MMPI

---

[1] Only 26 of the 33 subjects completing the study (see Chapter 4) had complete data for all the variables analyzed.

that was elevated beyond normal limits was the *MF* scale for both men and women (see Chapter 10). The mean demonstrated "sex-role flexibility," scoring high on this scale, while the women tended to be more stereotypically feminine (scoring low on this scale).

Procedure

Before the experimental sessions began, subjects were given the SPSHS:I as well as the Harvard Group Scale of Hypnotic Susceptibility, Form A (HGSHS:A) and the Stanford Hypnotic Susceptibility Scale, Form C (SHSS:C). These three scales as a group comprise the entire range of phenomena ordinarily used in experimental studies of hypnosis, including ideomotor phenomena, hypnotic fantasy and dreams, hypermnesias and age regressions, analgesias, negative and positive hallucinations, amnesias, posthypnotic phenomena, and cognitive and affective distortions. Thus, subjects had become familiar with standardly defined laboratory hypnosis.

Subjects practiced self-hypnosis alone in a room, in 1-hour daily sessions. As described in earlier chapters, they were encouraged to experiment with self-suggestions and with procedures for inducing and remaining in trance, in addition to using techniques learned during heterohypnosis. During the 4 weeks of the experiment, subjects kept daily journals in which they detailed the contents of their self-hypnotic experiences. They were instructed to make entries in their journals every day immediately following their self-hypnotic sessions. The entries were to include the date, the time of day, the duration of trance, self-suggestions attempted (and whether or not these suggestions were successful), and critical reflections on each aspect of the self-hypnotic experience. The descriptions of the self-hypnotic sessions in these journals served as the raw data from which imagery production ratings were made. Subjects were told to monitor their self-hypnotic depth with the slightly revised[2] version of the ENCS (Tart, 1972, 1979) three times per self-hypnotic session: after the induction, sometime during the middle of trance, and before termination of trance. Subjects recorded these depth scores in their journals.

In order to minimize experimenter effects, monitoring of the subjects during the 4-week period was limited to weekly telephone calls and biweekly meetings. No suggestions were given during these meetings as to the content

---

[2] The wording on the ENCS was changed in three minor ways: (1) to refer to self-hypnotic rather than heterohypnotic suggestions; (2) to change all "I" statements (referring to a specific hypnotist) to a collective "we" (the group of researchers doing the self-hypnosis research); and (3) to encourage the subjects to write down the numbers for the depths of their "states" after each self-hypnosis session rather than to call them out orally during the session (two sentences were appended to the ENCS for this purpose).

of the journals. Throughout the month-long experiment, the subjects' self-hypnosis experiences were thus essentially self-directed.

The Variables

Susceptibility was measured using the total scores on the SPSHS:I. The SPSHS:I was specially constructed for use with highly hypnotizable subjects (Weitzenhoffer & Hilgard, 1967), and as such was ideally suited for distinguishing levels of susceptibility within our sample. Among these highly hypnotizable subjects, the distribution of scores was skewed toward the high end of the scale. Only two subjects scored at the very low end of the scale, and when these outliers were removed, the resulting distribution more closely approximated the normal curve (skewness = $-.92$). The range of scores was from 13 to 26 (the two lowest scores removed were 5 and 8).

The general construct of Imagery Production was measured by combining two subscales: reality-oriented and primary-process imagery. These two separate measures of imagery were obtained by coding all the journals, first for reality-oriented imagery and then for primary-process imagery. For each subject, the journal entry for each session was scored on a scale of 0 to 2 for each subscale.

Reality-oriented imagery, the first subscale, was operationally defined as the extent to which a subject produced imagery that seemed real to him. Criteria for evaluating the reality value of imagery included attention to detail, statements pertaining to the reality of the imagery, perception of imagery on more than one sensory channel, and whether affect was associated with the imagery. As for primary-process content of imagery, the second subscale, a subject obtained a high score on this subscale for a session if the subject produced imagery and the imagery was nonrealistic, fantastic, or dreamlike, as described earlier (see Chapter 10 for details). Nonrealistic imagery often seemed very "real" to a subject, just as the nonrealistic content of dreams often seems very real to the dreamer during the dream.

After two judges reached 85% agreement for both aspects of imagery on five journals, a single judge went on to score the remainder of the journals. Neither judge was aware of the subject's susceptibility scores, nor were judges aware of the specific hypotheses being tested. Each subject was given a reality-oriented imagery score and a primary-process imagery score for each hypnotic session. The scores were averaged over all sessions to yield a single score for each scale for each individual.

The high correlation between these two subscales (Pearson $r = .72$) indicated that they were part of the same general construct. Thus, they were combined into a single score by taking the first principal component of the two imagery scores, using the covariance matrix. This single imagery score accounted for more than 87.4% of the total variance of the original scores and was normally distributed. Sex differences were highly significant ($t = 2.956$, $p = .007$), with females scoring higher than males.

Self-reported Self-Hypnotic Depth was measured using a slightly revised version of the ENCS (footnote 2 details the revisions). The ENCS is defined for a range of 0 to 40. Although the instructions leave the scale open-ended for depths beyond 40, no description was given to subjects as to what depth greater than 40 would be like subjectively. Because the scale was left open-ended, several of the subjects went beyond 40 in at least one of their depth reports, with a few going well beyond. These few outliers created a distribution that was highly skewed. Two very clear outliers (average depth scores of 99.4 and 137.1) were removed from the analysis.

A single summary depth score needed to be constructed for each subject in order to provide a basis of comparison with the susceptibility and imagery scores. Unlike hypnotic susceptibility, which is a stable trait (E. R. Hilgard, 1965; Piccione & Hilgard, 1987), depth may fluctuate throughout the course of the hypnotic session (Tart, 1970). An average of the scores within a session would give a rough measure of the average depth during that session. Such a score would tend to fall about midway between 0 (the waking state) and the greatest depth achieved in that session. However, the greatest depth score from a session would give a rough estimate of the greatest depth achieved during that session. In a study of depth, it would be imperative to focus on the maximum depth achieved, since average depth would be contaminated by the fluctuations in depth during a single session. Thus, a summary depth score was obtained for each subject by averaging the highest score reported for each session across all sessions. Utilizing the average of the daily maximum scores was appropriate, since no statistically significant changes in depth scores occurred over the course of the experiment. There did appear to be an upward trend in maximum depth scores over the 4-week period of the experiment, but it was not strong enough to warrant the conclusion that there is a typical upward trend in maximum depth scores.

The average maximum depth scores (with the two outliers retained in the sample) formed a positively skewed distribution that differed significantly from a normal distribution (Shapiro–Wilks $W = 0.718$, $p < .01$; see Shapiro & Wilks, 1965, for a description of W). With the outliers removed, the distribution of scores for the final sample ($n = 22$) was not significantly different from the normal curve. The skewness dropped from 2.6 to 0.19. The mean score for the final sample was 31.58 with a standard deviation of 11.97. Scores ranged from 10.31 to 53.96.

Sex differences in average maximum depth scores were highly significant (Wilcoxon rank-sum test, with correction for continuity, $z = 3.060$, $p = .002$, two-tailed), with females achieving higher maximum depth scores than males.

RESULTS

As can be seen in Table 11.1, the Pearson correlation of susceptibility with the average greatest depth scores was high in magnitude and highly significant (Pearson's $r = .61$, $p = .002$). The imagery scores and the greatest depth scores correlated highly as well (Pearson's $r = .649$, $p < .001$). The correlation for the imagery scores with the susceptibility scores was also strong, but not as powerful as the other two correlations (Pearson's $r = .494$, $p < .02$). As can be seen from Table 11.1, both sexes followed the same pattern.

The correlations were performed using the individual measures of imagery production (reality-oriented and primary-process) separately. The correlation pattern was exactly the same, with both kinds of imagery correlating strongly with depth (.59 and .61) and with susceptibility (.43 and .46). The kinds of imagery did not affect either depth or susceptibility differentially.

In addition to these single correlations, multiple correlations were calculated corresponding to multiple regressions, with depth as the dependent variable and imagery, susceptibility, and the multiplicative interaction of imagery and susceptibility as the independent variables. The results of the most important of these regressions are summarized in Table 11.2. As suggested by the R^2 values of the correlation coefficients given above, the best single predictor of depth scores was imagery production. Adding the susceptibility variable resulted in the best two-predictor model, with $R^2 = .535$. Thus, the imagery score and the susceptibility scores together accounted for an estimated 53.5% of the variance in the depth scores. This represented an absolute increase of 11.9% in the total variance accounted for over that accounted for by the imagery variable alone. This increase was significant, $F(1, 20) = 4.87$, $p = .04$. Moreover, the estimated beta coefficients on both of the nonconstant terms in this model were significant. Adding the interaction

TABLE 11.1
Pearson Correlations of Depth, Imagery, and Susceptibility

	Depth (ENCS)	Imagery
Susceptibility (SPSHS:I)		
Total	.61 ($p = .002$)	.494 ($p = .02$)
Males	.55 ($p = .06$)	.41 ($p = .18$)
Females	.60 ($p = .06$)	.43 ($p = .20$)
Imagery		
Total	.649 ($p = .001$)	
Males	.60 ($p = .03$)	
Females	.47 ($p = .17$)	

Note. Final $n = 22$ (12 males, 10 females).

TABLE 11.2
R^2 **Values for Hierarchical Regression Models**

Model 1: Imagery as sole predictor of depth (ENCS).
$R^2 = .4157$.

	df	Sum of squares	Mean square	F	p
Regression	1	1251.54	1251.54	14.23	.0012
Error	20	1759.19	87.96		
Total	21	3010.74			

	Beta	Std. error	Type II sum of squares	F	p
Intercept	31.04				
Imagery	12.46	3.34	1251.54	14.23	.0012

Model 2: Imagery and susceptibility (SPSHS:I) as predictors of depth (ENCS).
$R^2 = .535$.
Improvement over previous model: R^2 change $= .1193$. $F = 4.87$ ($p = .04$).

	df	Sum of squares	Mean square	F	p
Regression	2	1610.80	805.40	10.93	.0007
Error	19	1399.94	73.68		
Total	21	3010.74			

	Beta	Std. error	Type II sum of squares	F	p
Intercept	3.26				
SPSHS:I	1.32	0.599	359.26	4.88	.04
Imagery	8.76	3.46	472.22	6.41	.02

Model 3: Imagery, susceptibility (SPSHS:I), and their interaction as predictors of depth (ENCS).
$R^2 = .541$.
Improvement over previous model: R^2 change $= .0058$. $F = 0.22$ (not significant).

	df	Sum of squares	Mean square	F	p
Regression	3	1628.14	542.71	7.07	.002
Error	18		1382.60	76.81	
Total	21		3010.74		

	Beta	Std. error	Type II sum of squares	F	p
Intercept	0.88				
SPSHS:I	1.41	0.64	374.83	4.88	.04
Imagery	−3.68	26.42	1.49	0.02	.89
Interaction	0.57	1.21	17.34	0.27	.64

TABLE 11.3
Partial Correlations of Depth, Imagery, and Susceptibility

	Depth (ENCS)	Imagery
Susceptibility (SPSHS:I)	.35 ($p = .03$) (controlling for imagery)	.11 ($p = .52$) (controlling for ENCS)
Imagery	.40 ($p = .01$) (controlling for susceptibility)	

term resulted in the only possible three-factor model, with $R^2 = .541$, which represented a nonsignificant increase in the R^2. The absolute increase in the percentage of variance accounted for by adding the interaction term was only 0.6%. Thus, the best regression model for predicting depth scores was the two-factor model.

Another way of looking at the relationship among depth, imagery, and susceptibility is to examine the partial correlations between these variables (see Table 11.3). The partial correlation of depth scores and imagery scores, with the linear influence of susceptibility scores removed, was smaller than the simple correlation between depth scores and imagery scores, but was still significant (partial $r = .40$, $p = .01$). Similarly, the partial correlation of depth scores and susceptibility scores, with the linear influence of imagery scores removed, was smaller in magnitude than the simple correlation, but it too was still significant (partial $r = .35$, $p = .03$). However, the partial correlation of imagery scores and susceptibility scores, controlling for the effects of depth scores, was so low in magnitude that it fell well below the level of significance (partial $r = .11$, $p = .52$). Thus, although there were real linear relations between depth scores and imagery scores and between depth scores and susceptibility scores, the apparent linear relationship between imagery scores and susceptibility scores was due to the linear relationship of each of these two variables to depth scores.

DISCUSSION

Our results clearly support the notion of the multidimensional nature of trance depth with respect to self-hypnosis. Before discussing the specific interrelationship of our three variables, let us turn to the measure of depth itself, the ENCS. One of the major criticisms of self-report measures of self-hypnotic depth, such as the ENCS, is that there is no consistency of scaling across subjects. However, given that (1) the subjects had a common base of hypnotic experience, due to the administration of the same susceptibility scales and instructions pre-experimentally, and (2) state reports in the range of 0 to 40 were well defined in the instructions given to the subjects at the beginning of the experiment, state reports across subjects in this range can reasonably be considered to be on the same scale. Although some subjects deviated by going beyond the high end of the scale, the mean and standard deviation indicate that this was not the general trend.

Another criticism of self-report scales of hypnotic depth is that estimates made by subjects are not really spontaneous, as specified in the instructions, but instead are "pegged" on the success or failure of hypnotic phenomena that occur just before or just after the depth report is given. Studies that involve subjects' giving depth reports immediately after items on susceptibility scales are especially vulnerable to this criticism (see, e.g., Hatfield, 1961; Field, 1966; E. R. Hilgard & Tart, 1966; Tart, 1970; and Perry & Laurence, 1980). In the current study, however, depth reports were given totally separately from the administration of the susceptibility scale. Thus subjects could not base the reports of their self-hypnosis performance on items of the SPSHS:I.

The correlations found between the variables clearly lend validity to the ENCS as a measure of self-hypnotic depth. They also support Shor's concept of the multidimensional nature of hypnotic depth. Given the simplicity of the measure of imagery (a 3-point scale), these correlations are quite high, indicating that the depth scale (the ENCS) measured, to some extent, the vividness of imagery. The correlation between the ENCS and the SPSHS:I indicates that the ENCS also measures susceptibility. The correlation between the imagery scores and the SPSHS:I scores, although smaller than the correlations above, suggests a relationship between these two variables as well. However, despite the correlation, there is no evidence of a direct linear relationship between these two variables. The partial correlation, excluding linear relationships with the depth scores, failed to reach significance. The apparent relationship between susceptibility and imagery, at least in this study, can be explained by the strong relationship of each of these variables to the depth variable, not to each other. In other words, if depth scores were held constant, no relation would be seen between susceptibility and imagery production. In contrast, partial correlations of depth scores with each of the other two variables, partialing out the third, remains significant. The relations of imagery and susceptibility to the depth scale are real.

Thus, the average greatest ENCS scores are linearly related to both susceptibility and imagery. There are several possible models that would account for these relations. First, depth of hypnosis may be achieved through any of several paths (Shor, 1962; E. R. Hilgard, 1965), so that a high score on a measure of either of the two paths would indicate that a high degree of depth was reached. Second, depth of hypnosis may be the result of a condition where all of the dimensions of depth must be present. Such a conjunctive model is suggested by McBain (1954), who hypothesizes that "goodness of imagery [is] a necessary but not sufficient condition for the attainment of the deeper stages of hypnosis" (p. 37). For the present study, this model implies that a high depth score would result only if both imagery and susceptibility were profound. Third, depth of hypnosis may simply be the result of the additive effects of the dimensions of depth. In the present study, a high score would result if either imagery or susceptibility were profound, but a higher score would result if both were profound. The fourth possibility follows the additive-effects model but states that beyond these effects there may be a potentiating or synergistic effect when both are present. Our data support the third model of simple additive effects more strongly than the multiple-paths model, the conjunctive model, or the synergistic model.

The results of this study show that the ENCS can be used as a measure of at least two dimensions of self-hypnotic depth, hypnotic susceptibility and the ability to produce vivid imagery. However, the generalizability of these findings is limited. The sample consisted of 22 highly hypnotizable subjects. Therefore, conclusions drawn as a result of this study can be made only with regard to self-hypnosis as practiced by highly hypnotizable subjects. While it has been shown (Barber, Dalal, & Calverley, 1968) that subjective reports by hypnotic subjects tend to vary with the form of the questions asked, Barber et al. (1968) also found that this instability is less evident among highly hypnotizable subjects. This suggests that subjective reports of hypnotic subjects, including reports of depth, are more reliable if obtained from more deeply hypnotizable subjects.

In addition, we found in our pilot studies (see Chapter 3) that highly hypnotizable subjects are better able to make phenomenological distinctions with regard to self-hypnosis than are less hypnotizable subjects. Thus, the ability to use self-report scales of depth in a consistent and valid manner may be restricted to highly hypnotizable subjects.

Generalizability may be further restricted in that this sample was a highly curious, intellectually oriented group. Because they were highly hypnotizable, they may also have enjoyed self-hypnosis more than people might generally. Also, the issue of experimenter effects may be relevant (Johnson, 1981), in that the devotion these subjects showed to the experimental process may in part have been based on rapport with us, the experimenters (despite the fact that contact was kept in a minimum). These may have been reasons why our subjects were willing to devote 1 hour a day for 30 consecutive days to self-hypnosis.

With regard to sex differences, it is clear from the correlation matrix that both sexes follow the same patterns with respect to the real relationships between depth and imagery, and depth and susceptibility. This is the case despite the fact that the female scores were significantly higher on both the measure of imagery and that of depth. There may ultimately be hidden sex differences that this study failed to uncover because of the small number of cases. In light of this, future research should consider the effects of sex differences.

In a follow-up study, four major improvements could be made. First, measures of imagery *within* trance could be coded on a more refined scale, but only if the format of the subjects' journals were more standardized. In our exploratory study, it was advantageous *not* to standardize them. This more refined measure of imagery *within* self-hypnotic trance would also need to be compared to the more standard measures of imagery (e.g., Betts, 1909) used in the field of hypnosis. This would further our understanding of imagery production by developing a method for assessing it *within* hypnosis. It would also increase the strength of the results, since imagery would be more comprehensively measured and clearly separated from the measure of depth. Second, a greater number of self-reports of depth could be obtained from subjects, so that changes in depth both within a single self-hypnosis session and between sessions for a single subject, as well as differences between subjects, could be investigated. Third, subjects spanning the full range of susceptibility could be included in the study. Fourth, the subjects who—as unpaid volunteers—completed all phases of this study may have been a highly self-selected sample. Controlling for personality and selection characteristics would increase generalizability.

CONCLUSION

This study has shown that self-reports of self-hypnotic depth when averaged across a number of sessions are valid indicators of self-hypnotic depth among highly hypnotizable subjects. Thus, their usefulness, until now confined to heterohypnosis, is greater than previously realized. Self-reported depth scales are easily taught and do not interfere with the self-hypnotic experience in the way that behavioral measures might. In self-hypnosis, self-reports of hypnotic depth can be used by subjects to monitor their own depth, so that depth can be more precisely controlled. This ability should tend to increase subjects' self-confidence, perhaps making self-hypnosis easier for them. For the researcher or clinician, self-reports of self-hypnotic depth recorded in journals, as in this study, give the investigator valuable information regarding the depth of subjects' self-hypnosis, so that progress can be monitored without interfering with the self-hypnosis experience.

Furthermore, our study shows that both hypnotic susceptibility and the ability to produce realistic and/or primary-process imagery in self-hypnosis are related to self-hypnotic depth. However, the apparent relationship between self-hypnotic imagery and heterohypnotic susceptibility seems to be based on the relationship of each of these to self-hypnotic depth.

ACKNOWLEDGMENT

We wish to thank Betty Johnson and Mary Hallowitz for valuable assistance in the revision of this chapter.

CHAPTER 12

Self-Hypnotic Absorption and Personality

Since Shor (1959) first introduced the dimension of absorption as an aspect of hypnotic experience, advances in both research and theory have linked it to the core features of hypnosis. Studies have related it to hypnotic susceptibility (Ås, 1963; P. G. Bowers, 1978; Davis, Dawson, & Seay, 1978; Finke & McDonald, 1978; J. R. Hilgard, 1965, 1970; Spanos & McPeake, 1975; Yanchar & Johnson, 1981), fading of the General Reality Orientation (Shor, 1960, 1962), and trance depth (Tellegen & Atkinson, 1974). More recently, Crawford (1982) found that absorption was strongly related to hypnotic susceptibility, to vividness of imagery in the waking state, and to positive-affect daydreaming styles. She also found sex differences in these measures, with females scoring higher than men on the measure of absorption and on the vividness of imagery. Rønnestad (1989) found that although low- and high-autonomy subjects did not score differently on Tellegen's Absorption scale (Tellegen & Atkinson, 1974; see below), absorption predicted hypnotic depth better for high- than for low-autonomy subjects. In addition, Rønnestad's findings, like ours, demonstrate the positive relationship absorption has to the three ego functions that Fromm (1977, 1979; see also Chapter 4, this volume) earlier had pointed out as being important aspects of hypnosis: shifts toward Ego Receptivity, and increases in expansive attention and in primary-process thinking.

Two scales of absorption have been developed: the Absorption scale of the Differential Personality Questionnaire (DPQ; Tellegen & Atkinson, 1974) and a sociological measure by Swanson (1978). Both measure the capacity of becoming "imaginatively involved" in everyday waking-state experiences. Absorption as measured by these scales has been explored in relationship to other personality variables. Swanson's measure was associated with roles individuals took in their families. That is, "agents" (group members who are more identified with the collective interests of the group—e.g., in the family, the firstborn) are more likely to engage in absorbing experiences;

this is particularly true of those whose families are geared toward collective goals rather than individual interests. O'Grady (1980) found absorption, as defined by Tellegen and Atkinson (i.e., as becoming imaginatively involved in a waking experience), to be a distinct personality trait, relatively unrelated to such variables as locus of control, anxiety, and social desirability. It was, however, mildly correlated with the Repression–Sensitization Scale (Byrne, Barry, & Nelson, 1963). This scale measures a tendency to "repress" (i.e., to use such "avoidance" defenses as denial) versus a tendency to "sensitize" (i.e., to utilize "approach" defenses such as intellectualization). Thus, absorption has been measured as a trait or disposition that is closely allied to susceptibility, and has been found to relate to certain abilities (e.g., the production of vivid imagery) and certain personality traits (e.g., characteristic defenses such as denial or repression).

The intent of the study reported in this chapter was to measure Absorption/ Fascination levels in self-hypnotic trance rather than in the "waking" state, or after a heterohypnotic experience. We consider absorption as part and parcel of the structure of any hypnotic experience (see Chapter 4). However, we explored absorption in a way different from that of Tellegen and Atkinson. We examined the ability to become totally engrossed in and fascinated by whatever experiences one is involved in *during the self-hypnotic trance*. Individual differences in the capacity for Fascination/Absorption, culled from our subjects' self-hypnosis diaries, are related to the capacity for imaginative involvement as measured by the Absorption scale of the DPQ (Tellegen & Atkinson, 1974). If these two are related, then the measure of absorption in self-hypnosis should relate also to hypnotizability in much the same way as the Absorption scale does. Other questions about the nature of absorption in self-hypnosis were explored: (1) How does it relate to other aspects of the trance (vividness of imagery in trance, trance depth); and (2) is there a particular personality style that is conducive to obtaining a greater degree of absorption in self-hypnosis?

METHOD

Procedures

Four hundred twenty-five volunteer subjects—mostly students at the University of Chicago—were screened for hypnotic susceptibility using various standard heterohypnotic scales (see "Susceptibility," below). The Rorschach and the Minnesota Multiphasic Personality Inventory (MMPI) were used to screen out psychotic trends. (See Chapter 4 for a detailed account of the selection procedures.) Fifty-eight subjects began the month-long experiment. For various reasons, 43% of them dropped out, leaving 33 subjects who completed the entire experimental procedure. Of these 33 subjects, the 30 with no missing data (17 males and 13 females) constituted the sample for this study.

The personality measures were administered before the subjects began practicing self-hypnosis. Subjects obtained some experience with hetero-hypnosis through administration of the Revised Stanford Profile Scales of Hypnotic Susceptibility, Form I (SPSHS:I; Weitzenhoffer & Hilgard, 1967), which was given before the experiment began. The SPSHS:I was readmin-istered at the end of the experiment, and Form II (SPSHS:II) was given midway through the experiment, to assess changes in susceptibility due to practicing self-hypnosis. Subjects also monitored their hypnotic depth with a slightly revised version of Tart's (1972, 1979) Extended North Carolina Scale (ENCS) three times during each self-hypnotic session.

Each subject practiced self-hypnosis alone in a nearly stimulus free environment for 1 hour daily, over a period of 4 weeks. After each hour, the subject recorded his experiences in a diary, noting ENCS scores there as well. At the end of the 4 weeks, each subject completed a series of questionnaires detailing his experiences over the month (see Chapters 4 and 5).

Measures

The measures described below represent a subset of those used in the earlier study (see Chapter 4).

SUSCEPTIBILITY

As noted above, subjects were selected for high hypnotizability by a score of 9 or above (out of 12) on the Harvard Group Scale of Hypnotic Susceptibility, Form A (HGSHS:A) and on the Stanford Hypnotic Susceptibility Scale, Form C (SHSS:C). In addition, each subject was administered the SPSHS:I twice and the SPSHS:II once.

PERSONALITY

Jackson's (1974) Personality Research Form (PRF), Form AA, and Shostrum's (1972) Personal Orientation Inventory (POI) were administered prior to the experimental period. The first is an omnibus personality measure of a set of traits. The second is a measure of self-actualization and its subaspects.

The 10 subscales of the POI were created by Shostrom (1972) to reflect different aspects of self-actualization. We conducted a factor analysis to arrive at a single category representative of the self-actualizing personality (see

Chapter 9). One strong factor, which we called the Actualized Personality Factor, emerged from the principal-components analysis with a varimax rotation. It accounted for 52% of the variance in the POI items.

Coding the Diaries

Each daily entry in the subjects' diaries was coded for Absorption/Fascination, Ego Receptivity versus Ego Activity, and Imagery (reality-oriented as well as primary-process content). These scores were then averaged for each subject across the days of the experiment, yielding five separate scores.

ABSORPTION/FASCINATION

Absorption/Fascination was judged by two raters from the entries an individual made into his diary, and was scored as either present or absent during all or part of each daily self-hypnosis session. An individual was scored as being absorbed for a day if he stated in the diary that the day's self-hypnosis experiences were fascinating and engrossing. Aesthetic elements and a childlike wonder were also considered to be parts of this experience, but their presence alone was not sufficient to indicate Absorption/Fascination. When an individual became intrigued by and highly involved with what was transpiring during self-hypnosis, then Absorption was scored as present for that day. These scores were then summed and divided by the number of days in the experimental period to yield an average Absorption/Fascination score. After interrater reliability of 81% was obtained by two independent raters, one rater scored all the journals for Absorption/Fascination.

The following two passages were instances of Absorption/Fascination being judged as present for the session reported:

> ". . . I remember vividly a total involvement with the exploration of the light."

> "These images continued to appear as if they were being generated effortlessly by my mind. I found this stream of images and patterns intriguing and satisfying. . . . The experience as a whole was quite absorbing."

The DPQ (Tellegen & Atkinson, 1974) was administered to a subsample of our subjects both before and after the experiment. One of the subscales of this inventory is the Absorption scale. It represents a refined version of the original Tellegen–Atkinson Absorption scale (1974). It consists of 37 self-descriptive items that refer to experiences of being absorbed or deeply involved in a variety of activities. No significant change in the level of

Absorption as measured by this scale was found across the 4-week period. The scores on this "trait" subscale were used to help validate our measure of the "state" of Absorption/Fascination in self-hypnotic trance.

EGO RECEPTIVITY VERSUS EGO ACTIVITY

As noted in Chapter 9, Ego Receptivity in self-hypnosis was defined as an openness to inner experience in which unconscious or preconscious material emerged freely. Ego Activity was defined as a mode of mental activity that was directed by the subject (e.g., making decisions, giving oneself suggestions), allowing self-hypnosis to be structured rather than free-floating. Ego Receptivity and Ego Activity were scored according to the relative amounts of each present during a single self-hypnosis session. These scores were not independent of each other, since a relative increase in one would necessarily entail a decrease in the other. A judgment of the approximate percentage of time spent in these modes was made for each day. Interrater reliabilities were 84% (Ego Receptivity) and 81% (Ego Activity).

IMAGERY

Imagery was coded in two ways, both on a 3-point scale (from 0 to 2). Reality-oriented imagery was defined as the extent to which a reality-based visual image, often accompanied by sensory experiences, seemed real to the subject (see Chapter 10 for full details). Interrater reliability was 85%. Primary-process imagery was defined as imagery that was nonrealistic, fantastic, or dreamlike (again, see Chapter 10 for a full discussion). The two kinds of imagery were not rated as mutually exclusive. Interrater reliability for primary-process imagery was 85%.

DEPTH OF SELF-HYPNOTIC TRANCE

Each subject was asked to report his depth of trance three times per session, using a slightly revised version of the ENCS. Occasionally subjects included fewer (and sometimes more) state reports. Since depth of trance is known to fluctuate during hypnosis, perhaps the best estimate of the greatest depth achieved would be the greatest depth reported during each session. This score, and the three scores given during each session (just after induction, during the middle, and before the end), were averaged across the 4-week period, yielding four summary scores for each subject. It was deemed appropriate to average these scores, since there was no significant difference between scores at the beginning of the experiment and at the end, although the trend was an upward one (i.e., the scores tended to increase).

RESULTS

Table 12.1 displays the frequency distribution of the level of absorption, averaged across the experimental period. Since no pattern of experiencing differentiated the earlier days from the later ones, using the average score across days was appropriate. A majority of subjects (60%) did feel totally engrossed or fascinated by what was transpiring during trance at least at some time during the 4-week experiment; two of the subjects felt this kind of involvement almost one-third of the time. It is also important to note that 40% of our subjects were *not* found to be sufficiently immersed in the experience to be judged as being absorbed. The frequency distribution was roughly the same for both sexes, although there was a trend for females to be more frequently engrossed and fascinated by their experience than males, but not significantly so. Since the frequencies depicted in Table 12.1 do not represent a normal distribution, nonparametric statistics were utilized in the analyses that follow.

Before we discuss the correlations of this variable with other aspects of self-hypnosis, it is necessary to establish its construct validity. As can be seen in Table 12.2, self-hypnotic absorption was found to be related to the Tellegen measure of absorption (the DPQ Absorption scale), particularly when this measure was administered at the termination of the experiment. This would indicate that those who had the "trait" of absorption as measured by the DPQ were also likely to utilize this capacity while in self-hypnosis.

As mentioned above, previous studies have linked levels of absorption measured *outside* of the trance to hypnotic susceptibility. Absorption in trance has been assessed before, but only anecdotally. Therefore its correlates are unknown, but it does seem likely that Absorption/Fascination in trance would also be correlated with susceptibility. This in fact was true for our sample: Absorption/Fascination *during* self-hypnosis correlated with suscep-

TABLE 12.1
Frequency Distribution of Self-Hypnotic Absorption/Fascination

Percentage of time absorbed/fascinated, averaged over the experimental period	n	Percentage of total n
0 (no absorption during the experiment)	12	40%
1–7%	6	20%
7–15%	8	26.6%
15–22%	2	6.6%
22–29%	1	3.4%
29–36%	1	3.4%
Total	30	100%

TABLE 12.2
Chi-Square Analysis of the Relation of Self-Hypnotic Absorption/Fascination to Waking-State Absorption (DPQ Absorption Scale)

DPQ Absorption scale	Self-hypnotic Absorption/Fascination	
	0^a	$>0^b$
Before the experiment		
Low[c]	4	3
High[d]	3	5
χ^2	0.56 ($p = .21$)	
After the experiment		
Low	7	1
High	1	7[e]
χ^2	9.00 ($p = .002$)	

[a] No Absorption during the experiment.
[b] Any level of Absorption above 0.
[c] Scores below the mean.
[d] Scores greater than or equal to the mean.
[e] Differences in the number of cases before and after the experiment are due to missing data.

tibility as measured by the SPSHS:I and SPSHS:II. It also seems likely that Absorption/Fascination in self-hypnotic trance would correlate with perceived depth of trance as measured on the ENCS. As can be seen in Table 12.3, all four of the measures of depth correlated with our measure of Absorption/ Fascination. Thus, Absorption/Fascination as measured in self-hypnotic trance seems to possess construct validity, in that it relates to susceptibility and to self-hypnotic trance depth in much the same ways that the more traditional measures of the trait of absorption do (Crawford, 1982; Finke & McDonald, 1978). Construct validity is further established by a number of strong correlations to other measures of the self-hypnosis experience (see Table 12.3). As might be suspected, those subjects who were able to experience vivid images, particularly images with much primary-process content, became more deeply absorbed during the trance itself.

One of the primary concerns of this study was the relationship between Absorption/Fascination in trance and personality traits. Table 12.4 presents these results. Clearly, those subjects who were able to become totally engrossed in their self-hypnotic experiences were likely to take risks, seemed to need little external support and nurturance, and had little concern for social recognition and status. In addition, they showed a strong tolerance for ambiguity and could therefore accommodate to unfamiliar and uncertain situations (such as self-hypnosis). The correlation between the PRF measure of Social Desirability and Absorption can be interpreted in light of the current literature

TABLE 12.3
Spearman Correlations of Absorption/Fascination with
Other Self-Hypnosis Variables

Self-hypnosis measures	Absorption/ Fascination	
	r	p
Imagery		
Reality-oriented	.27	.13
Primary-process	.46	.01
Susceptibility		
SPSHS:I (first administration)	.50	.009
SPSHS:I (second administration)	.40	.04
SPSHS:II	.33	.11
Depth		
ENCS (beginning of session)	.63	.0002
ENCS (middle of session)	.54	.002
ENCS (end of session)	.58	.0008
ENCS (greatest depth)	.51	.003
Ego modes		
Ego Activity	−.44	.01
Ego Receptivity	.53	.002

TABLE 12.4
Spearman Correlations of Absorption/Fascination with
Personality Variables

Personality measures	Absorption/ Fascination	
	r	p
Jackson PRF		
Succorance	−.61	.0006
Cognitive Structure	−.50	.006
Harmavoidance	−.40	.03
Social Recognition	−.40	.03
Social Desirability	.38	.04
Shostrom POI		
Actualized Personality Factor	.65	.0004
Variables heavily loading on this factor (most of the subscales loaded on this factor, which accounted for 52% of the total scale variance for this sample)		
Inner-directedness	.59	.001
Spontaneity	.59	.001
Self-actualizing values	.58	.001
Self-acceptance	.53	.006

on Social Desirability, which sees it as a personality characteristic closely allied to ego strength. Thus, a profile emerges of the highly absorbed subject as an independent individual who can take risks, who is little concerned with status, and who also possesses a good deal of ego strength.

Furthermore, as shown by the correlations to the POI Actualized Personality Factor, the individual more likely to become deeply absorbed during self-hypnosis is also likely to be more self-actualized—to have high self-regard, to be more spontaneous, to be more inner-directed, and to be more aware of his emotions. These correlations give evidence of convergent validity, since both personality measures yielded similar results.

DISCUSSION

Most often Absorption has been measured as a *trait*—one that can be manifested in many waking situations as well as in trance-like conditions. Here we examined the state of Absorption/Fascination by assessing it directly, *in the state of self-hypnosis itself.* This study did successfully measure the state of being absorbed in self-hypnosis. Furthermore, this "state" measure was clearly related to the capacity or "trait" of Absorption as measured while awake. Thus we have demonstrated that those who have the capacity to be imaginatively involved in their waking activities tend to use this capacity to become absorbed in self-hypnosis. The research undertaken here represents a beginning, since our measure of Absorption/Fascination was a global estimate of its presence or absence. It did not assess variation within the state (i.e., degree of Absorption/Fascination attainable). In addition, the rater's judgment of Absorption/Fascination was based on the reports of the self-hypnotic experiences as chronicled in the diaries. It is likely that more of the subjects in future studies will be judged to be absorbed, should more detailed and process-oriented measures be developed. Future research in this area might measure absorption in an ongoing way and assess various levels attained.

At first we conceived of Absorption as a structural variable of self-hypnosis—the background, so to speak, against which the phenomena intrinsic to the self-hypnotic experience could unfold (see Chapter 4). The current study has gone on to develop this concept further by establishing that self-hypnotic phenomena such as Imagery, Depth, and Ego Receptivity are likely to be present when one is fascinated and absorbed in self-hypnotic trance. Absorption that is associated with the fading of the General Reality Orientation provides the backdrop for self-hypnotic phenomena. Absorption/Fascination is a powerful aspect of the state itself. It is found when core aspects of trance are present in self-hypnosis.

This study also demonstrates that Absorption/Fascination in self-hypnosis is clearly related to hypnotic susceptibility. This parallels findings relating the trait of Absorption/Fascination to hypnotic phenomena (Crawford, 1982; Finke & McDonald, 1978; J. R. Hilgard, 1979; Kihlstrom, Register, Hoyt, Albright, Grigorian, Heindel, & Morrison, 1989; Tellegen & Atkinson, 1974). Patricia Bowers (1978) found that Absorption correlated with imagery vividness, hypnotizability, creativity, and effortless experiencing. However, she also found that effortless experiencing accounted for much of the common variance and that the relationship between hypnotizability and absorption dropped to insignificant levels when effortless experiencing was controlled for. Here too, one underlying phenomenon may account for the relationship between Absorption/Fascination and all the other aspects of the self-hypnotic experience. This concern is taken up in Chapter 13.

The most important findings of this study demonstrate that a certain personality style is conducive to becoming absorbed and fascinated during self-hypnosis. The results paint a portrait of a self-actualized individual who takes risks, has a high tolerance for ambiguity, needs little external validation and support, and is open to experience. This parallels other research in the area of personality and hypnosis, such as the relationship of risk taking and imaginative involvement (J. R. Hilgard, 1979). A recent study (Rønnestad, 1989) demonstrated the mediating effects of personality on the relationship between the trait of Absorption and the depth achieved during trance. For the highly autonomous individual, Absorption and its various dimensions predicted greater depth than for the less independent subject. It is interesting to note that our findings for subjects in hypnotist-absent self-hypnosis were more powerful than those of Rønnestad, who used hypnotist-present self-hypnosis and heterohypnosis. In general, the findings in the heterohypnotic literature are not as powerful as those reported by us here. This may be due to the fact that more behavioral indices of Absorption/Fascination were utilized; having the trait of Absorption does not necessarily indicate a willingness actually to become absorbed, particularly in the less structured situation of self-hypnosis. However, a person who is highly self-reliant and willing to experiment is much more likely to do so. If O'Grady (1980) had utilized an *in vivo* measure of absorption, perhaps he would have found evidence for a relationship to personality.

The implication of this study for treatment is this: Self-hypnosis as a therapeutic technique may be used most effectively with those who are self-reliant, autonomous, and self-actualizing. This kind of person is more likely to be absorbed in the experience of self-hypnosis and therefore more likely to enjoy vivid imagery, a deep state of trance, and a heightened sensitivity to internal processes (Ego Receptivity). For the more dependent, less self-actualized individual, heterohypnosis may be more effective, at least until such time as the patient's self-confidence and self-actualization have been enhanced and he has gained some self-reliance.

CHAPTER 13

Overview: The Relationship of Structural, Content, and Personality Variables in Self-Hypnosis

In the four preceding chapters, we have examined different aspects of self-hypnosis, relating them to each other or to certain personality variables. Chapter 9 has examined the various modes of the ego in self-hypnosis, and Chapter 10 has analyzed imagery production in self-hypnosis. In both chapters we have also investigated the influence of specific personality factors. The research presented in Chapter 11 has validated the Extended North Carolina Scale (ENCS; Tart, 1972, 1979) by demonstrating a strong positive relationship between self-hypnotic depth and susceptibility and self-hypnotic imagery. Chapter 12 has focused on self-hypnotic Absorption/Fascination and its relationship to other self-hypnotic phenomena as well as to personality characteristics. In this chapter we examine the relationship between the set of four variables describing and delineating the "state" of self-hypnosis, and the set of four personality or "trait" variables. We begin with the self-hypnosis variables and explore how these variables relate to one another, as well as which of them are most crucial to the self-hypnotic experience. A second set of research questions addresses how the personality and susceptibility variables interact with each other. Finally, we explore the relationship between personality and susceptibility on the one hand and self-hypnosis on the other.

Through the first set of questions about the self-hypnosis variables, we can develop a model for self-hypnosis. The model proposed here is a hierarchical one examining the relationship of two structural variables (Ego Receptivity and Absorption/Fascination) and one content variable (Imagery Production) to Self-Hypnotic Depth. The overall quality of the self-hypnotic experience is reflected in the subject's own rating of the depth of his self-induced trance. That is, the subject's own rating of the depth of trance in self-hypnosis is viewed as a function of the general experience he is having in self-hypnosis. This is a particularly powerful measure, since this rating is not a deliberate one, but has its source in the unconscious (see Chapter 11). The direct determinants of depth of trance to be explored are the structure and content of that experience. "Content" here refers to the production of reality-oriented and primary-process-oriented imagery. "Structure" refers to the state of mind most conducive to depth—in this case, Ego Receptivity and Absorption/Fascination, the essential conditions under which self-hypnotic imagery can unfold. The intensity of the imagery produced is perhaps the best predictor of the profundity of the experience. The more vivid, affect-laden, and fantastic the imagery, the deeper the trance should be.

In order to test this model, a number of specific research questions have been generated:

1. Do the self-hypnosis variables form a cohesive construct? That is, do they demonstrate significant relationships to each other?

2. What is the relative strength of each of the self-hypnosis variables in terms of the total variance?

3. Does structure (Ego Receptivity and Absorption/Fascination) significantly affect self-hypnotic depth? If so, which of these two variables has a more significant effect?

4. Does imagery production alone influence trance depth? If so, is imagery production influential based simply on the structure laid down by Ego Receptivity and Absorption/Fascination, or is there an effect beyond the structure of the experience? Which represents the most significant contribution to depth—structure or content?

Once the model of self-hypnosis has been elucidated, the interrelationship of the personality and susceptibility variables is examined. In particular, the question of the relationship of susceptibility to other personality variables needs scrutiny. To this end, the following research questions have been formulated:

5. Do the personality variables form a cohesive construct? That is, do they demonstrate significant relationships to each other?

6. What is the relative strength of each of the personality and susceptibility variables in terms of the total variance of this group of variables?

Finally, the relationship between personality variables and the self-hypnosis variables is explored by answering the following questions:

7. Do personality characteristics and heterohypnotic susceptibility enhance self-hypnosis? If so, which of the two has the stronger effect?

8. Do certain personality variables differentially affect specific self-hypnosis variables?

METHOD

The selection of subjects, the procedures, and the variables have been described in detail in earlier chapters (specifically Chapters 4 and 11).

Subjects

In earlier chapters, we have shown that our subjects evidenced a strong theoretical orientation, a high level of curiosity, and disregard of the opinions of others. In addition, the men demonstrated "sex-role flexibility," while the women tended to be more stereotypically feminine (on the Minnesota Multiphasic Personality Inventory [MMPI]). Throughout the month-long experiment, the subjects' experiences in self-hypnosis were essentially self-directed. The 22 subjects in this study were selected according to the procedure described in Chapter 11.

The Variables

Two new variables were created for this study by combining variables described in earlier chapters.

COMPOSITE SELF-HYPNOSIS

The new Composite Self-Hypnosis variable was derived by summing the standard scores of the following variables: Self-Hypnotic Depth (as measured by a slightly revised version of the ENCS), Ego Receptivity, Absorption/Fascination, and Imagery Production. A summary depth score was obtained by averaging the highest score reported for each session across all sessions (see Chapter 11). Ego Receptivity was defined as an openness to inner experience in which unconscious or preconscious material emerged freely. Its frequency was determined by rater's assessment (see Chapter 9). Absorption/Fascination was also based on rater's judgment. An individual was scored as being absorbed if he indicated in the diary that the experiences in self-hypnosis that day were fascinating and engrossing (see Chapter 12). Imagery Production was measured by combining two subscales: reality-oriented and primary-process imagery. Reality-oriented imagery was defined as representational imagery in which the subject *vividly* imagined things or situations that can exist in reality (e.g., swimming in the ocean with a group of friends). Primary-process imagery was defined as nonrealistic or fantastic imagery — that is, not in accordance with the laws of nature (e.g., sliding on a moonbeam).

Such nonrealistic imagery, however, usually seemed very real to the subject in trance. The high correlation between these two subscales (Pearson r = .72) suggests that they are part of the same general construct (see Chapter 10).

COMPOSITE PERSONALITY

The new Composite Personality variable represented a linear combination of the standard scores of the following variables: Outgoingness, Impulse Expression, the Actualized Personality Factor, and Susceptibility. Outgoingness and Impulse Expression were combinations of subscales from Jackson's (1974) Personality Research Form (PRF), Form AA. Outgoingness (which we arrived at by combining the PRF variables Dominance, Exhibitionism, and Harmavoidance) measured the degree of expansiveness and willingness to take risks. Impulse Expression (PRF variables Cognitive Structure, Order, Change, Impulsivity, and Harmavoidance) gauged the availability of an individual's impulse life (see Chapter 10). Shostrum's (1972) Personal Orientation Inventory (POI) was summarized into a single category representative of the self-actualizing tendency, which we called the Actualized Personality Factor, by using factor analysis to create a factor score (see Chapter 9). Susceptibility was measured using the total scores on the Revised Stanford Profile Scales of Hypnotic Susceptibility, Form I (SPSHS:I). Since our sample was selected for high hypnotizability, subjects scoring at the low end of the scale skewed the distribution and were consequently removed (see Chapter 11).

RESULTS

Our first research question asks whether the self-hypnosis variables form a cohesive construct. That is, do these variables bear some relationship to one another; do they covary? Table 13.1 displays the correlation matrix of self-

TABLE 13.1
Intercorrelation of Self-Hypnosis Variables and Hypnotic Susceptibility

	Ego Receptivity	Absorption	Imagery	Depth
Susceptibility (SPSHS:I)	.44*	.30	.45*	.59**
Ego Receptivity		.44*	.67***	.42*
Absorption/Fascination			.21	.31
Imagery Production				.60***

Note. n = 22 (12 males, 10 females).

* $p \leq .05$; ** $p \leq .01$; *** $p \leq .001$.

hypnosis variables. From this it is clear that the variables were all positively intercorrelated, but that they were also distinct and separate. None correlated above .67, and the mean level of correlation was .44. The strongest correlation was that between Imagery and Ego Receptivity, followed closely by the correlation between Imagery and Depth. The weakest correlations were those between Absorption/Fascination and Imagery and between Absorption/Fascination and Depth. Thus, it appears that Imagery was central to self-hypnosis in our sample, boasting the two highest correlations, and that Ego Receptivity followed close behind with the largest number of significant correlations. Ego Receptivity thus accounted for more of the overall variance in the Composite Self-Hypnosis variable than any of the other variables. Depth also contributed strongly to the Composite Self-Hypnosis variable and was most strongly allied with Imagery Production. Absorption/Fascination represented the weakest link in the group. Taken as a whole, the variables seem to form a cohesive construct, since all were positively and significantly intercorrelated (with the exception of Absorption/Fascination).

A more precise rendering of the covariance of variables comprising self-hypnosis was obtained through factor analysis. In order to obtain the rank ordering of each of these variables' contribution to the overall variance of self-hypnosis, a principal-components analysis was performed on the standard scores of each of the variables. The results are displayed in Table 13.2. Again, Ego Receptivity and Imagery Production were clearly the most powerful of these four variables, with Depth demonstrating a moderate contribution to the overall variance and Absorption/Fascination showing the least influence. This answers the second research question: The rank order of the self-hypnosis variables, indicating their relative strength, is Ego Receptivity, Imagery, Depth, and Absorption/Fascination.

The third research question concerns the relation of self-hypnotic structure to the Depth achieved. Table 13.3 displays the regression equations. Ego Receptivity significantly affected Depth (Equation 1, $p = .02$), whereas Absorption/Fascination seemed to have little influence on the Depth achieved (Equation 2, $p = .55$). Ego Receptivity predicted an additional 11.54% of the variance in Depth beyond the effects of Absorption/Fascination (Equa-

TABLE 13.2

Factor Loadings of the Standardized Self-Hypnosis Variables (Principal-Components Analysis)

Variable	Factor loading
Ego Receptivity	.8572
Imagery Production	.8427
Depth (ENCS)	.7627
Absorption/Fascination	.5911

TABLE 13.3
Regression of Depth onto Structural Variables

Equation 1: Ego Receptivity as sole predictor of Depth (ENCS).
$R^2 = .2418.$

	df	Sum of squares	Mean square	F	p
Regression	1	727.99	727.99	6.38	.02
Error	20	2282.75	114.14		
Total	21	3010.74			

	Beta	Std. error	Type II sum of squares	F	p
Intercept	21.04				
Ego Receptivity	12.46	2.42	727.99	6.38	.02

Equation 2: Absorption/Fascination as sole predictor of Depth (ENCS).
$R^2 = .1265.$

	df	Sum of squares	Mean square	F	p
Regression	1	380.99	380.99	2.89	.10
Error	20	2629.75	131.49		
Total	21	3010.74			

	Beta	Std. error	Type II sum of squares	F	p
Intercept	28.42				
Absorption/Fascination	39.59	23.26	1251.54	2.89	.10

Equation 3: Ego Receptivity and Absorption/Fascination as predictors of Depth (ENCS).
$R^2 = .2565.$
Improvement over Absorption/Fascination model: R^2 change = .1300. $F = 3.32$ ($p = .08$).
Improvement over Ego Receptivity model: R^2 change = .0147. $F = 0.38$ ($p = .55$).

	df	Sum of squares	Mean square	F	p
Regression	2	772.25	386.13	3.28	.0599
Error	19	2238.49	117.82		
Total	21	3010.74			

	Beta	Std. error	Type II sum of squares	F	p
Intercept	21.34				
Absorption/Fascination	15.70	25.62	44.26	0.38	.55
Ego Receptivity	5.23	2.87	391.27	3.32	.08

tion 3), and this approached statistical significance. In summary, Ego Receptivity is clearly the more powerful of the two structural variables, demonstrating both a powerful direct influence on Depth and a nearly significant effect beyond Absorption/Fascination. Absorption/Fascination, however, shows no significant direct effect and virtually no additional influence on Depth beyond that already shown by Ego Receptivity.

TABLE 13.4
Regression of Depth onto Imagery and Structural Variables

Equation 1: Imagery as sole predictor of Depth (ENCS).
$R^2 = .4157$.

	df	Sum of squares	Mean square	F	p
Regression	1	1251.54	1251.54	14.23	.0012
Error	20	1759.19	87.96		
Total	21	3010.74			

	Beta	Std. error	Type II sum of squares	F	p
Intercept	31.04				
Imagery	12.46	3.30	1251.54	14.23	.0012

Equation 2: Ego Receptivity and Absorption/Fascination as predictors of Depth (ENCS).
$R^2 = .2565$.

	df	Sum of squares	Mean square	F	p
Regression	2	772.25	386.13	3.28	.0599
Error	19	2238.49	117.82		
Total	21	3010.74			

	Beta	Std. error	Type II sum of squares	F	p
Intercept	21.34				
Absorption/Fascination	15.70	25.62	44.26	0.38	.55
Ego Receptivity	5.23	2.87	391.27	3.32	.08

Equation 3: Ego Receptivity, Absorption/Fascination, and Imagery as predictors of Depth (ENCS).
$R^2 = .4512$.
Improvement over Imagery model: R^2 change = .0355. $F = 1.27$ ($p = .38$).
Improvement over Ego Receptivity and Absorption/Fascination model: R^2 change = .1947. $F = 6.38$ ($p = .02$).

	df	Sum of squares	Mean square	F	p
Regression	3	1358.33	452.78	4.93	.01
Error	18	1652.41	91.8		
Total	21	3010.74			

	Beta	Std. error	Type II sum of squares	F	p
Intercept	31.35				
Absorption/Fascination	24.45	22.88	104.86	1.14	.30
Ego Receptivity	−1.32	3.62	12.21	0.13	.72
Imagery	12.75	5.05	586.08	6.38	.02

The fourth research question asks how both structure and content affect Depth in self-hypnosis. From Table 13.4 it is clear that imagery in and of itself had a very powerful effect on depth (see Equation 1, $p = .0012$), despite the low n of cases. The structural variables together also affected Depth, but they clearly were not as powerful (Equation 2, $p = .0599$). However, Imagery affected Depth beyond the effects of the combined structural variables. This indicates that the influence of Imagery upon Depth is not entirely based on the structure of the self-hypnotic trance achieved, but that Imagery generates a sense of Depth in its own right.

Now that the relationship of the factors of self-hypnosis has been clarified, the variables affecting this self-induced altered state need to be examined. Table 13.5 displays these results. First of all, it is clear that the personality variables form a cohesive construct. Five out of six of the intercorrelations of these variables were significant. The Actualized Personality Factor from the POI boasted the strongest correlations, all of which were powerful and statistically significant. Outgoingness also correlated strongly with the other three variables. Thus, the Actualized Personality Factor and Outgoingness were much more strongly correlated with the Composite Personality variable. Impulse Expression correlated moderately well with the other variables, the strongest correlation being that with the Actualized Personality Factor. Part of the self-actualizing tendency measured by this factor is the ability to be spontaneous. We would expect Impulse Expression to correlate strongly with this self-actualizing tendency. This high correlation thus establishes some construct validity. Susceptibility demonstrated the least correlational power, but the correlations were still quite strong. The Composite Personality score represented all four of these variables well.

The results displayed in Table 13.6 address our seventh research question. The best predictor of the state of self-hypnosis (the Composite Self-Hypnosis variable) was heterohypnotic susceptibility. However, the Actualized Personality Factor represented a very close second. Impulse Expression also influenced the self-hypnotic state, while Outgoingness seemed to be only mildly related. The relationship between the Composite Personality and

TABLE 13.5
Intercorrelation of Personality and Susceptibility Variables

	Outgoingness	Impulse Expression	Susceptibility (SPSHS:I)	Actualized Personality Factor (POI)
Composite Personality	.80***	.75***	.72***	.88***
Outgoingness		.43*	.52**	.59**
Impulse Expression			.28	.66***
Susceptibility (SPSHS:I)			.47*	

*$p \leq .05$; ** $p \leq .01$; *** $p \leq .001$.

TABLE 13.6

Correlation of Personality and Susceptibility Variables with the Composite Self-Hypnosis Variable

	Composite Self-Hypnosis
Composite Personality	.57**
Outgoingness	.24
Impulse Expression	.44*
Susceptibility (SPSHS:I)	.58**
Actualized Personality Factor (POI)	.54**

* $p \leqslant .05$; ** $p \leqslant .01$.

Composite Self-Hypnosis factors was a surprisingly strong one. Personality factors, particularly the self-actualizing tendency, thus have a powerful influence on the state of self-hypnosis. In addition, most people who have the ability to become hypnotized by someone else can also hypnotize themselves successfully.

Table 13.7 displays the correlation matrix of the individual self-hypnosis variables and the individual personality variables. Heterohypnotic Susceptibility again demonstrated the highest number of strong correlations; the strongest relationship was with self-hypnotic Depth. Outgoingness showed the least influence on any of the self-hypnosis variables. The Actualized Personality Factor seemed to exert the strongest influence on Absorption and Ego Receptivity, but it had little effect on Imagery and only a minor effect on Depth. Impulse Expression followed this same pattern but with less powerful effects.

There are some illuminating differences in the patterns of correlations. Heterohypnotic Susceptibility was most strongly related to the more primary aspects of self-hypnosis: Ego Receptivity, Imagery Production, and Depth. The relationship to the Depth measure, which assessed the overall quality of the self-hypnotic experience, was most powerful. There was, on the other hand, no significant relationship between Susceptibility and Absorption/

TABLE 13.7

Intercorrelation of Personality, Susceptibility, and Self-Hypnosis Variables

	Ego Receptivity	Absorption/ Fascination	Imagery	Depth
Outgoingness	.20	.18	.09	.23
Impulse Expression	.39*	.61***	.13	.16
Susceptibility	.44*	.30	.45*	.59**
Actualized Personality Factor	.48**	.59**	.23	.34*

* $p \leqslant .05$; ** $p \leqslant .01$; *** $p \leqslant .001$.

Fascination. Therefore, the ability to engage in heterohypnosis is the personality characteristic that relates most strongly to the general self-hypnotic experience.

When it comes to a particular aspect of self-hypnosis, that of being engrossed or fascinated during self-hypnosis, a number of personality factors seem to make a difference. Specifically, the ability to tolerate or express one's impulse life (Impulse Expression) and the degree of self-actualization (the Actualized Personality Factor) were strongly correlated with being absorbed in self-hypnosis. Although the Actualized Personality Factor was also related to Ego Receptivity and to Depth, its strongest relationship by far was with Absorption/Fascination. Thus, the ability to engage in heterohypnosis is most strongly related to the general content and structure of the self-hypnotic experience, but not to the specific aspect of self-hypnosis found when one is engrossed or fascinated. The personality variables of Self-Actualization and Impulsivity, on the other hand, have less to do with self-hypnosis generally, but are more related to being totally absorbed in the experience. Having an openness to life and to one's impulses allows one to be more fully involved in self-hypnosis.

DISCUSSION

The results delineated above indicate that, in terms of the "state" variables we measured, Ego Receptivity and Imagery Production dominate the self-hypnotic experience. Absorption/Fascination in self-hypnosis seems to be less crucial to the overall experience (note that this is Absorption as measured *in* trance). Self-reported Depth is also an important aspect of the experience, although not as powerful as either Ego Receptivity or Imagery Production.

Looking at the factors comprising Depth in self-hypnosis, we have already discovered (see Chapters 4 and 5) that structure and content are both essential to achieving a deep self-hypnotic trance. We have now found more specifically that Ego Receptivity (one of the structural conditions) and Imagery Production (a content variable) are significant factors in attaining a powerful self-hypnotic experience (i.e., one where significant levels of depth are achieved). Although both Ego Receptivity and Imagery influence depth, Imagery has an effect beyond that laid down by this structural variable. That is, maintaining an ego-receptive mode in self-hypnosis defines the limits of that experience; the content, in the form of imagery, is not simply a function of the structure, but exerts an influence in its own right. Thus, the state of mind (Ego Receptivity) conducive to trance depth seems to lay the foundation of the experience, while the imagery that is created carries the subject that much deeper. This perspective further illuminates why the correlation between Ego Receptivity and Imagery Production was so powerful: Ego Receptivity and Imagery go hand in hand.

The second structural variable we measured, self-hypnotic Absorption/ Fascination, seems to have little influence on the level of depth achieved. Why does this variable play such a small role in self-hypnosis? Our measure of this variable represents an *in vivo* measure of Absorption—the degree attained and then reported in the diaries. Although it is related to the Tellegen and Atkinson measure (see Chapter 12), the two are really very different. Tellegen and Atkinson's scale is administered in the waking state and represents a personality *trait*, a *capacity* for imaginative involvement in a number of situations and circumstances. On the other hand, our measure of Absorption/Fascination is a measure taken in an altered state, that of self-hypnosis, and does not represent a general capacity. A subject was considered to be in this state when he specifically mentioned the fading of the General Reality Orientation or chronicled a particularly engrossing or fascinating occurrence during self-hypnosis. Rather than necessarily representing the ongoing backdrop for the unfolding of imagery, Absorption/Fascination more often marked an unusually intriguing and involving session or portion of a session. The finding that this occurred with less regularity than Ego Receptivity and Imagery therefore makes sense.

Let us turn now to the "trait" variables. The Composite Personality variable represents a summary of the four personality variables assessed (Outgoingness, Impulse Expression, the Actualized Personality Factor, and Hypnotic Susceptibility). As the results indicate, susceptibility is least like the other "traits"; it had the lowest correlation with each of the individual personality variables and with the composite variable. This may in part be due to differences in assessment procedure. That is, the Susceptibility measure is generated by scoring specific tasks in heterohypnosis, whereas the other measures are paper-and-pencil tests of personality traits. However, with the exception of imaginative involvement (J. R. Hilgard, 1979) and the trait of Absorption (Tellegen & Atkinson, 1974), Susceptibility has not yet been *consistently* related to other personality variables, despite frequent attempts by many researchers (see Kihlstrom, Register, Hoyt, Albright, Grigorian, Heindel, & Morrison, 1989). There have been a number of studies showing that hypnotizability is related to relative mental health, as measured by the Rorschach (H. Spiegel, Fleiss, Bridger, & Aronson, 1975; Lavoie, Sabourin, & Ally, 1976; Zlotogorski, Hahnemann, & Wiggs, 1987). Other studies have positively correlated suggestibility and the need for change with hypnotizability (Ås & Lauer, 1962; Ås, 1963). The fact that we did find correlations between our personality variables and hypnotizability is significant. What we discovered is that an individual who is extroverted and self-actualized tends to be susceptible in heterohypnosis. The spontaneity and openness to experience characteristic of the self-actualized person, coupled with an outgoing, seeking tendency, enhance the ability to become hypnotized with a hypnotist present.

Perhaps the most significant question we addressed is this: What kind of an individual experiences successful self-hypnosis? Do the same personality variables that influence heterohypnosis also enhance the ability to engage in self-hypnosis?

Self-actualization is as important in affecting the self-hypnotic experience (measured by the Composite Self-Hypnosis variable) as we found it to be in influencing heterohypnotic susceptibility. However, when it comes to self-hypnosis outgoingness is less important, while being internally attuned to one's impulse life becomes more crucial. Thus, the kind of person who is open to experiences will achieve success both in heterohypnosis and in self-hypnosis. The critical difference is that the more outgoing personality does better in heterohypnosis and the more internally attuned personality achieves a more profound self-hypnotic experience. An outgoing style enables the individual to focus on factors in the relationship with the hypnotist, while an internal responsivity allows one to focus on what transpires within. This empirically confirms Fromm's conjecture that in self-hypnosis there is more receptivity to factors arising from within, and that in heterohypnosis more attention is directed to the interaction with the hypnotist (Fromm, 1979, p. 92).

As might be suspected, heterohypnotic susceptibility has the strongest influence on self-hypnosis. If we consider hypnotizability as a trait—more specifically, as a capability for engaging in heterohypnosis—then it would be likely that this trait would correlate with the ability to engage in self-hypnosis. However, it may also be the case that method variance would contribute to the strength of the correlation. That is, the ability to engage in heterohypnosis is measured by the hypnotist's scoring of specific hypnotic tasks *in vivo*. All of our self-hypnosis measures were based on reports in the diaries of *in vivo* occurrences. It is likely that these two kinds of *in vivo* measures would be more highly correlated and would correlate less strongly with paper-and-pencil measures.

In summary, the kind of person who enjoys and can produce more powerful self-hypnotic experiences is sensitive to her impulse life, is self-actualized, and demonstrates the ability to engage in heterohypnosis.

Do the specific personality variables (including susceptibility) affect the various aspects of self-hypnosis differentially? Susceptibility seems more crucial to Depth than to the other aspects of self-hypnosis, although its correlations with Ego Receptivity and with Imagery were strong. Susceptibility thus is influential not only for structure and content, but even more so for the indicator of the overall self-hypnotic experience, Depth. The remaining personality traits that correlated with the Composite Self-Hypnosis variable—Impulse Expression and the Actualized Personality Factor—were correlated highly ($r = .66$, $p \leq .001$). Thus it is not surprising that they followed the same pattern with respect to the four subfactors of self-hypnosis. What is surprising is that the pattern differed from that of the Susceptibility correlations. While Susceptibility seemed to have the strongest relationship to self-hypnotic Depth, the Actualized Personality Factor and Impulse Expression most strongly influenced the structural variables, particularly self-hypnotic Absorption/Fascination. Heterohypnotic Susceptibility had no significant relationship to our measure of Absorption/Fascination in self-hypnosis.[1] Thus, the capacity for heterohypnosis is related to the ability to engage in self-hypnosis and to have a successful experience. We believe that a general capacity to engage in an altered state is what underlies the ability to engage in either self-hypnosis or heterohypnosis. However, when it comes to a specific type of very involving experience, only those individuals who are more spontaneous and self-actualized and who are more attuned to their impulse life seem to become fascinated and deeply absorbed in their self-hypnotic trances.

There remain two questions involving the relationship of personality to heterohypnosis and self-hypnosis. The first is this: Why did we find such a clear relationship between these personality variables and self-hypnosis when analyzing the journals, but not when the questionnaires were analyzed earlier (see Chapters 4 and 5)? However, our questionnaire findings do parallel our later findings from the journals. The ability to engage in self-hypnosis was found to be related to spontaneity, openness to feelings, curiosity, and an aesthetic sense in our earlier research. Perhaps the journals, because they represent an ongoing account of the phenomenology of self-hypnosis, could bring out the fact that self-hypnotic experiences vary according to personal style; perhaps the questionnaires, either because they were standardized or because they gave only a retrospective account, could not do this.

The second question is this: Why did we find such a clear relationship between personality and heterohypnotizability? As mentioned above, other researchers have discovered few factors or personality traits (i.e., absorption, imaginative involvement, and need for change) linking personality to hypnotizability. Given the somewhat unusual characteristics of our sample—namely, their strong sense of curiosity and their lack of concern for the opinions of others, along with their sex-role flexibility—these results need replication in other populations. Furthermore, the correlations involve only those at the high end of the scale on hypnotizability. Perhaps when one is already quite hypnotizable, one's personal style may contribute more to

---

[1] As mentioned earlier in this chapter, this measure is an *in vivo* measure of Absorption/Fascination *in self-hypnosis*. Although it is related to the Tellegen and Atkinson (1974) concept of absorption, it is not synonymous with it. Thus, while susceptibility correlates strongly with the Tellegen and Atkinson measure in many earlier studies (see Kihlstrom et al., 1989), it should not necessarily correlate with Absorption/Fascination in self-hypnosis.

one's ability to engage in hypnosis. These results may be less powerful when the full range of hypnotizability is used.

The results obtained through these analyses are quite important. Most of our highly hypnotizable subjects were able to use the lack of structure in self-hypnosis to create rich and varied imagery and to allow themselves to be receptive to their internal environment. Furthermore, the self-actualized individuals with access to their impulse lives were the ones we found to be able to create such lively and vital self-hypnotic experiences. These strong results replicate the findings of our earlier research by utilizing the daily, ongoing (rather than retrospective) accounts of those involved. We are now on even firmer ground. Future research can provide an even deeper base for the delineation and comprehension of the phenomenon of self-hypnosis, and thereby can increase its effectiveness in clinical practice. The next two chapters of this book describe clinical applications of self-hypnosis that we have already explored.

PART THREE

CLINICAL APPLICATION

CHAPTER 14

Self-Hypnosis as a Therapeutic Aid in the Mourning Process

The following words were written in a letter to her husband by a grieving woman, a month after his death.

> "I have discovered something about the pain of separation, the loss of a loved one with whom one has shared life as intimately and joyfully as you and I. It is not a thing that happens in a finite, frozen moment of time. It is a process, going on over days and weeks and months, perhaps years. The pain is not time-bound, occurring at a moment, then receding. It is like the flow and ebb of tides, now receding a moment from consciousness, now overwhelming one with unbearable pain and longing."

Half a year later, this woman, whom we shall call Louise, participated as a subject in our experimental study on self-hypnosis and found herself working through the mourning process in daily self-induced trance states. In the present chapter, using selected passages from her diary, we discuss the potential value of hypnosis—and particularly self-hypnosis—for the facilitation of the mourning process; we also discuss self-hypnosis in connection with the theoretical literature on mourning.

THE PHASES OF MOURNING

Mourning has several phases, which must be worked through and which usually take about 2 years. Most authors divide the mourning process into three stages (see Table 14.1).

An earlier version of this chapter was published under the same title in 1982 by Erika Fromm and Marlene R. Eisen in the *American Journal of Clinical Hypnosis, 25*, 3–14. Reprinted by permission of the coauthor and the journal editor.

TABLE 14.1
The Mourning Process

Author	Stage 1	Stage 2	Stage 3
Freud (1917/1957b)	Denial of reality of loss.	Hypercathexis of memories of beloved. Also hyperactivity.	Detachment of libido.
Klein (1940)	Immobilization of ego. "Gating out" external world. Fleeing inward. Attempts to revivify dead.	Giving up idealized image of deceased without losing his love and trust.	Regaining of trust in outside objects. Reparation and preservation of self; finding new object. Creative, growth-promoting.
Pollock (1961, 1977)	Intense grief.	Hyperactivity.	Growth-promoting, liberating, creative state.
Silverman (1975)	Impact.	Change of sense of self and of world. Recoil.	Recovery.
Bowlby (1973)	Protest and denial.	Disorganization and despair.	Reorganization.
Arieti & Bemporad (1978)	Attempts to revivify the dead.	"Rearrangement" of ideas.	Separation.
van der Hart (1981)	Collecting of symbols and materials symbolic of relationship.	Burning or interring ceremony (funeral).	Ceremonial dinner with friends.

Freud, in his seminal paper "Mourning and Melancholia" (1917/1957b), speaks of the need on the part of the bereaved initially to deny the reality of the loss of the love object—a reality so painful that it threatens the very integrity of the self. The fact that Louise wrote a letter to her dead husband is an example of such massive denial. Says Freud: "This opposition can be so intense that a turning away from reality takes place and a clinging to the object through the medium of hallucinatory wishful thinking" (p. 244). The dead person is glimpsed in a crowd, "seen" standing in a dark room; a sniff of familiar cigar smoke sends the spirits soaring, followed by deep sadness, as reality imposes itself. Each single one of the memories and expectations in which the libido is bound to the object is brought up and hypercathected and then decathected. Detachment of libido thus is accomplished in slow, piecemeal fashion. If the ego, at the very time of the death of a beloved one, had to deal with the total reality of object loss, it might feel overwhelmed. Therefore, in small increments, memories and situations of expectancy connected to the object are subjected to reality testing and to the process of giving them up, until one can accept the fact that the beloved person no longer exists.

Silverman (1975) uses the disaster framework to speak of the stages of mourning—namely, impact, recoil, and recovery. Bowlby (1973) also divides grief work into three stages: (1) protest and denial, (2) despair and disorganization, and (3) reorganization. Parkes (1971) states that with the repeated failure to achieve reunion with the dead, the intensity and duration of the search diminish. Lindemann (1944) feels that the duration of grief depends on the success with which the bereaved carries out her mourning work: emancipation from her bondage to the deceased, readjustment to the environment from which the deceased is missing, and re-establishment of new attachments to important others in the world of the living.

Melanie Klein (1940) describes the process by which the adult mourner regains trust in external objects and values. The mourner gives up the idealized image of the deceased without losing his love and trust. Dependence on the lost object based on love becomes an incentive to reparation and preservation of the self, and, by identification, of the lost object. It is essentially creative and growth-promoting. Pollock (1961) also sees mourning as a growth process of adaptation to loss and bereavement, having three sequential stages and phases; these involve the undoing of the old object relationship and the getting ready for new relationships with reality-present figures. He states that resolution and outcomes of the mourning process "can be freedom, revitalization and, in gifted individuals, creative products" (Pollock, 1961, p. 18). In a later paper he calls this the "mourning–liberation process" (Pollock, 1978, p. 479). Louise's mourning work in self-hypnosis showed all of these characteristics.

Kübler-Ross (1969) states that fantasies of communication with the dead person, or daydreams about him, isolate the mourning individual from reality and from the living, providing time out for healing; she adds that trying to force the person out of isolation is a disservice. Drawing him out slowly, gradually, and just being there, are more helpful.

van der Hart (1981), a Dutch psychotherapist, uses symbols in a carefully thought-out three-step "parting ritual" to help patients with their mourning.[1] In a preparatory phase, the ritual and how it can help in the mourning work is explained to the patient. The first major step is a "reordering phase," in which the therapist lets the patient collect and make the materials that are symbolic of the relationship the patient has had with the deceased person. For instance, the bereaved is asked to write daily letters for a while to the beloved departed, or to make drawings of or write poems about her or events they had shared. Souvenirs or presents received, and the dead person's clothing, are collected; then, as a second step, the therapist and the bereaved together bury or burn these objects in a ceremony symbolizing the patient's saying farewell to the beloved one. After the symbolic "funeral" or "cremation" the mourner takes a bath, followed by a ceremonial dinner with friends or family; these acts symbolize the mourner's turning again toward the living and the changing of his social relations, in which old friends or new friends will occupy important places.

Some such symbols and ceremonies, Louise—not knowing about van der Hart's work—had invented for herself. In the beginning of her mourning, she wrote letters to her departed husband, as shown above. In the end she went with a group of friends on a vacation.

THE FIRST HALF OF THE JOURNAL: DENIAL, PANIC, AND SADNESS

In Louise's self-hypnosis journal, many of the images recorded in the beginning involved memories and experiences shared with her deceased husband, John. Initially, when she imagined herself being somewhere with her husband, the affect would be positive (denial of death); invariably, however, the image shifted in some way, and joy turned to sorrow or panic (imposition of reality). On the second day, Louis imaged four people in a gondola in Venice, a city she had visited with John. Suddenly, they turned into faceless, wooden forms. She wrote:

---

[1] van der Hart (1981) employs similar three-step techniques to help patients sever affectionate ties to living people with whom they have a masochistic relationship.

"I felt a real sense of something akin to panic. I had taken a gondola ride with John and two friends in Italy 3 years before. Was one of those wooden, faceless figures me? It is as if parts of my past have been erased like the faces on those figures."

On Day 5, Louise saw herself on a swing. John was on another swing next to her. She had a pleasant, comfortable feeling. Suddenly, she became aware that the other swing, though still moving back and forth, was empty. A great sense of loss and sadness overcame her.

Using hypnotically induced imagery, the individual can re-experience, decathect, and reintegrate thoughts and memories related to object loss in self-adjusted increments, according to her individual needs.

With reference to this technique for grief resolution, Melges and DeMaso (1980) describe the use of guided imagery with patients suffering from severe, prolonged grief reactions. They guide their patients into a sequence of images that facilitate a process of reliving, revising, and revisiting experiences related to the loss as though they were taking place in the present. They have found that this serves to mobilize anger, weeping, and forgiveness and to undo binds. Both processes can be helpful in dealing with acute grief.

The healing power of fantasy is dramatically portrayed in segments from the self-hypnosis journal under discussion. Louise recounted how often she had fantasies of sharing experiences with John as if he were still alive, or of joining him in death because the pain of living without him was so great. One particularly vivid image on Day 9 expresses her ambivalence about life and death.

"Walking down the road, I saw old people all bent over, walking slowly in front of me. I had a hard time getting by them, because they kept weaving back and forth. I felt I knew them, but I couldn't recognize them. In front of them was a group of children laughing and waving. I waved back at them, though I thought I saw my own face among them. John was standing at the end of the road, arms stretched forth in greeting. It felt good to see him, but I knew I couldn't . . . couldn't get by all the people. I sensed the inevitability of my waiting . . . my need to remain with the living."

Freud describes the ambivalent pull of Thanatos and Eros in the mourning period and states that "the ego, confronted as it were with the question of whether it should share this fate [death], is persuaded by the sum of narcissistic satisfactions it derives from being alive, to sever its attachments to the lost object" (1917/1957b, p. 255).

Two days later, the imagery described in Louise's diary shows that she preconsciously realized, first with sadness and then with resignation, that she could not and must not join John in death, but must "start all over" and build for herself a new life again, though that might be difficult ("rocky") in the beginning. She wrote:

> "Went into a theatre—suddenly I was alone in a large, darkened theatre—mood changed. Felt apprehensive as the curtain opened. John was sitting on a bench in a park, feeding pigeons, perhaps Lincoln Park in front of my parents' building. He looked up, smiled, and waved. I want to go to him, but couldn't get up from my chair. Image faded. I felt sad.
>
> "Next image also spontaneous—in strange carpet store. I wanted to buy a new carpet, but what really seemed to be happening is that I had been told that I was to start all over—the slate had been wiped clean. I was a tabula rasa—I only had basic abilities (to walk, talk, eat, etc.). But I had no past on which to build, nor any future. I had to find my own, and to start with a base—the carpet. The salesman spread out one rug and flowers suddenly sprouted up—shades of pink, blue, yellow, and green, all muted. I rejected that one. Next one had mountains, snow-peaked, a lake, blue skies, and puffy clouds—I wanted that one, but he snatched it away. Then he showed me one with small stones and rocks—they were wet, so it must have been a seashore—but so rocky! I turned away, but he insisted that this was the one I must have. I thought resignedly, 'I guess I don't really have a choice after all.'
>
> "The imagery, particularly the carpet sequence, was kind of incredible."[2]

In a later entry, on Day 26, Louise could let John go out of her life; at the same time, she knew that she could remain fond of his memory. She again imaged the road with the figure of John at the end. Only this time, people were standing on the sides waving her on. John reached for her hand; she started to go to him, but he waved her away and, still smiling, turned to go.

> "He seemed to say, without really talking, that I had to wait a while, but it would be all right. I did not feel terribly sad, I knew he was right. I waved and he waved back. We smiled at each other and I knew our hands were still holding . . . would always hold, no matter what happened."

In the first stages of grief, the ego is shocked by the suddenness and magnitude of the upset in equilibrium, and, as a defense, establishes a "warding-off structure" blocking further input (Klein, 1940). The intensity of this stage of mourning varies with circumstances and with the individual.

---

[2] Louise told us later that the flowered rug had reminded her of a rug her parents had had when she was a child, and that therefore she rejected it. She did not want to become a "child in her parents' house" again (i.e., be dependent on them emotionally).

As the individual "gates out" the external world, she flees inward. There is an attempt to recapture the dead person, to make him live again in dreams, daydreams, and fantasies. Attempts to revivify the dead are doomed to failure; the individual must begin to rearrange ideas and thoughts connected to the deceased (Arieti & Bemporad, 1978). At first, one associates the image of the dead person with those qualities and experiences that were pleasure-giving, so the memories become positive rather than painful. After a while it becomes possible for the mourner to give up the feeling that the deceased is totally indispensable for her. The mourner can then focus on the impact the lost beloved person had on other members of the family, and can become empathically available to them. This is a more reality-oriented way of continuing the effects of the life of the deceased and of extending these effects into the world of the living. Hypnotic suggestion is particularly valuable in this process of rearranging and altering connections between affect and thought. It is also useful in refocusing attention from a debilitating self-absorption to a renewed interest in the external world.

Sadness slows the mourner's activities and evokes a restricted motor response. It slows down mental processes and physical activities. When the point is reached where the mourner is able to accept the idea that the beloved dead person is really gone forever, former life goals and priorities that were based on the deceased's presence can be reorganized or changed. Pollock (1977) alludes to this when he says, "It is my belief that the mourning process is the transformational process that provides for adaptation and change" (p. 14). Mourning allows the individual who is reasonably healthy to re-establish balance intrapsychically, interpersonally, and socially. Parkes (1971) views grief as part of the realization that affectional bonds are broken and old models of the world and the self are given up. It is not the passage of time that heals, say Arieti and Bemporad (1978), but the rearrangement of ideas, which for some may require a considerable amount of time.

In the first half of her journal, Louise clearly went through this process—from intense self-absorption, with its attendant feelings of pain, panic, and helplessness, to a more positive state of mind in which the loved object was still sorely missed. At this midpoint, panic was replaced by a sense of the inevitability of loss, and sadness was experienced as one of the conditions of life. Memories were rehearsed with warmth and love, and aloneness became a time of intense experiencing, rather than the painful experience of loss and isolation. When we compared the images Louise produced at various points in the journal, we—like all other psychoanalytically oriented writers—could identify three different levels of functioning. Early images were self-involved; John appeared as real, sharing past joyful experiences with her but suddenly leaving her, which resulted in a panic for Louise. A second level involved rehearsal of memories about John, and the introduction of others (both dead and alive) who had been important in Louise's life. On a third level, we recognized efforts to remobilize and recathect the real world. In the later images, there were renewed contacts with significant others, a return of empathy, and efforts at integrating loss and reality in the present.

Early images included the following. On Day 5 Louise wrote:

> "Riding in a canoe[3] . . . John was in the boat with me, riding the rapids. The boat turned over. John disappeared. I looked for him with an increasing sense of panic. I saw my son on shore holding John's clothes. I felt panic and sadness. I did not want to come ashore. Tried to suggest diving—started alone—could not get into it. Swinging on swing back and forth. Nice feeling. John in swing next to me; vision of Florence spread out below.[4] . . . Suddenly John was gone. Other swing kept swinging with mine, but empty. Florence disappeared.
>
> "Then I became the pendulum in the clock tower in Venice, high above San Marco Square. Alone. I looked down, saw pigeons perched on a scarecrow, pulling out straw. People, like little automatons, marched around . . . like dolls on a track, stretched out like a maze around the square. Was the scarecrow John or me? I wanted to tell the birds to stop, but I was so high in the tower, I couldn't be heard."

In interpreting this latter image, Louise wrote:

> "The image was very strong as was the affect of isolation and helplessness. Caught up in my own role (as pendulum), I could not reach out to have any effect on what was happening below."

This statement accurately reflects the mourner's state during the first stage of mourning: Louise was helpless to effect the desired change in reality. The canoe image, and John's appearance on and sudden disappearance from the swing next to hers, both contained the wish to keep the deceased with her, followed by feelings of isolation and helplessness—a fate over which Louise at this point had no control at all.

Images from the middle section of the journal suggest a different level of involvement in the grief work. Several themes appeared again and again: a sense of inevitability; feelings of loneliness, hyperactivity, and dissociation; but also thoughts about starting over again. On Day 10, for example, Louise

---

[3] Louise had enjoyed many water sports (canoeing, deep sea diving, etc.) with her husband when he was still alive.

[4] Louise and her husband had taken a lovely trip to Italy together some years before, as noted earlier.

imaged herself on a train, going very fast through beautiful mountain scenery. She wished John were there to share the experience with her, as he had done in the past when they went on camping trips in the mountains. But she was also aware that he could not be there, and the train (life?) would continue to carry her along without stopping. There was still a feeling of not having much control over her own fate.

From findings of an extensive project on widowhood done at Harvard, Silverman (1975) draws the conclusion that as the widow passes through the grief process, she changes her sense of self, and the very nature of her world becomes different in the process. Louise, in the carpet sequence described earlier, seemed to be dealing with the knowledge that her world as she knew it was no longer functioning for her, and she must begin to reconstruct it. But there still was an overshadowing of fatalism, of the inevitability of what would be. A world that can snatch a beloved mate away is not as safe and dependable as one might have believed. One is not as powerful, cannot control one's life as one had hoped one could.

Freud (1917/1957b) and later Pollock (1961) speak of hyperactivity that sometimes follows the period of initial, intense grief. This is also reflected in Bowlby's (1973) second stage, where disorganization is a characteristic. On Day 13, Louise described an image of "being liquid . . . changing shape constantly." She reported being "busy holding my shape." On Day 14 she saw two "selves, one severe, middle-aged . . . working too hard; the other, younger, more frivolous," complaining that she needed to exercise and have fun. On Day 17, she had a series of revivifications of panic situations from her childhood. Then she experienced an image of herself "running down and then backing up a hill . . . like a movie running forward and backward." All of these images had the quality of hypomanic activity and disorganization.

As feelings returned with greater intensity, Louise began to experience her loneliness. This affective state evoked sadness rather than the panic that had caused her mind to flee from the overwhelming reality of loss experienced in earlier self-hypnosis sessions. On Day 18 she imaged John beside her in a boat. Then he was gone. In the background calliope music played; suddenly she was on a merry-go-round, a very little girl, with her grandfather beside her. Then he in turn was gone. Now she was an adult, riding alone, and the music sounded like a broken record. This was followed by an image of a goldfish with long eyelashes ("it is me," she wrote, "swimming around and around in a little bowl . . . all alone"). Louise began to cry.

In the earlier boat scene, John's loss was met with panic. Now Louise's response was sadness. But in the goldfish fantasy, there was also a hint showing that Louise was beginning to get ready to make contact again with life and other people—particularly with men. Although the goldfish was alone in its little glass bowl, it also looked out through the glass, and it had long eyelashes that could be batted flirtatiously.

THE SECOND HALF OF THE JOURNAL: MOVING BACK TO LIFE

In the second half of her journal, Louise began to recapture with sadness memories of moments shared with John, but there was also an accompanying pleasure. On Day 19, she reported the following session:

> "This sentence kept marching through my mind: 'Back with John to the beginning,' like a chant. Quick glimpses of our first date, when he fixed my earrings, the airport on the way to our honeymoon, walking in ancient ruins, steps of the pyramid. I felt tears welling up, my body felt stiff and heavy, statue-like. . . . This gives way almost immediately, to another image: Going diving. The water was very clean . . . a coral garden with huge gorgonians, like leafless branches stretching upward. . . . Everything was blue-green with glints of gold. I was anxious to reach bottom. All alone, but that seemed just great. There was a sense of exhilaration and excitement. I was almost drunk with the beauty and peaceful solitude."

In her interpretation, she wrote of this session:

> "Though it brought tears and a great sense of loss, the memory scan today was warm and positive. I had the feeling that my memories are a treasure, not a burden. What a nice feeling! Not wallowing in the sadness of loss, but relishing what I can retain of a beautiful relationship. Instead of feeling isolated and lonely, I could revel in the beauty and undemanding pleasure of solitude."

On Day 20, Louise had a vivid image in which she symbolically relived John's death from within her own body, and thereby came to a new level of acceptance. In her journal, Louise described it as follows:

> "Suddenly, I felt myself in the hospital with an oxygen mask, I.V., the whole thing.[5] My breathing became heavy and painful, my chest hurt. I could feel my heart pounding. My body felt swollen and immovable. My head rolled from side to side, and the fingers of my right hand moved in grasping motions. I saw the straw coming toward my mouth. I knew if I sucked it, it would be all over.[6] I felt a sense of relief, escape from all the tubes, all the pain. I took the straw to my mouth and felt myself sinking into blackness, peacefully. . . . It flashed in my mind that I better hang on or I really will die . . . but then, I knew it wasn't true. There was in this re-enactment a feeling that his death was,

---

[5] Identification with the beloved deceased.

[6] John had aspirated his own fluids after sucking water through a straw. Louise had held the glass.

for him, escape from unbearable pain. There was no sadness, perhaps because I was feeling his feelings, not mine. As I write this I feel a great sense of sadness for my loss—but in the imagery it was *his* feelings I was experiencing, and they expressed a need to escape from that tortured body.

Arieti and Bemporad (1978) describe the third stage of the mourning process as the separation period, which involves intense scanning of the elements of the relationship, and an evaluation of the mourner's acts and feelings with respect to the deceased; the mourner may emerge from this period as an integrated, revitalized person. Louise described several sessions during which she imaged such a series of shared moments, with feelings ranging from deep sadness to warm remembering.

As Louise worked through her grief, new themes appeared in her images: Humor began to surface.

"I saw myself as a bird. I tried to fly, but all the boys (my children) were on my back in a tower. It made flying hard. I picked Steve [married son] off with my beak, and he flew away joined by four other birds [his family]. Then I picked Marc off [college-bound son]. He flew away with books in his beak. Dave [in high school] flew off by himself, circling around, not leaving, but flying on his own. Ron [8-year-old] stayed, but weighed very little."

The next image in this same session started off with humorous affect, but the mood changed.

"At an art fair, I was invisible. I could become the moving part of any art work. I became a face in one and stuck my tongue out; a foot in another and wiggled my toes. Crowds walked by, pointing to my 'animated' pictures. Then I saw my kids, searching frantically, but they couldn't find me, and I couldn't communicate with them! I felt so sad . . . alienated from my children."

Alienation from children during the mourning process, when energy is all directed inward, is a theme often encountered in the surviving parent. For the first 2 weeks of her journal, Louise only saw the children as roadblocks in her efforts to rejoin John. Now she began to get in touch with their needs, their sadness. Her first reactions were egocentric in nature; that is, at first she was only concerned with her own loss. But as the mourning process evolved, her egocentricity diminished. She began to feel her children's grief, for they, too, had experienced a deep loss. She wrote:

"Fleeting thought of tomorrow being Father's Day . . . our first without John. Ron's face [the youngest] floated into consciousness, looking incredibly sad."

Louise's images began to have philosophical meanings attached to them, dealing with issues of connectedness to the world of the living, the meaning of life. Suffering can become productive (Klein, 1940). It can liberate new levels of creativity (Pollock, 1977). Painful experiences of all kinds can stimulate growth, or even bring hidden talents to the surface. Some people may take up painting or writing or become productive in a variety of different ways. Others begin to look at the world differently—to be more appreciative of people and things, more tolerant, wiser. The adult can use hypnotically induced imagery to reconstruct the internal conflicts, to clearly identify them, and to find resolution, just as the young child uses fantasy games or daydreams. The observing ego, and perhaps the therapist as well, are available to assist in the important task of reality testing. A sense of self-worth can grow from mastery of pain and can lead to a revitalizing of one's own inner resources and an increasing sense of independence.

Louise's moving from the self-absorption of the first level of mourning to a "world view" was demonstrated toward the end of her journal. On Day 25 she imaged a huge egg.

> "Little wriggly things popped out, lots of rubbery eggs. Baby turtles crawled from them and marched to the sea. They crawled over logs and rocks, sometimes falling over, but righting themselves and marching on. At the shore, a large fish with open jaws gulped them down. I felt sad for their efforts, only to see them devoured. I thought of that as analogous to human life: marching forward, climbing obstacles, falling, rising, all of that . . . only to be devoured by death in the end."

And on Day 27:

> "I saw my brother and myself as kids, on a fence watching cowboys breaking bucking broncos. Then I was on a bucking horse myself, an adult again, hanging on for dear life; wanting to fall off because it was so uncomfortable, but afraid the fall would be worse. Next, I was on the deck of a ship, dressed in floating chiffon.[7] A man approached. We started dancing very slowly, very formally. I tried to see his face, but couldn't. I wanted him to be John, but he wasn't. I felt cold, yet it was nice, in a funny way, to be dancing with measured tread with this formal stranger."

Louise wrote, "I think my dancing partner was death, and perhaps the bucking bronco was life." We disagreed with the first part of her tentative interpretation—partly because it seemed to us to be too conventional, and partly because on the preceding day Louise had written in her diary:

---

[7] This was a repetitive image, Louise reported, from her adolescence.

"The recurring image of John on the road also seemed to have changed form. Now I have come to terms with the fact that—even without the excuse that there are people who need me—I will live, and not too unhappily, until it is my turn to go."

We thought that Louise's dancing with a man whose face she could not yet see represented the wish for a new relationship with a man, as yet a stranger, and her preconscious feelings that it would now be possible for her again to establish enjoyable, satisfying relations in life.

Louise came to terms with the concept that life is a challenge, and that though the loss of her beloved John would leave a permanent scar, there were important connections with significant others that she could activate or reactivate.

FOLLOW-UP AND FINAL COMMENTS

Self-hypnosis proved extremely helpful to Louise as she progressed through the stages of mourning the death of her husband following surgery. Through 4 weeks of daily self-hypnosis sessions, Louise systematically and spontaneously imaged her way from intense, self-absorbed pain and panic, in which there was little if any investment in the outside world (her children, family, and friends), through a period of renewing contact with her own feelings and with significant others, to an acceptance of sadness and loss. This acceptance was accompanied by a renewed attachment to life and the living, and a new faith in her own inner strength and resources.

The mourning process was near completion at the end of the 4 weeks of daily self-hypnosis. In 1982, nearly 8 years later, Louise reported that she still had occasional moments of deep sadness when a feeling or experience re-evoked a precious shared moment from her life with John. However, she spent those 8 years growing and expanding in her personal and professional life. She remarried, and her profoundly meaningful relationship with her present husband was enriched by her past experiences. She felt that her work with self-hypnosis played an important part in the healthy resolution of mourning.

One of the affective states of the mourning process as identified by Freud (1917/1957b), Kübler-Ross (1969), and many others is anger. There was no anger represented in the images described by Louise in her journal. However, in discussing this issue in a follow-up interview, Louise reported that she had turned her anger toward the hospital and the doctors, who she felt had contributed in some way to her husband's death through carelessness or lack of concern. In retrospect, she felt that this anger had had a purgative value, though perhaps no justification in reality. Pollock (1961) states that anger in the mourning process is restitutive, in the sense that it indicates the recognition of separation. This anger has some similarity to the narcissistic rage of the child who thinks: "Something is happening to me and I have no control over it . . . I am furious at my parents who are letting it happen." When the rage is discharged diffusely (toward institutions or agents instead of toward the loved object), says Pollock, frustrations and feelings of helplessness may be avoided or overcome.

Hypnosis has certain characteristics that make it particularly effective in dealing with the mourning process. Because hypnosis is a regression in the service of the ego (Gill & Brenman, 1959; Gruenewald, Fromm, & Oberlander, 1979), the mind tends to work with thoughts and feelings closer to the primary-process level than to the secondary-process level of the continuum between primary and secondary process (Fromm, 1979, pp. 92–93; see also Fromm, 1978–1979). Primary process is characterized by fantasy, imagery, and irreality; secondary process by logic and full reality orientation. Because in the early stage of mourning, the bereaved individual flees into fantasy in any case (the fantasy that the deceased really is not gone), hypnosis may be particularly effective in helping the bereaved. In hypnosis, imagery can be guided (by the therapist or by the patient), and accompanied by reality testing in fantasy and thought for insight and understanding. Successful mourning eventually leads to a new set of expectations and realities that no longer encompass the lost object. With hypnosis this can be done faster than in the ordinary mourning process; typical thought associations rather easily can be changed, removed from their usual contexts, and rearranged. This process of dissociation and reassociation, described by Milton Erickson (1980) and others, can facilitate the decathexis of and detachment from the lost object, which need to be achieved in the resolution of the mourning process. Painful thoughts and feelings, and increasing glimpses of a changing reality, can be exposed in tolerable proportions and worked through in self-hypnosis or heterohypnosis more thoroughly and more quickly; this helps the injured self of the mourner to heal more rapidly. From the images, the ego can gain important insights. It can consciously accept revealing materials, or can return these images and feelings to unconscious awareness until it is able to deal with them constructively. In Louise's journal, images were repeated, sometimes in slightly altered form, usually with very different affect; these images showed how her ego processed thoughts and feelings in an ever more integrative fashion with the passage of time.

For example, on Day 20, the day on which she relived John's death, Louise also saw herself swinging on a rubber tire, high in the air, suspended from space. Looking down on a sea of people reaching up, "I felt elated at the thought of being beyond their reach," she wrote. "I was a little girl, sitting in that tire, laughing at the grasping world below . . . who couldn't touch me." Note the similarity in the form of this image and the pendulum in the clock tower at the beginning of the journal. High above the crowd, out of reach, instead of experiencing isolation and helplessness, she experienced elation and joy, the power of separateness. Images of sea and sand also abounded in later sessions, but with an affect very different from that earlier in the mourning process, when John's absence from a formerly shared experience made her feel hollow and sad. On Day 23, Louise saw herself sitting on a rocky ledge overlooking the sea. She experienced a great sense of peace.

> "I saw children playing in the sand below . . . friends waved greetings. . . . I responded warmly, but remained on my perch, . . . relishing the solitude, which was not isolation. People were there, available when I chose to join them, but I could also be alone with myself."

Experiencing this evolving process through self-hypnosis provides a window inward for the grieving individual. Louise described the satisfying awareness of her changing perceptions as she continued to monitor her emotional state through self-hypnosis—her sense of the changes taking place, of being more in control of her feelings and of her life.

An interesting aspect of the self-hypnosis journal discussed here is the evolution of the process of mourning as Louise moved from images and affects of self-absorption, panic, and helplessness, to awareness of the feelings of her children, to a world view in which death and sorrow were seen as an inevitable part of life, and eventually to a point where she was ready to reinvest her libidinal energy joyfully in a new love object (her new husband) and in a new, creative job. Memories became a treasure rather than a burden, and the gratifications of independence and solitude superseded the sense of loneliness and helplessness.

It is our contention that self-hypnosis, as an altered state that stimulates primary-process imaging and intense absorption, provokes affective rather than intellectual responses, and therefore can be uniquely effective when therapeutically used with mourning subjects. It provides an avenue for turning, step by step, from intense grief and preoccupation with the dead love object to creative liberation from grief and the finding of new love objects. In the first period, heterohypnosis and self-hypnosis can help feed the dependency yearnings of the traumatized psyche and/or the feeling of being helpless and lost. Self-hypnosis can be utilized to promote a sense of mastery and to move more quickly than would otherwise be possible from the first intensely painful stages of mourning to a joyful reattachment to the world of the living.

CHAPTER 15

The Clinical Use of Self-Hypnosis in Hypnotherapy: Tapping the Functions of Imagery and Adaptive Regression

COMBINING SELF-HYPNOSIS WITH HETEROHYPNOSIS: THE THERAPEUTIC RATIONALE

The aim of this chapter is to demonstrate how the use of self-hypnosis incorporated into hypnotherapy facilitates the understanding of conflicts and defenses, and promotes healthier, more functional adaptations and coping. Combining heterohypnosis and self-hypnosis in the special way to be described here proved particularly effective for patients who on the whole had fairly substantial ego strength, but who had not been able to come to a satisfactory, mature balance between their dependency and their independency needs. We asked ourselves whether we could help such patients by intertwining heterohypnosis and self-hypnosis and by having the therapist act as a dependable parent figure, who is available when desired and is supporting, but who also enjoys and encourages the patient's efforts to develop and use her own resources.

As described in detail in Chapter 4, in the University of Chicago self-hypnosis study subjects practiced self-hypnosis daily for 1 month and kept careful diaries. Evaluation of the diaries brought to light the intensity and complexity of imagery in self-hypnosis and its particular relevance to the subjects' own psychic processes (see especially Chapter 10). In addition, a variety of interesting and creative uses for this altered state emerged, including

---

An earlier version of this chapter was published under the same title by Marlene R. Eisen and Erika Fromm in the October 1983 issue of the *International Journal of Clinical and Experimental Hypnosis, 31*, 243–255. Copyrighted by The Society for Clinical and Experimental Hypnosis, October 1983. Reprinted by permission of the first author and the journal editor.

problem exploration and resolution. The imagery reported was very rich, was quite idiosyncratic, and seemed to be of constructive, growth-producing value for many of the individuals (though the experiment had not been run for therapy purposes). We therefore felt that the incorporation of self-hypnotic imagery into heterohypnotically induced trance experiences could provide a rich source of therapeutically valuable material, and adapted the experimental process to the therapeutic milieu.

METHOD

Knowledge of hypnotic techniques was introduced through heterohypnosis. Each patient's initial session with the therapist was spent in obtaining a history and learning something about the patient's problems, preferences, fears, and so on. Often, a simple ideomotor induction was performed to introduce hypnosis. In the second session, the patient was guided through a full heterohypnotic trance, with induction and deepening techniques using both ideomotor suggestions and imagery. At that point, the idea of self-hypnosis as an adjunct to therapy was introduced. Patients were asked to practice at home in self-hypnosis the hypnotic techniques to which they had been exposed, in particular the creative production of imagery. Hypnosis was presented as a skill, which they could learn through heterohypnosis and then refine for themselves through practice and reinforcement in self-hypnosis. The idea was introduced that through self-hypnosis one could take a more active role in the therapeutic process. The patients were encouraged to maintain diaries of their self-hypnotic experiences, so they would be available for use in heterohypnotic sessions with the therapist. Imagery sequences that were particularly meaningful to the patient were repeated in hetero-hypnosis, with suggestions from the therapist (when appropriate) for expansion, clarification, and interpretation.

The method of guided imagery (Leuner, 1969) is close to our approach. In fact, in many heterohypnotic sessions we use guided imagery, usually focusing on the patient's own images. But in the self-hypnotic sessions the imagery is unguided. In addition, we utilize affect bridges to depotentiate, dissociate, and realign emotional responses connected to the patient's images. We employ these affect bridges via free association, while Watkins (1971) uses affect bridges to induce age regression.

ILLUSTRATIVE CASE MATERIAL

Four cases are presented here. All four patients came into therapy specifically seeking hypnotic intervention for a series of problems ranging from headaches and tics to agoraphobia and general anxiety. All were highly verbal, intelligent people, who (with one exception) were functioning successfully in most aspects of their personal lives. They were good to excellent heterohypnotic subjects, with a positive mental attitude toward therapeutic intervention, stemming from past experiences.

Favorite rituals for entering trance and deepening in heterohypnosis were selected by the patients and readily adapted to self-hypnosis. After three or four sessions, most patients induced their own trance states *in* the therapeutic session and directed their own imagery, with the therapist intervening only when appropriate. They also practiced self-hypnosis on their own four times a day, each time for about 20 minutes. Eventually, most patients reported that they used self-hypnosis more frequently for brief periods to meet specific needs. For example, Andy, who had a facial tic, learned to control his contortions by closing his eyes and touching two fingers to his temple for a moment or two. Betty, an agoraphobic, was able to image a bubble in which she walked safely through crowds when panic began to set in. Spontaneous retrieval of therapeutic images was a common experience.

Using Heterohypnosis and Elaborating on Patients' Own Self-Hypnotically Originated Imagery

SELF-NURTURING IMAGES AND SPLITTING OF ROLES

It is interesting to note that most of our subjects used self-hypnosis in a self-nurturing way, giving themselves loving, accepting messages, with the adult-self often hugging and caring for the child-self in imagery. Modeling of the giving, deeply caring therapist undoubtedly played some role in the emergence of these images. Usually the patient evoked the image of the sad, lonely little child spontaneously in self-hypnosis, not so much as an age regression but as a vividly evoked image from the past. The therapist then often suggested in heterohypnosis that the adult-self join the child and care for it, providing the nurturing it needed and could not get elsewhere.

Andy reported a self-hypnotic image in which his 2-year-old self sat beneath a tree, abjectly miserable, lonely, dirty, and with a diaper full of feces. This may have been a spontaneous age regression along an affect bridge (Watkins, 1971) in self-hypnosis, or it may have been imagery. The hypnotherapist then suggested to Andy in heterohypnosis that he, the adult, sit with the 2-year-old and comfort him. At first Andy was disgusted, but he held the child, washed it, and replaced the dirty diaper. He did this over and over again in imagery. Then one day in a therapy session, while re-experiencing the image in heterohypnosis he suddenly grinned broadly. "The little fellow is clean and smiling," he said. "I really enjoy holding him now." After the trance experience, he described himself as content and peaceful, a unique emotional state for him.

This splitting of roles in trance—being both adult and child—is not uncommon. Ina, in therapy for anxiety attacks, often became her child-self. In one self-hypnotic image, she was a child sitting on a stool, manipulating strings attached to a gate in a thick wall that rose about her world. The gate was a large face, her own adult face—very much like the Wizard's face in *The Wizard of Oz*. There were children playing behind her, and a fairy castle up a hill, but she could not leave her place or the face would sag lifelessly. In heterohypnosis, she reimaged her wall and, at the therapist's suggestion, attempted (with limited success) to release the strings and play for a while. After the trance experience, she said she came to realize that she had to work hard to be comfortable with her adult-self. The "adult mask" she wore in public was a cover-up for the little girl busily trying to keep things in control underneath.

HETEROHYPNOTIC GUIDED INSIGHT UTILIZING AFFECT-LOADED SELF-HYPNOTIC IMAGERY

Ina was particularly adept at creative imagery. She had complained early in therapy of a heavy pressure on her chest that constricted her breathing. This upset her primarily because she was in the last stages of pregnancy and hoped to deliver using the Lamaze method. She reported that when she tried in self-hypnosis to image the pressure, as she had been taught to do in heterohypnosis, she found a creature sitting on her chest. It had an old Chinaman's face, very wise, bobbing on a spring like a jack-in-the-box. But instead of a box, there was a dinosaur, dressed in harlequin clothes like a clown. In a heterohypnotic trance, when this figure was reimaged, Ina declared, "The wise old man is a fraud. He is covering his old bones with a clown suit. It is dealing with the archives, old rotting stuff." The therapist asked what the figure represented. "My mother . . . You know she is taking Chinese because they are going to China. It is so dumb, and they keep cropping up [popping up?], dragging me back to the old stuff." This patient, the less favored of identical twins, saw her parents as a unit always acting against her. Her father, a college professor, had physically abused her when she was small, at her mother's instigation. Her image combined her parents— father as fraudulent wisdom, mother as "old bones"—who she felt continued to seek out, find fault with, and then reject their daughter. Once she could rid herself of this image by destroying it in trance, she was able to identify the negative-affect link to her parents as she saw them in her childhood; to accept the validity of her feelings; and, as an adult, to establish a more viable, mature relationship with her parents as they (and she) existed currently.

In trance, pathological images of self and others can be recognized and restructured and become integrated into higher-level representations and healthier ego structures. The case of Jane provides us with a good example of the use of rich self-hypnotic imagery and the full creative interweaving of self-hypnosis into the heterohypnotic therapy process for the purpose of gaining insight.

Jane came into therapy with an infertility problem. She was an extremely compulsive, constricted person, who expressed horror at the thought of spontaneous behaviors. Yet in trance, when encouraged by the hypnotherapist to open up and "let go," her images became rich, fluid, and expressive. Many of her images occurred in trance in the office; she induced her own trance and directed her own imagery, describing her experiences as if they were very real at the moment. It was like listening to a fairy tale vividly told. Apparently, Jane used the permission-giving aspect of hypnotherapy to fully experience creative abilities normally held severely in check. Jane's parents had divorced when she was a young child, and her mother, a physician, had kept her in bed for a year and a half with an alleged case of rheumatic heart disease. Eventually the father, who was denied access to his daughter during this time, demanded a medical report, which failed to confirm the diagnosis. Jane remained with her mother for many years, however, finally breaking away at great emotional cost to make her own life. She married in her early 40s and immediately devised an elaborate system for attempting to get pregnant, which ritualized and severely structured her sex life with her husband.

The following is an example of Jane's self-hypnotic imagery: "I am in a cave-like place, a dark room, deep in the ground. There are many tunnels. I will go straight ahead." At first she was fearful; then she made her way through a tunnel, which led to a place on the side of a mountain, surrounded by lush vegetation. Below was a beautiful green valley. She said it looked like her "secret place," the meadow of the mind she had escaped to in youthful fantasy. She descended into the valley, but found it less inviting than it had appeared from a distance. She had to fight to keep going. The valley itself was not wide open, but thick with jungle-like growth, with narrow pathways in many directions. She chose one that went off to one side. The going was difficult, accompanied by a feeling that she was being dragged under water. (This was a recurring image in her trance fantasies, which she said reminded her of how her mother always tried to "suck her in.") She found herself in a grotto-like room under the mountain. She saw a creature, ugly and nasty, breathing fire and reaching for her with its claws. She gave it a "withering look" and it retreated to its shelf, still fussing and fuming, but harmless.

When this fantasy was reimaged in response to the therapist's suggestion in heterohypnosis, she said, "It reminds me of my father. He really isn't so dangerous after all." Jane experienced a series of images during self-hypnotic trance, all variations on the theme of the "dangerous" mother and father, whom she learned to overcome through courageous struggle. As her parents became less threatening, she was able to give up the ritualized, protective structures she had built around herself. Her initial surprise and embarrassment at the richly creative images her mind drew were replaced by pleasure and pride. She began to plan tête-à-têtes with her husband and to enjoy their relationship in a more spontaneous manner. She was even able to take a vacation from the fertility clinic, at which she had been seen regularly. Through her vivid imagery, Jane came to know and appreciate the free, spontaneous aspect of herself she had so strongly denied, and to be more comfortable with it and with herself.

This example illustrates how deeper aspects of awareness are activated to the extent that the person becomes committed to the hypnotic experience. Self-hypnosis establishes a mental set that seeks out and accepts new experiences and altered perceptions, even a whole new set of realities. This increased Ego Receptivity to inner experiences—which, as we have shown in earlier chapters (particularly Chapters 4 and 9), is greater in self-hypnosis than in heterohypnosis—opens the floodgates of creativity for the cognitively complex individual (P. G. Bowers & Bowers, 1979).

The Use and Elaboration in Self-Hypnosis of Heterohypnotically Induced Fantasies

SUPPORTIVE: THE THERAPIST SUGGESTS IMAGES WITH STRONG POSITIVE VALENCE

Sometimes the patient is afraid of the grandiose fantasies stimulated by idealized self-images occurring in self-hypnosis. When these images are suggested by the therapist in heterohypnosis, however, they are not experienced as being so dangerous, and they may be effectively utilized in the therapeutic process.

When the therapist in heterohypnosis suggested to Ina that she was a princess doll in a toy store, who, with her magic wand, could bring all the toys to life and control them at will, her initial response was to flee from the suggested image. Later she did allow the image to develop, however, and obviously enjoyed it thoroughly. She reported at the next session that she had found the princess doll image particularly satisfying. It had recurred persistently in self-hypnosis, and she was aware of how much more comfortable and "happy" she had felt in relations with others during the week. In heterohypnotic trance, she remembered how often her parents had admonished her not to brag about her accomplishments, not to "fuss" over her appearance, and so forth, because it would upset her less healthy, less attractive twin sister. She re-experienced the consolation and self-soothing she had felt when lying in her room as a child, separated from a rejecting family, ranging the world of fantasy in her creative mind. She had often seen herself as the very princess doll she had imaged when the suggestion was made to her in heterohypnosis, but she had felt guilty about the sheer grandiosity of the image. Having been given permission, she was able to re-evoke the image with great pleasure.

BALANCING: IN HETEROHYPNOSIS THE THERAPIST
COUNTERACTS THE PATIENT'S IMAGES OF STRONG
NEGATIVE VALENCE

When the patient, in self-hypnosis, creates images with a strong negative valence—images of the "bad self" and/or the "bad parent"—the therapist, via heterohypnosis, can counter with idealized self and object images, which the subject can then integrate into a more realistic representation. The princess doll is one example. Another would be the suggestion to see the self in a mirror "just as you would like to be." Split-screen or split-mirror images—bringing the ideal and the present image into juxtaposition, and then attempting to integrate them—are other useful metaphors. Sometimes the patient evokes the idealized self in self-hypnosis, and a reality-testing counterimage in heterohypnosis can be helpful.

Andy, in a self-hypnotic session, saw himself as a knight on a white charger, with a cape flowing from his shoulders. He reported feeling strong and in control. When the image was revivified in heterohypnosis, the therapist suggested that Andy could take off his wonderful costume, while retaining the strong feeling that went with it. Andy found this suggestion very helpful. He recalled how, as a child, he would fantasize being a powerful king or knight, and how sad he felt when he was wrenched back into the real world, where he felt so completely ineffectual.

Betty, whose mother had rejected her after divorcing her father, had a strong negative image of herself as unlovable. This image had been reinforced by painful memories of sexual abuse at the hands of "a friend of the family," over a prolonged period from the ages of 9 through 13. Betty suffered from agoraphobia, making it difficult for her to shop or perform other family tasks. In this case, the therapist suggested to the patient in heterohypnotic trance that she image nurturing her child-self. Betty used the image in self-hypnosis to establish positive feelings about herself. She reported in a later heterohypnotic session that her child-self was really quite sweet and good. The sense of reward (positive feelings) derived from self-nurturing provided her with hope that solutions to her other problems were available to her.

Betty was a good candidate for self-hypnosis. She needed to experience her autonomous self in a positive way, to know that she did not have to be a helpless, compliant little girl to get her needs met. In re-experiencing the sexual encounters with the "family friend" in heterohypnotic age regression, she discovered that the pleasurable feelings accompanying the pain and guilt did not make her an evil child. These feelings had been repressed, along with a strong negatively valenced self-representation involving her body, sexuality, and intimate relations with men. At a follow-up 2 years later, Betty no longer suffered from agoraphobia and had faced cancer and the threatened dissolution of her marriage with courage and wisdom. Perplexing or traumatic early life experiences can lead to ego strength in individuals that enables them later to deal with life's problems. This capacity could be seen in Betty and other patients, in the resourceful way they utilized imagery to construct solutions for their problems.

The Therapist as Benign Guide in the Patient's Adaptive Regression

The therapist as "benign guide" helps the patient connect the imagery evoked in trance to his psychic dilemmas. In the therapeutic intervention, the interaction between self-hypnosis and heterohypnosis becomes an elaborate intertwining of images and interpretations. Once the imagery begins, it seems to expand and intensify. In heterohypnosis, the therapist might suggest that recurrent themes from self-hypnosis will become lucid, and that thoughts related to such themes, as they are recorded in the diaries, might also come to the surface during moments of relaxation (e.g., when one is daydreaming, or when attention is focused on something else such as driving a car, or during hypnagogic or hypnopompic states). The patient is encouraged to include these random thoughts (free associations) in the diaries, along with self-hypnotic material and dreams (if she does not keep a separate dream journal). These core themes and their meanings are then available for revivification and interpretation in heterohypnotic trance and in discussion in the therapeutic setting.

The idea that patients are doing their own work, guiding their own therapy, is consistently reinforced. In heterohypnosis, images from self-hypnosis are re-evoked, with the suggestion that symbolic meaning will become manifest. At times in heterohypnosis the therapist will suggest images that are drawn from cues in the patient's self-hypnotic material. At other times the hypnotherapist may give the patient a metaphor with which the patient and the therapist then may work creatively back and forth in heterohypnosis and in self-hypnosis. For instance, the image of a mask as an external symbol of an aspect of the self was suggested by the hypnotherapist to Andy, the patient with headaches and tics. Andy had been taught in heterohypnosis that he could bring on as well as suppress his headaches in trance by raising and lowering his arm. As he began to control his headaches and tics in self-hypnosis, the therapist suggested that he image a mask containing the somatic symptoms and his distorted body image.[1] This mask, said Andy, picking up the metaphor, walled him off from the world of real relationships. The therapist suggested that he remove the mask. He replied, after trying unsuccessfully, that he could not; there was nothing behind the mask. It would be "like the picture of Dorian Gray, either nothingness or something too ugly to look at." Later in self-hypnotic sessions, and finally in heterohypnosis, he did remove the mask, with great difficulty; he said it was not a face mask, but covered his whole body. When he had removed it, he said he now felt "more wonderful than I ever dared hope."

When the therapist suggests an image, the patient may or may not accept it. Often, when the image is accepted, the patient picks up on it as if it were originally his own. In fact, if the therapist and the patient have established a strong therapeutic alliance, chances are that the image did grow from the therapist's empathic reading of cues from the patient, and the image is ego-syntonic. What the patient does with the image is guided by his own psychic processes. The suggestion is then made that the image be re-experienced in self-hypnosis.

Patients often induced their own trance states and directed some of their own fantasies in the therapy sessions with the hypnotist. It seemed important to us to let them do just that, because these patients were struggling to free themselves from overwhelming regressive/dependent longings. All had established elaborate rituals in their lives to protect them from the "danger" of spontaneous reactions. The ritual of hypnosis gave them a viable structure for dealing with "new" psychic material. After the therapist via heterohypnosis gave them the idea of nurturing the child within themselves, the child that had arisen spontaneously in self-hypnotic imagery, the patients were often able to use their own creative imagery in giving up the idealized and at the same time feared parental imago. Their case histories had shown merging between child and parent, resulting in disturbances of cohesiveness (Kohut, 1971) or in a precariously established self (Freud, 1914/1957a). Enhanced by the empathic, supportive relationship with the therapist, the patients developed a feeling of control over their own lives, an increased awareness of the separateness of self from mother, and a new sense of the value they had in the eyes of others and the roles they could play in the world. As a result, they showed improved self-esteem, acquired purpose and ideals, and found a new sense of direction. Through imagery, Jane pulled away from the water threatening to engulf her and stared down the dragon; Andy pulled off the mask that separated him from seeing himself as he really was; and Ina pulled away from the creature in the marsh, part wise fraud,

---

[1] In Ina's case, the mask image (the Wizard of Oz-like face) came up first in the patient's self-hypnosis imagery; in Andy's case, it was first suggested in heterohypnosis, by the therapist.

part "old bones." By recognizing and destroying the negative-affect links to these threatening and disapproving introjects, the patients were able to integrate self and object representations at a higher, more mature level. Because the sense of mastery growing out of such intrinsically rewarding experiences is so satisfying, it reinforces similar adaptive behavior in the future. Many of our subjects in follow-up contacts have reported using self-hypnosis at critical moments in their lives to good advantage.

CONCLUSION

In the four cases presented in this chapter, patients became active partners in the therapeutic alliance, utilizing autonomously directed and controlled creative imagery in self-hypnosis. The hypnotherapeutic method described here allows the therapist to act as a benign guide who helps the patient to identify recurrent themes and metaphors, and, through heterohypnosis and free association, to work with the patient to discover the relevance of the symbols that have appeared in imagery. The therapist also serves as a transitional self-object, a mirroring, empathic parent figure (Kohut, 1971), or a "good-enough mother" (Winnicott, 1971). Self-hypnosis is a process that enhances the autonomous functioning of the patient. Heterohypnosis provides the safely dependent relationship out of which independence can grow. In the same way in which the toddler during the separation–individuation period (Mahler, Pine, & Bergman, 1975) establishes a sense of "me" and "not-me" by alternatingly venturing away and running back to a consistently nurturing, good mother, and a sense of self-confidence through the mother's proud glances and admiring or approving exclamations about his exploits (Kohut, 1971), and in a way similar to that in which the toddler seeks out a blanket or teddy bear when he gets hurt (Winnicott, 1958, 1971), our patients used a combination of the therapist's and their own self-nurturing images to serve these functions. This enabled them to resolve conflicts and to move toward the developmental goals they had set for themselves.

According to Kernberg (1976), the internal world of object relations includes affect links from early childhood, and object introjections and identifications. From our material it would seem that images, symbols, and metaphors for object representations occurring in hypnosis may derive from anywhere along the chain linking introjects and identifications of homologous affect. The power of hypnotic trance, and particularly of self-hypnosis, can send the mind on a search along any affect-linked chain from a contemporary issue to its analogue in the individual's personal history. Object images that remain relatively unmodified in the unconscious are less affected by structuralization and therefore not normally integrated into higher structures. They remain available in their primitive form to be called up in trance states.

Our own theoretical orientation is psychoanalytic (neo-Freudian), and we look at our cases from the viewpoints of ego psychology (coping and mastery), object relationship theory (dependency needs vs. autonomy), and self theory (self-worth and self-actualization). Thus, we try to help our patients to learn to master their problems, to become independent while on the other hand allowing themselves to have adult dependency needs fulfilled, and to realize their full potential. The techniques described here, however, can equally well be used by therapists belonging to other schools of thought. Experience has taught us that good psychotherapists coming from widely differing theoretical orientations actually often do the very same things—though for different reasons.

PART FOUR

CONCLUSIONS

CHAPTER 16

Implications for Treatment

What practical conclusions can we draw from our findings with regard to teaching self-hypnosis to our patients?

INTRODUCING SELF-HYPNOSIS

We think it is advisable initially to give persons who want to learn self-hypnosis a couple of experiences of heterohypnosis, so that they may learn what kind of suggestions for induction and deepening procedures they can use in the beginning. In addition, this allows the patients to familiarize themselves with the "feel" of hypnosis in general and to experience some phenomena common to both heterohypnosis and self-hypnosis. Our research has shown that Absorption and the fading of the General Reality Orientation provide the structure for both types of hypnotic experiences. It has also shown that the subjective sense of depth is another important aspect of self-hypnosis, which can be experienced and measured in self-hypnosis as well as in heterohypnosis by means of Tart's Extended North Carolina Scale (ENCS).

In order to experience self-hypnosis fully, patients should be prepared for the differences between heterohypnosis and self-hypnosis. They should be given training in the ability to "let go," and to become more ego-receptive to imagery. They must also come to understand that whereas attention is concentrative in heterohypnosis, they must allow for the use of a different type of attention in self-hypnosis—namely, free-floating, expansive attention. That is, we need to explain to our patients that they should allow themselves to "experience effortlessly" and not try so hard, a concept P. G. Bowers has developed (1978, 1982–1983). Many patients need that instruction or permission. The patients should also be told to expect greater fluctuations in trance depth in self-hypnosis.

WAYS OF USING SELF-HYPNOSIS

Depending on the personality structure of the patient and the purpose of the therapy, there are four or five ways of using self-hypnosis effectively.

1. The therapist can teach patients to practice true hypnotist-absent self-hypnosis at home and, if possible, in their offices. The case of Louise, who in self-hypnosis came to terms with her grief and the mourning of her husband (Chapter 14), exemplifies the working through of problems and the creative coping an individual can accomplish in brief self-hypnotic hypnotherapy.

2. In self-hypnosis, in the hypnotherapeutic hour, the therapist can intertwine heterohypnosis and hypnotist-present self-hypnosis for a patient's benefit. Several examples illuminating this technique are given in Chapter 15.

3. The therapist can also encourage a patient to do self-hypnosis at home, alone, and then to bring the material that came up in self-hypnosis into the hypnotic or nonhypnotic waking therapy hour, where the patient and the therapist will interpret the material together. This is a good technique to use with patients who fear that they might lose their independence, no matter how permissive the hypnotist is.

4. The therapist can let a patient make tapes in the patient's own voice, in the hypnotherapy hour. The patient can then, at home, listen to those tapes and use them self-hypnotically for induction and deepening, relief of pain or tension, and other therapeutic purposes. He must be warned not to let other people use these tapes.

5. The therapist can make a tape, in the therapist's voice, for a patient to take home and to use for induction and deepening purposes or when the patient needs to feel the therapist is "with" her. To make a tape is particularly advisable for dependent, emotionally needy patients and patients who do not trust their own ability to induce self-hypnosis; for tense and anxious patients or patients suffering from pain; or for other therapeutic purposes. Before being given such a tape, however, the patient must agree never to let others use it.

In our opinion, the last-named technique above (paragraph 5) really should not be called self-hypnosis. It is heterohypnosis by means of a tape. However, many clinicians conceive of it as being self-hypnosis.

SUCCESS IN SELF-HYPNOSIS: THERAPIST AND PATIENT FACTORS

Many hypnotherapists have tried to teach patients to use self-hypnosis at home, but have found that in the majority of their cases patients fail to practice it and prefer to get all the help they need in heterohypnosis. Other therapists are more successful in keeping their patients working with self-hypnosis. This undoubtedly is due to some degree to tactics these therapists use. A hypnotherapist who, for the first few weeks, asks patients encouragingly at every visit whether they have employed the new tool they have learned may succeed better in keeping the patients on the narrow path of practicing self-hypnosis than the therapist who simply teaches patients self-hypnosis but then shows no special interest in their use of it.

But the most important factors with regard to teaching patients self-hypnosis are personality factors that lie within the patients themselves. When a therapist is deciding whether to teach a patient self-hypnosis, these factors must be considered seriously. Hypnotizability, of course, is one of them. Patients who show low heterohypnotic hypnotizability (i.e., the patients who have no talent in the field of hypnosis) will hardly have a chance to be successful in using self-hypnosis, except perhaps when they want to conquer physical pain—in other words, when there is a very special motivation. But beyond (hetero)hypnotizability, we have found that even among highly hypnotizable individuals there are some who will not be able to use self-hypnosis successfully.

What are the required personality characteristics? Our research has shown that those people who do best in self-hypnosis are individuals who take risks, are autonomous, need little external support or validation, and are self-actualized individuals. This makes good sense. They are the people who like to do things for themselves, independently. They are not rigid, are rather impulsive and outgoing, have a high tolerance for ambiguity, are open to experiencing and enjoying vivid fantasy and imagery, and can allow themselves to let go and become aware of feelings and memories that arise from within. They have high Ego Receptivity to stimuli rising from their own preconscious and unconscious. In addition, they can become fascinatedly absorbed in their own imagery and fantasies and in problems they may currently be working on. They may employ their fascination with imagery for dissociative purposes—for instance, to remove themselves from the physical pain they are suffering.

For more dependent, less autonomous patients, however, heterohypnosis may be a better choice until the point has been reached at which the patients' self-confidence and desire for at least partial independence have increased so much that they feel safe enough to try self-hypnosis.

We feel that, at least initially, self-hypnosis should not be taught to very sick borderline patients and psychotics. They need the "holding environment" (Winnicott, 1965) that the "good-enough" other, the hypnotherapist, can provide to help them not to be overwhelmed by affect or by unconscious material that may push to the surface when they are alone in the self-hypnotic state. At a later stage of therapy, when through the interpersonal relationship with the hypnotherapist they have developed more ego strength, the therapist can consider teaching them self-hypnosis. Self-hypnosis then can be used to make them become aware of the mature parts in themselves, and one can suggest to these patients then that the mature part of the ego can hold and soothe the frightened child part and prevent it from being overwhelmed. But in general, we would advise therapists not to teach self-hypnosis to borderlines and psychotics, or only for the purpose of helping such patients to help themselves feel relaxed and comfortable; definitely not for uncovering purposes. With these categories of patients, uncovering should only be done, if at all, in the presence of the protective hypnoanalyst.

To all other kinds of patients—the great majority of all patients—self-hypnosis may safely be taught. The hypnotherapist who teaches it should always stress that in self-hypnosis Ego Receptivity characteristically increases when a person does not try so hard to make things happen, but just relaxedly and effortlessly lets imagery come up. He can also tell the patient that imagery represents the voice of the preconscious and unconscious, which, when it comes into awareness in trance, more often than not can be a real, powerful, and creative ally in the patient's attempts to gain relief from pain and/or achieve insight and full emotional health.

CHAPTER 17

Summary and Thoughts for Future Research

This chapter is divided into four sections. In the first, the experiential research on self-hypnosis represented in this volume is compared to the more behavioral approaches. This is followed by a summary of our results and then by suggestions for future research. The chapter ends with a concluding statement.

EXPERIENTIAL VERSUS
BEHAVIORAL APPROACHES

The definition of hypnosis, and therefore of self-hypnosis, varies according to the assumptions that are made and to the perspective that is taken. For both hypnotist and subject, the expectations of what hypnosis is like defines the parameters of the hypnotic experience, just as expectations, attitudes, and beliefs in general delimit and control our perceptions and behavior to a certain degree. Selective attention to certain aspects of situations and occurrences enhances specific experiences, whereas selective inattention relegates other experiences to the sidelines or even precludes them as possibilities. Consequently, the definition one gives to self-hypnosis delineates the relevant phenomena for inquiry into this construct.

There are basically two definitions of self-hypnosis in the field today, which involve two basic modes of assessment. The first approach defines self-hypnosis as hypnotic experiences induced and maintained through self-directed responses. Its exponents hold that the subject is engaging in self-hypnosis as long as the subject is directing his own hypnotic activity, regardless of whether the task is suggested by the hypnotist or even regardless of whether the hypnotist is present or absent. Taking heterohypnosis as its baseline, this definition is operationalized as a specific set of *behaviors* that are readily observed and recorded. In heterohypnosis, the Stanford Hypnotic Susceptibility Scales (SHSS) are built up on this behavioristic principle, as

is the Harvard Group Scale of Hypnotic Susceptibility (HGSHS), which is
a rewording of the SHSS:A. Shor's (1978) Inventory of Self-Hypnosis (ISH)
in turn is a rewording of the HGSHS, which also assesses behaviors, but
with a subjective approach: The subject scores his own (behavioral) self-
hypnotic responses. The ISH has been used in two inquiries by Johnson
and his collaborators[1] (Johnson & Weight, 1976; Johnson, Dawson, Clark,
& Sikorsky, 1983).

The second approach, originated by Fromm (1975a,b,c; see Chapter 3)
and exemplified in the research reported in this volume, defines self-hypnosis
as hypnotic experiences engendered by self-directed suggestions as well as
by self-directed responses. The focus of investigation here is on the purely
experiential aspects of self-hypnosis rather than the behavioral ones. Shor
(1979) also came to advocate the phenomenological approach for the measurement of hypnotic phenomena. Thus, he advocated two types of experiential
approaches. The first, the subjective approach, is based on the subject's own
judgment and rating of his experiences. The second, the phenomenological
approach, enlists the subject as a collaborator in surveying the experience
and in delineating its underlying structure and dimensions.

From the experiential standpoint, different definitions of self-hypnosis
(and heterohypnosis) can be viewed as involving different *kinds* of hypnotic
experiences, based on the relative involvement levels of self (the subject)
and other (the hypnotist) in the experience. At one end of the spectrum,
the phenomena are *qualitatively different* from experiences at the other end.
Both ends of the spectrum do share certain aspects of the hypnotic
experience—namely, those concerning structures and processes involved
in this altered state of consciousness.

Thus we propose hypnosis to be conceived of as falling along a spectrum
or continuum of initiation. Whether self-hypnosis or heterohypnosis emerges,
or a combination of both, depends upon who initiates or directs or suggests
different aspects of the experience. The continuum is depicted linearly in
Figure 17.1. At any point during trance, one can locate the kind of experience
along the continuum. However, during a particular trance, the relative amounts
of involvement fluctuate. Although they can cluster at one position along
the continuum, they do not remain static. For example, a permissive hypnotist
can periodically be silent during trance to allow the subject to get more
involved with her own private thoughts, fantasies, and suggestions (Point
1). However, when the hypnotist is giving suggestions and describing what
happens, he may move the experience more toward the hypnotist-initiated
end of the continuum (Point 5). Notice that heterohypnosis is not necessarily

---

[1] Johnson utilized experiential checklists in his research as well; his approach cannot be considered
purely behavioral.

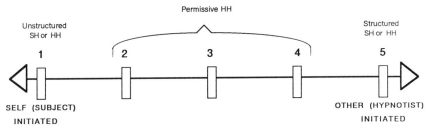

FIGURE 17.1. Linear continuum of self (subject) and other (hypnotist) involvement in both heterohypnosis (HH) and self-hypnosis (SH). 1 = unstructured hypnosis (SH or HH); 2 = unstructured permissive hypnosis; 3 = semistructured permissive hypnosis; 4 = structured permissive hypnosis; 5 = structured authoritarian hypnosis.

found at the hypnotist-initiated end of the spectrum, nor is self-hypnosis necessarily located at the self-directed end.

The continuum represented in Figure 17.1 can more accurately be depicted in a two-dimensional plane (Figure 17.2). Neither the self (subject) nor the other (hypnotist) entirely predominates at the extremes of the spectrum. The self cannot entirely initiate the experience, because a person's beliefs and expectations about hypnosis have been shaped and colored by the culture in which he lives, by his previous exposure to various kinds of hypnosis,

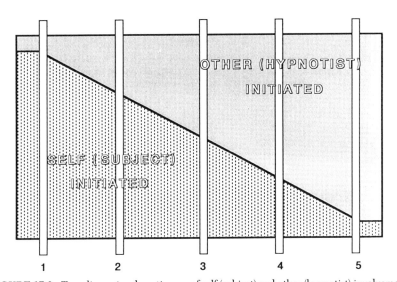

FIGURE 17.2. Two-dimensional continuum of self (subject) and other (hypnotist) involvement in both heterohypnosis and self-hypnosis. 1 = unstructured hypnosis (SH or HH); 2 = unstructured permissive hypnosis; 3 = semistructured permissive hypnosis; 4 = structured permissive hypnosis; 5 = structured authoritarian hypnosis.

and by his interactions with the hypnotist/examiner. The other cannot completely control the experience, since no matter how forceful and authoritarian the hypnotist is, there still remains a part of the self (the hidden observer or just the idiosyncratic aspects of the fantasies or images) that is involved.

Research in self-hypnosis can now be discussed in terms of this continuum. The two lines of research differ with respect to set, setting, and the types of suggestions utilized. "Set" refers to the notions, beliefs, and attitudes that one brings to the hypnotic experience. The hypnotist and subject both "agree" on what will be involved in the experience, and together define the steps that need to be taken to achieve those experiences. Our subjects in the research described in this book were pre-experimentally given a standard set—that of "laboratory-defined hypnosis"—and might be considered to be at Point 5 on the continuum. However, they were told they could use their heterohypnotic experiences as a starting point and were encouraged to explore further in their own ways what phenomena might appear in self-hypnosis. This therefore opened up the possibility for all to experience self-hypnosis at Point 1. At this end of the spectrum, the set forming the boundary of the experience of hypnosis was left up to each subject. Such clearly is not the set in the behavioral approach, in which the experimenter requires the subjects to do what he tells them to do.

"Setting" refers to the situation in which the hypnotized individual finds himself. It is obvious that an individual can achieve a deep state of hypnosis with little structure and in the absence of a hypnotist. The crucial distinction here is the *kind* of hypnosis achieved. At Point 5 an individual can, in the presence of the hypnotist, use the structure provided to create an experience very much attuned to what the hypnotist is suggesting. In the absence of hypnotist and structure, an individual creates an experience based on directions provided by the self (Point 1). However, self-hypnosis (with the hypnotist absent) is not necessarily to be found at Point 1, nor is heterohypnosis (even with the hypnotist present) necessarily to be found at Point 5, although both are certainly more likely to be found at these points. In the presence of an authoritarian hypnotist who intrusively attempts to direct and structure as much of the experience as possible, a subject can still engage in a self-directed experience despite the intrusions. And a subject without a hypnotist and without structure imposed from the outside can vividly imagine the presence of both, and create a very rigidly defined and constricted experience based on suggestions and responses enacted "as if" both were very much present. Three of our research subjects took precisely this latter approach and produced very poor and boring self-hypnotic experiences, despite the fact that they were highly hypnotizable. Again, when it comes to setting, it is ultimately the *kind* of hypnosis engaged in that is crucial to the subject's experience.

Suggestions clearly can be more, or less, self-initiated or other-initiated. The suggestions at Point 5 might be given by the hypnotist, or might be given by an imagined hypnotist with the subject modeling the suggestions she has already heard. A combination of the two would involve the hypnotist's giving a specific suggestion and the subject's in some ways changing that suggestion and reformulating it before responding to it.

The implication here is that the ego is divided into three parts (the experiencing ego, the observing ego, and the directing or suggesting ego) during heterohypnosis and even frequently during waking consciousness. As mentioned in Chapter 2, these three parts are very apparent in the state of self-hypnosis, where the directing ego has a stronger, very clearly defined, and specific role. In the waking state and in heterohypnosis, this directing ego is present without the awareness of the individual. Often it simply is inactive and allows an external suggestion to be responded to. At other times it may filter or censor the suggestion.

The remarks about set, setting, and suggestion made above can help clarify the findings in current research in self-hypnosis.

Sacerdote (1981) thought that all hypnosis is derived from heterohypnosis, while Ruch (1975) reduces all hypnosis to self-hypnosis. Ruch found no distinct differences between self-hypnosis and heterohypnosis experimentally, but he was comparing them both at Point 5. Sacerdote believes that heterohypnosis is what is experienced first and becomes the model on which self-hypnosis is based. Johnson (1979) and Johnson et al. (1983) have also compared hypnotist-present self-hypnosis and heterohypnosis both at Point 5. From a behavioral viewpoint, the comparability of stimuli (matching stimuli based on specific behaviors, comparably structured in time) is maximized at Point 5. From a purely phenomenological viewpoint, it makes little sense to compare hypnotist-absent self-hypnosis at Point 5 to hypnotist-present heterohypnosis at Point 5, because there will be few, if any, real differences except those that are due simply to the physical presence of the hypnotist. In order to understand the differences between the two states, it makes much more sense to compare self-hypnosis at Point 1 with heterohypnosis at Point 5, making the heterohypnotic experience the baseline. Here some distinct differences can (and did, in our research) emerge, based on the *experience* of the individuals involved.

Having made these points, we can now more completely reply to Johnson's (1981) criticisms of our approach. Heterohypnosis has generally been known through the vast amount of traditional standardized research done in this century on the basis of behavioral measures. Johnson (1981) has voiced three basic concerns from this behavioral point of view: (1) intent of the study and definitions of self-hypnosis, (2) insufficient comparisons and artifactual results, and (3) generalizability.

The first issue involves the distinction between defining self-hypnosis as including both subject-initiated suggestions and subject-directed responses, on the one hand, and defining it as including simply subject-directed responses, on the other. Johnson's argument that the self-directed response is a sufficient condition for defining self-hypnosis is based on three points: (1) This is the "traditional" approach; (2) clinical self-hypnosis involves primarily self-directed execution of therapist-taught tasks; and (3) it therefore makes sense to compare highly specific and structured tasks in both self-hypnosis and heterohypnosis. The assumptions we made, the definitions created, and the methodology employed were based on the intent of our inquiry: to chart the phenomenology of self-hypnosis, and then to ascertain some of the differences between these phenomena and standard, behaviorally judged heterohypnosis. However, our research was exploratory and used heterohypnosis more as a point of departure than as a standard of comparison. Although some of the self-hypnosis research prior to 1981 utilized the self-directed response definition, we have moved experimental research on self-hypnosis toward the clearly phenomenological approach. Our purpose was to push the definition of self-hypnosis to its limits—to study what self-hypnosis *could* encompass and to stretch the definition—rather than simply to adopt the traditional view. Furthermore, we wanted to put more of the "self" into self-hypnosis, and consequently opted for the self-initiated suggestions approach.

While it is true that traditional clinical self-hypnosis involves modeling heterohypnosis (Sacerdote, 1981) or performing specific techniques learned in the sessions with the therapist, such techniques represent only the beginning. In order for self-hypnosis to become an effective tool, it needs to be assimilated by the self and in turn to be shaped by the subject's own personality characteristics. It may be useful to give a self-hypnosis tape to a client at the beginning of treatment, but it soon loses its "magic." Soskis (1986) discourages the use of tapes and strongly encourages the independent use of self-hypnosis, so that the subject can benefit from the self-enhancement and the self-regulatory thrust. Basically, Johnson (1981) advocates comparing self-hypnosis at Point 5 to heterohypnosis at Point 5. But at Point 5, what we consider to be true self-hypnosis is constricted. Instead, we preferred to use standard laboratory-defined heterohypnosis simply as a point of departure in our research, leaving the self-hypnotic experience open to new possibilities (Point 1).

As to Johnson's second point: Johnson (1981) argues that our subjects' self-hypnotic and heterohypnotic experiences were not matched one-for-one or comparably structured in time. If our primary aim had been to compare the performance of specific tasks in self-hypnosis and heterohypnosis, which is his goal (Johnson et al., 1983), then methodological rigor in these respects would have been paramount. Our research, however, was exploratory, endeavoring to open new vistas. Matched comparisons of specific features can be attempted in future research based on our findings.

Johnson's statement that the results of self-hypnosis involving expansive attention and of self-hypnotic experiences differing from heterohypnosis are the result of demand characteristics can also be challenged. Although our subjects were encouraged to go beyond the structures and experiences exemplified in their heterohypnotic sessions, a number of subjects did not do so. In addition, these subjects were *less* autonomous than those that did go beyond. This defies the expectation that the more dependent subjects would follow instructions more explicitly. Also, two-thirds of the questions on the Comparative Questionnaire *failed* to demonstrate a difference. While we have focused in Chapter 4 mainly on the questions that did show these differences, they did not represent the majority of the questions asked. That some of our subjects did go beyond heterohypnosis some of the time therefore is not artifactual, but represents a genuine finding.

Finally, according to Johnson, our sample does not allow generalizability, since only highly hypnotizable and highly motivated (curious and involved) subjects were used. He feels that this indicates we are not concerned with the "normative" experience. Our preliminary research (see Chapter 3) indicated that only the highly hypnotizable subjects could articulate the phenomenological differences between self-hypnosis and heterohypnosis, and that their self-hypnotic experience would be fuller and richer than that of less hypnotizable subjects. It is true that the use of only highly hypnotizable subjects limits the generalizability of our findings. But it was necessary to employ such a sample in order to ascertain the contours and chart the boundaries of the self-hypnotic experience. Now that we have done so, the full range of motivation and hypnotizability can be explored, and "normative" aspects can be delineated.

RESEARCH SUMMARY

A comprehensive summary of our research over the last 17 years involves a blending of different directions and distinctions. As we have mentioned in Chapter 2, the direction and focus of our research changed in accordance with the unfolding of our results. Our first interest was to examine self-initiated self-hypnosis, using behavioral heterohypnosis as the baseline. Later, as we moved to analyzing the diaries, the dimensions and parameters of self-hypnosis became less salient, while some very interesting personality considerations moved to the forefront.

As we look back, the research seems to fall into three distinct phases yielding comparable results. The first phase (see Chapter 3) involved conceptualization and preliminary or pilot studies. In the second phase (see Chapters 4–6), we created and analyzed extensive questionnaires based on ideas we had gleaned from the results of the pilot studies. In these questionnaires the subjects were asked to judge how much or how little of various phenomena they had experienced. This represents the subjective approach discussed above. The third phase (see Chapters 7–13) focused on the diaries and represented the phenomenological approach (Shor, 1979). Throughout these phases, the clinical implications and applications were being formulated and expressed. Some of these were delineated in detail in the two clinical papers republished here as Chapters 14 and 15.

In the first phase, it was readily apparent that both vivid, reality-oriented imagery and primary-process imagery were at the heart of the self-hypnotic experience, even more so than in standard heterohypnosis. Also, the split among the experiencing, observing, and directing parts of the ego came to light. Ego Receptivity, while not operationalized experimentally, was a salient feature and could be distinguished clearly from Ego Passivity. Two aspects of personality seemed to be influential: (1) Some subjects were able to structure their own self-hypnotic experience, while others stuck closely to their het-erohypnotic experience; and (2) some subjects were able to readily incorporate self-hypnosis into their life style, while others lost motivation rather quickly and wanted to drop out after a couple of weeks.

During the second phase, these working hypotheses were explored more fully, and other questions were formulated in detail. Results indicated that the fading of the General Reality Orientation and Absorption provided the structure for both self-hypnosis and heterohypnosis, whereas Ego Re-ceptivity, free-floating attention, and fluctuations in trance depth characterized self-initiated self-hypnosis. Ego Activity was also clearly present in self-hypnosis, as was a shifting or mixture of Ego Receptivity and Ego Activity. Not all attention was expansive; selective concentration provided a backdrop for the experience. In terms of the content, vivid, idiosyncratic imagery again was powerfully salient, with personal memories and adventures emerging with great frequency. Although a number of subjects specifically attempted age regression in self-hypnosis, most felt that they were more successful with age regression in the structured heterohypnotic situation. Time distortion was a part of the self-hypnotic experience as well. Longitudinally, Ego Re-ceptivity, Imagery, confidence in the ability to enter and maintain trance, and Trance Depth increased over time, while anxiety and doubt decreased. The personality results were mixed, although it was clear that individuals with a seeking, open, spontaneous stance toward life were more successful in self-hypnosis.

In the third phase, the constructs delineated in the first two phases were explored in greater detail in the diaries. During this period, the phe-nomenological approach was utilized. Through systematic analysis of our subjects' experiences—as documented in their own words in the diaries they kept—the results emerged with greater power and clarity, and could be related to personality factors that appeared on the Personality Research Form (PRF) and the Personal Orientation Inventory (POI).

The frequency and function of Ego Activity and Ego Receptivity and the alternations between them were clarified. Ego Activity occurred more frequently than Ego Receptivity and provided the structure for the unfolding of self-hypnosis. Ego Receptivity allowed the facets of the self to emerge by providing the context to allow them to bubble up from the unconscious. Although more Ego Activity was actually found in self-hypnosis, Ego Receptivity was what seemed to be at the heart of the experience. The rhythm of alternation between Ego Activity and Ego Receptivity was dictated by the needs of the individual subjects, who at times needed structure and guidance in the face of overwhelming affect, while at other times they could work through some of the emotions salient in their unconscious and preconscious lives. One of the most important findings was that a specific cluster of personality traits influenced the experience. Independent subjects who were at ease with themselves, and who were spontaneous and open to experience and to their emotions, were able to allow more Ego Receptivity in self-hypnosis. When Ego Activity predominated heavily over Ego Receptivity, the experience became dull and constricted. The rigid, nonspontaneous, and externally oriented individuals tended to have this torpid type of self-hypnotic trance.

As for self-hypnotic Imagery, we found that both reality-oriented and primary-process imagery were at the core of self-hypnosis, particularly for females. Although Ego Receptivity and Imagery went hand in hand, Imagery was the sine qua non of self-initiated self-hypnosis, in that it influenced trance depth beyond the influence of Ego Receptivity. Again some striking sex differences emerged, and again personality characteristics were found to be influential primarily for the women in the sample. The more available a subject's impulses were, and the more outgoing and the more self-actualized the subject was, the more profound and vivid the subject's Imagery was.

The assessment of self-hypnotic Trance Depth with the Extended North Carolina Scale (ENCS) was demonstrated to be quite effective. Though trance depth seemed to indicate the overall quality of the experience, it was a less central variable than either Ego Receptivity or imagery production. Personality characteristics were also less influential here, though the pattern paralleled the findings with Ego Receptivity and Imagery: The more spontaneous, outgoing, and self-actualized individuals experienced greater Trance Depth in self-hypnosis.

We also measured how engrossed and involved our subjects became *during* trance (i.e., an *in vivo* assessment); we called this variable self-hypnotic Absorption/Fascination. While related to the *trait* of absorption as measured by a scale of the Differential Personality Questionnaire (DPQ; Tellegen & Atkinson, 1974), this was a very different measure; it occurred less frequently than other aspects of self-hypnosis, since it was a specialized feature. Not every self-hypnotic trance was completely absorbing and filled with wonderment. When the self-hypnotic trance was heightened to this extent, the influence of personality characteristics became the most profound. Again, the individuals who were self-actualized and who readily experienced impulses found themselves absorbed and fascinated more easily.

Finally, when the self-hypnosis variables were summarized into one composite measure and the personality variables were also combined, a very strong relationship between the two sets emerged. This very important finding deserves further scrutiny. Why did we find personal style to make such a difference, when research previously has been hard put to find a relationship between hypnosis variables and personality traits? A number of ways in which our research differs from that of others may shed some light on this question.

One of the most important disjunctions with past research is our methodology. We assessed the self-hypnotic experience via the phenomenological method, which allowed us to tap its richer and more varied aspects. The specific behavioral aspects of self-hypnosis were less important to us and therefore occupied a less central focus. Furthermore, we were examining a specific type of self-hypnosis—the kind that was self-initiated, rather than simply the self-directed execution of hypnotist-initiated tasks. This allowed more of the self to emerge, making for more individual differences in the experience. Consequently, personal style could have more of an impact. Finally, each of the aspects of self-hypnosis (Ego Receptivity, Imagery, Depth, Absorption/Fascination, etc.) was assessed separately by "objective" judges, and a great number of data points were analyzed. Hypnotizability assessment involves much fewer instances of behavior. It is likely that the increased frequency of response over a period of time heightened the accuracy of the measures.

In summary, our research has taken a different approach and emerged with some new and exciting results; the subjective and the phenomenological methods produced corresponding findings. The later research confirmed and validated the earlier, more exploratory findings through a more painstaking and refined method that tapped more profound aspects of the phenomenon of self-initiated self-hypnosis. The level of correspondence with the earlier findings may provide some of the convergent validity (Campbell & Fiske, 1959) that is so essential to scientific endeavor. However, given the exploratory nature of our research, there are a number of caveats and guides for future research. These are taken up in the next section.

FUTURE RESEARCH

Considerations for future research include the following: (1) enlarging and randomizing the sample, (2) comparing the phenomena of heterohypnosis and self-hypnosis to those of the waking state, (3) combining behavioral and phenomenological approaches, and (4) specific areas of focus.

Sample Considerations

The small size of our sample, while allowing a wealth of idiographic analyses, nonetheless limits nomothetic considerations. It is appropriate for exploratory research. But such a small sample (33 subjects in all; 30, 27, 26, or 22 in some analyses) limits statistical inference and generalizability. Future research should be conducted on larger samples.

These samples should also be randomized to include the full range of hypnotizability and motivation. In order to heighten the differences between self-hypnosis and heterohypnosis, only highly hypnotizable subjects were used in our final sample. Earlier, the pilot project (see Chapter 3) had demonstrated that the differences were highlighted in the highly hypnotizable individuals. Therefore, such individuals were selected for the final pool of subjects. Future research needs to explore the differences in the population at large, to be certain that the effects we found are not simply artifacts due to a rarefied sample. A more normative experience can now be the focus of investigation. In addition, utilization of the entire range with a large number of cases should permit separate analyses of subjects at the high and the low ends of the hypnotizability spectrum. The subjects at the low end of the spectrum could be used as controls.

Sex differences (see Chapter 10) need to be consistently explored as well. Since we found Ego Receptivity and Imagery to be at the heart of self-hypnosis, and since we also discovered sex differences in these two areas—and furthermore, since we found different personality characteristics influencing Imagery in men and in women—it becomes imperative in all future research on self-hypnosis to examine gender differences. This means that, in addition to having a large number of subjects along the spectrum of hypnotizability, each distinct level must have a high enough number of men and women to afford comparability. That is, women at the low end of the scale need to be compared to women at the high end, as well as to the men at both ends of the scale.

Motivational and personality characteristics also need to be randomized. An unpaid subject who for 4 weeks spends 1 hour daily in self-hypnosis is indeed a rare individual. When we take into account that almost half of our original sample dropped out of the experiment at various points, the remainder, our experimental group comprised entirely of volunteer and unpaid subjects, must have been very highly motivated. A comparison of personality differences between those who stayed in and those who dropped out of the experiment would shed some light on whether this sample actually was an unusual one.

Personality differences between our highly susceptible subjects and the population at large were not substantial. Results on the Minnesota Multiphasic Personality Inventory (MMPI) revealed that the subjects were more emotionally stable than the normative sample. Our results also revealed sex-role flexibility for males. The PRF showed our University of Chicago subjects of the mid-1970s to be substantially higher than the norm on understanding (curiosity and intellectuality), to be more sensitive and more aesthetically oriented, and to have little concern for the opinions of others. Although these were not large departures from the norm, they may have affected the outcome.

One final consideration regarding the sample involves the historical context in which the experiment was conducted. It was a period following the political unrest and social ferment of the 1960s. Those high-minded individuals who were interested in political change also seemed to gravitate toward an interest in expansion of the limits of the mind (and thus to experiments in hypnosis). Would a sample taken at a time less characterized by idealism, interest in social change, and the popular search to understand the inner workings of the mind react the same way to self-hypnosis and demonstrate the same results found in our sample?

Standards of Comparison

In Chapter 5 we have discussed the elements of self-hypnosis proper, without reference to heterohypnosis or to changes in self-hypnotic responsivity over time. Chapter 13 and other chapters demonstrate the relative frequency of occurrence of the different aspects of self-hypnosis (e.g., Imagery, Ego Receptivity). Unfortunately, there is no standard of comparison; that is, nothing is known with regard to the frequency of imagery in the waking state or in heterohypnosis. Although certain phenomena occur more frequently in self-hypnosis than in heterohypnosis, we do not know how much more frequently. Future studies can remedy this situation by instructing a group of subjects to report daily over consecutive stretches of time on the occurrence of such phenomena in the waking state, in heterohypnosis, and in self-hypnosis.

Combination of Approaches

Research with the Chicago paradigm derives its theoretical base from the phenomenological perspective (see Chapter 4). As Orne and McConkey (1981) suggest, one must utilize behavioral measures along with phenomenological approaches to provide convergent assessment of the phenomenon of self-hypnosis. Convergent assessment can clarify the boundaries of self-hypnosis, throw into further relief the distinctions between self-hypnosis and heterohypnosis, and further specify the relationships between personality and hypnosis. Thus, in addition to administering retrospective questionnaires (the subjective approach) and rating or analyzing ongoing accounts of the subjects' experience (the phenomenological approach), observable and operationally defined behaviors need to be developed and assessed (the behavioral approach).

Creating behavioral indicators for self-initiated self-hypnosis is not a simple task. Shor's ISH is one method of assessing how much depth a subject can attain in self-hypnosis limited to relatively few hypnotic phenomena. As it is ultimately a variation of the SHSS:A, it spans a rather narrow range of phenomena. It does not tap such cognitive phenomena as Imagery and Ego Receptivity. Orne and McConkey (1981) suggest using changes in perception and control of pain or anxiety as indicators of self-hypnosis. With this in mind, experiments could be designed creating situations in self-hypnosis where more readily observable behaviors could be tabulated.

To standardize the stimulus, pain here would be *induced* rather than the result of ongoing pathology. This could be done by means of a tourniquet, the pressure of which would be controlled by an examiner located in another room. The subjects' videotaped behavior, body posture, and facial expressions could be compared to those of the same subjects under the same circumstances in the waking state and in heterohypnosis. All three situations would utilize videotape to record overt behaviors and statements about change in the level of pain experienced. Subjects who would be alone in a room in self-hypnosis could speak aloud throughout trance about the experiential changes, instead of recording the experience after the trance has ended. Simultaneously, physiological indicators could be used to measure changes in galvanic skin response, blood pressure, and pulse, not just during the administration of pain but for the entire duration of trance. Other hypnotic tasks, such as anosmia to various strengths of ammonia (as in the SHSS:C; see Weitzenhoffer & Hilgard, 1962), could be utilized, and the behavioral and physiological responses to them could be recorded on videotape. Differential responses in behavior and physiology might correlate with depth of trance. The same tasks along with physiological assessments could then be given to the same subjects in heterohypnosis and in the waking state, too, and videotaped and analyzed. Adding such techniques to the methodology of the phenomenological approach employed in our research could provide convergent validity.

Specific Areas

Certain specific areas of research can now be addressed: (1) comparison of the different kinds of hypnosis and the personality characteristics that are or are not influential, and (2) longitudinal aspects of self-hypnosis.

As we have stated earlier, our research not only explored and delineated the various aspects of self-hypnosis, but focused on a particular type— namely, self-initiated self-hypnosis. The unique involvement of the self that is made possible in hypnosis creates a special kind of experience. As might be expected with the unfolding of the self, certain personality characteristics foster this process while others inhibit it. To more fully comprehend the differences among the various kinds of hypnosis, comparisons on both an experiential and a behavioral level are in order. This would involve having the same subjects engage in more specific behavioral self-hypnotic tasks as well as give equal time to unstructured self-hypnosis, and then comparing the phenomenologies of both states by looking at both structural and content variables. For instance, different types of Ego Receptivity may be distinguished when the subject is directing attention to the hypnotist/other (Point 5 in Figure 17.1) versus the self (Point 1). Ego Receptivity at Point 5 may shade into Ego Passivity. At Point 1, it seems to require the presence of the directing ego to come to the forefront. The directing ego can periodically allow an alternation between Ego Activity and Ego Receptivity, according to the needs of the subject. This process may be easier in self-hypnosis, when the self is directly in contact with the subject's needs, than in het- erohypnosis, when the process is mediated through the direction of the hypnotist. Clearly, the self is more involved in the self-initiated form of Ego Receptivity, which may be more desirable from a clinical standpoint. However, Ego Receptivity at Point 5 and the presence of a structuring therapist may be more helpful when there is a fear of overwhelming affect, as there can be in an age regression. Our results indicated that while age regression occurred in self-hypnosis at Point 1, it did so less than in heterohypnosis at Point 5.

Likewise, the personality variables influencing other-initiated as opposed to self-initiated self-hypnosis could be examined. Individuals who were more self-actualized and attuned to their impulse life proved in our research to be more able to engage in self-initiated Ego Receptivity. Are there other correlates of hypnotist-initiated Ego Receptivity? Some researchers (Diamond, Gregory, Lenney, Steadman, & Talone, 1974; Rønnestad, 1989) have found that moderator analyses can clarify the relationship of personality to hypnosis. Such analyses may shed further light on the relationship between personality and self-hypnosis.

Over a short span of time (our experimental period of 4 weeks), there seems to be an enhancement of rather than a decrement in the experience of self-hypnosis. This may be due to the "active involvement" (Johnson et al., 1983) of the self or may simply be part of a learning curve. Are there specific structural (e.g., Ego Receptivity, etc.) or content (e.g., Imagery) variables that become further enhanced or possibly show a decline over the long haul? From a clinical standpoint, experiments spanning a longer period of time with less intensive self-hypnosis practice would be useful. Is there limited utility to the practice of hypnotist-absent self-hypnosis, and is there a need in such cases for periodic "reinforcement" by means of heterohypnotic sessions? What kind of therapeutic relationship variables are influential here? Is more self-initiated self-hypnosis easier to assimilate, and therefore practiced for longer periods of time, than self-hypnosis in which the experimenter or therapist assigns specific tasks to be done by the patient when alone? We now know that certain individuals (more autonomous and self-actualized) thrive on self-initiated self-hypnosis. How can self-hypnosis best be utilized to encourage individual development, so that subjects continue the therapeutic process not only after the end of the session, but also after termination of the therapy? Although Chapter 15 has suggested the interweaving of self-hypnotic and heterohypnotic techniques, the timing and sequencing of these techniques need further elaboration and specification.

CONCLUDING STATEMENT

The study of self-initiated self-hypnosis has clearly brought forth fruit. The phenomenological approach is the best strategy for highlighting the phenomena of self-initiated self-hypnosis and clarifying the relationship of personality to this particular altered state of consciousness. Crucial differences between self-initiated self-hypnosis and heterohypnosis have emerged, primarily in the field of the ego-receptive aspects involved in self-hypnosis. The more spontaneous, self-actualized, and open to internal impulses the subject is, the more likely it is that a fuller, richer self-hypnotic experience will unfold. We hope our research has further clarified that hypnosis and self-hypnosis are not unidimensional phenomena that can only be assessed through behavioral measures. We also hope our research has opened doors and shed some light on the varieties of hypnotic experience and the kinds of people who experience them.

References

Alman, B. M., with Lambrou, P. T. (1983). *Self-hypnosis: A complete manual for health and self-change*. San Diego: International Health.

Anderson, J. A. D., Basker, M. A., & Dalton, R. (1975). Migraine and hypnotherapy. *International Journal of Clinical and Experimental Hypnosis, 23*, 48–58.

Araoz, D. L. (1981). Negative self-hypnosis. *Journal of Contemporary Psychotherapy, 12*(1), 45–52.

Arieti, S., & Bemporad, J. (1978). *Severe and mild depression*. New York: Basic Books.

Arnold, M. B. (1946). On the mechanism of suggestion and hypnosis. *Journal of Abnormal and Social Psychology, 41*, 107–128.

Aronson, D. M. (1986). The adolescent as hypnotist: Hypnosis and self-hypnosis with adolescent psychiatric inpatients. *American Journal of Clinical Hypnosis, 28*, 163–169.

Ås, A. (1963). Hypnotizability as a function of nonhypnotic experiences. *Journal of Abnormal and Social Psychology, 66*, 142–150.

Ås, A., & Lauer, L. W. (1962). A factor-analytic study of hypnotizability and related personality experiences. *International Journal of Clinical and Experimental Hypnosis, 3*, 47–63.

Barber, T. X. (1979). Suggested ("hypnotic") behavior: The trance paradigm versus an alternative paradigm. In E. Fromm & R. E. Shor (Eds.), *Hypnosis: Developments in research and new perspectives* (2nd ed., pp. 217–271). New York: Aldine.

Barber, T. X., & Calverley, D. S. (1964). Definition of the situation as a variable affecting "hypnotic-like" suggestibility. *Journal of Clinical Psychology, 20*, 438–440.

Barber, T. X., Dalal, A. S., and Calverley, D. S. (1968). The subjective reports of hypnotic subjects. *American Journal of Clinical Hypnosis, 11*, 74–88.

Barr, H. L., Langs, R. J., Holt, R. R., Goldberger, L., & Klein, G. S. (1972). *LSD: Personality and experience*. New York: Wiley.

Benson, H., Arns, P. A., & Hoffman, J. W. (1981). The relaxation response and hypnosis. *International Journal of Clinical and Experimental Hypnosis, 29*, 259–270.

Bentler, P. M. (1963). Interpersonal orientation in relation to hypnotic susceptibility. *Journal of Consulting Psychology, 27*, 426–431.

Betts, G. H. (1909). *The distribution of and function of mental imagery* (Teachers College Contributions to Education No. 26). New York: Teachers College Press.

Binet, A., & Féré, C. (1888). *Animal magnetism.* New York: Appleton. (Original work published 1886)

Bowers, K. S. (1971). Sex and susceptibility as moderator variables in the relationship of creativity and hypnotic susceptibility. *Journal of Abnormal Psychology, 78,* 93–100.

Bowers, K. S., & Bowers, P. G. (1972). Hypnosis and creativity: A theoretical rapprochement. In E. Fromm & R. E. Shor (Eds.), *Hypnosis: Research developments and perspectives* (pp. 225–291). Chicago: Aldine-Atherton.

Bowers, P. G. (1978). Hypnotizability, creativity, and the role of effortless experiencing. *International Journal of Clinical and Experimental Hypnosis, 26,* 184–202.

Bowers, P. G. (1982–1983). On *not* trying so hard: Effortless experiencing and its correlates. *Imagination, Cognition and Personality, 2,* 3–13.

Bowers, P. G., & Bowers, K. S. (1979). Hypnosis and creativity: A theoretical and empirical rapprochement. In E. Fromm & R. E. Shor (Eds.), *Hypnosis: Developments in research and new perspectives* (2nd ed., pp. 351–379). New York: Aldine.

Bowlby, J. (1973). *Attachment and loss: Vol. 2. Separation: Anxiety and anger.* New York: Basic Books.

Brown, D. P. (1977). A model for the levels of concentrative meditation. *International Journal of Clinical and Experimental Hypnosis, 25,* 236–273.

Brown, D. P., Forte, M., Rich, G., & Epstein, G. (1982–1983). Phenomenological differences among self-hypnosis, mindfulness meditation, and imaging. *Imagination, Cognition and Personality, 4,* 291–309.

Brown, D. P., & Fromm, E. (1986). *Hypnotherapy and hypnoanalysis.* Hillsdale, NJ: Erlbaum.

Brown, D. P., & Fromm, E. (1987). *Hypnosis and behavioral medicine.* Hillsdale, NJ: Erlbaum.

Byrne, D., Barry, J., & Nelson, D. (1963). Relation of the Revised Repression–Sensitization Scale to measures of self-description. *Psychological Reports, 13,* 323–334.

Campbell, D. T., & Fiske, D. W. (1959). Convergent and discriminant validation by the multitrait–multimethod matrix. *Psychological Bulletin, 56,* 81–105.

Citrenbaum, C., King, M., & Cohen, W. (1985). *Modern clinical hypnosis for habit control.* New York: Norton.

Coe, W. C., St. Jean, R. L., & Burger, J. M. (1980). Hypnosis and the enhancement of visual imagery. *International Journal of Clinical and Experimental Hypnosis, 28,* 225–243.

Coué, E. (1922). *Self-mastery through autosuggestion.* London: Allen & Unwin.

Crasilneck, H. P., & Hall, J. A. (1985). *Clinical hypnosis: Principles and applications* (2nd ed.). Orlando, FL: Grune & Stratton.

Crawford, H. J. (1982). Hypnotizability, daydreaming styles, imagery vividness, and absorption: A multidimensional study. *Journal of Personality and Social Psychology, 42,* 915–926.

Dahlstrom, W. G., Welsh, G. S., & Dahlstrom, L. (1972). *An MMPI handbook: Vol. 1. Clinical interpretation.* Minneapolis: University of Minnesota Press.

Dahlstrom, W. G., Welsh, G. S., & Dahlstrom, L. (1975). *An MMPI handbook: Vol. 2. Research applications.* Minneapolis: University of Minnesota Press.

Dane, J. R., & Rowlingson, J. C. (1988). Hypnosis in the management of postherpetic neuralgia: Three case studies. *American Journal of Clinical Hypnosis, 31,* 107–113.

Davis, S., Dawson, J. G., & Seay, B. (1978). Prediction of hypnotic susceptibility from imaginative involvement. *American Journal of Clinical Hypnosis, 20*(3), 194–198.

Deikman, A. J. (1971). Bimodal consciousness. *Archives of General Psychiatry, 25,* 481–489.

Dengrove, E. (1976). *Hypnosis and behavior therapy.* Springfield, IL: Charles C Thomas.

Diamond, M. J., Gregory, J., Lenney, E., Steadman, C., & Talone, J. M. (1974). An alternative approach to personality correlates of hypnotizability: Hypnosis-specific mediational attitudes. *International Journal of Clinical and Experimental Hypnosis, 22,* 346–353.

Diamond, M. J., & Taft, R. (1975). The role played by ego permissiveness and imagery in hypnotic responsivity. *International Journal of Clinical and Experimental Hypnosis, 23,* 130–138.

Epstein, S. J., & Deyoub, P. L. (1983). Hypnotherapeutic control of exhibitionism. *International Journal of Clinical and Experimental Hypnosis, 31,* 63–66.

Erickson, M. H. (1980). Hypnotic investigation of psychodynamic processes. In M. H. Erickson & E. L. Rossi (Eds.), *Collected papers of Milton H. Erickson on hypnosis* (Vol. 3). New York: Halstead Press.

Erickson, M. H., & Rossi, E. L. (1977). Autohypnotic experiences of Milton H. Erickson. *American Journal of Clinical Hypnosis, 20,* 36–54.

Erikson, E. (1980). *Identity and the life cycle.* New York: Norton. (Original work published 1959)

Feinstein, A. D., & Morgan, R. M. (1986). Hypnosis in regulating bipolar affective disorders. *American Journal of Clinical Hypnosis, 29,* 29–38.

Field, P. B. (1965). An inventory scale of hypnotic depth. *International Journal of Clinical and Experimental Hypnosis, 13,* 238–249.

Field, P. B. (1966). Some self-rating measures related to hypnotizability. *Perceptual and Motor Skills, 23,* 1179–1187.

Field, P. B., & Palmer, R. D. (1969). Factor analysis: Hypnosis inventory. *International Journal of Clinical and Experimental Hypnosis, 17,* 50–61.

Finke, R. A., & McDonald, H. (1978). Two personality measures relating hypnotic susceptibility to absorption. *International Journal of Clinical and Experimental Hypnosis, 26,* 178–183.

Fischer, R. (1971). A cartography of the ecstatic and meditative states: The experimental and experiential features of a perception–hallucination continuum are considered. *Science, 174,* 897–904.

Forisha, B. L. (1978). Mental imagery and creativity. *Journal of Mental Imagery, 2,* 209–238.

Forisha, B. L. (1983). Relationship between creativity and mental imagery: A question of cognitive styles? In A. Sheikh (Ed.), *Imagery* (pp. 310–340). New York: Wiley.

Freud, S. (1953). The interpretation of dreams. In J. Strachey (Ed. and Trans.), *The *standard edition of the complete psychological works of Sigmund Freud* (Vols. 4 & 5, complete). London: Hogarth Press. (Original work published 1900)

Freud, S. (1957a). On narcissism: An introduction. In J. Strachey (Ed. and Trans.), *The standard edition of the complete psychological works of Sigmund Freud* (Vol. 14, pp. 73–102). London: Hogarth Press. (Original work published 1914)

Freud, S. (1957b). Mourning and melancholia. In J. Strachey (Ed. and Trans.), *The standard edition of the complete psychological works of Sigmund Freud* (Vol. 14, pp. 239–258). London: Hogarth Press. (Original work published 1917)

Friedlander, J. W., & Sarbin, T. R. (1938). The depth of hypnosis. *Journal of Abnormal and Social Psychology, 33,* 453–475.

Fromm, E. (1968). Transference and countertransference in hypnoanalysis. *International Journal of Clinical and Experimental Hypnosis, 16,* 77–84.

Fromm, E. (1972a). Ego activity and ego passivity in hypnosis, *International Journal of Clinical and Experimental Hypnosis, 20,* 238–251.

Fromm, E. (1972b). Quo vadis hypnosis: Predictions of future trends in hypnosis research. In E. Fromm & R. E. Shor (Eds.), *Hypnosis: Research developments and perspectives* (pp. 575–586). Chicago: Aldine-Atherton.

Fromm, E. (1975a). Autohypnosis and heterohypnosis: Phenomenological similarities and differences. In L.-E. Unestāhl (Ed.), *Hypnosis in the seventies* (pp. 24–28). Örebro, Sweden: Veje Förlag.

Fromm, E. (1975b). Autohypnosis. In L.-E. Unestāhl (Ed.), *Hypnosis in the seventies* (pp. 152–154). Örebro, Sweden: Veje Förlag.

Fromm, E. (1975c). Self-hypnosis: A new area of research. *Psychotherapy: Theory, Research and Practice, 12,* 295–301.

Fromm, E. (1976). Altered states of consciousness and ego psychology. *Social Service Review, 50,* 557–569.

Fromm, E. (1977). An ego-psychological theory of altered states of consciousness. *International Journal of Clinical and Experimental Hypnosis, 25,* 372–387.

Fromm, E. (1978–1979). Primary and secondary process in waking and in altered states of consciousness. *Journal of Altered States of Consciousness, 4*(3), 115–128.

Fromm, E. (1979). The nature of hypnosis and other altered states of consciousness: An ego-psychological theory. In E. Fromm & R. E. Shor (Eds.), *Hypnosis: Developments in research and new perspectives* (2nd ed., pp. 81–103). New York: Aldine.

Fromm, E., Brown, D. P., Hurt, S. W., Oberlander, J. Z., Boxer, A. M., & Pfeifer, G. (1981). The phenomena and characteristics of self-hypnosis. *International Journal of Clinical and Experimental Hypnosis, 29*(3), 189–246.

Fromm, E., & Gardner, G. G. (1979). Ego psychology and hypnoanalysis: An integration of theory and technique. *Bulletin of the Menninger Clinic, 43,* 413–423.

Fromm, E., & Hurt, S. W. (1980). Ego-psychological parameters of hypnosis and altered states of consciousness. In G. D. Burrows & L. Dennerstein (Eds.), *Handbook of hypnosis and psychosomatic medicine* (pp. 13–27). Amsterdam: Elsevier/North-Holland Biomedical Press.

Fromm, E., Litchman, J., & Brown, D. P. (1973, December). *Autohypnosis and heterohypnosis: Phenomenological similarities and differences.* Paper presented at the annual convention of the Society for Clinical and Experimental Hypnosis, Newport Beach, CA.

Fromm, E., Oberlander, M. I., Gruenewald, D. (1970). Perceptual and cognitive processes in different states of consciousness: The waking state and hypnosis. *Journal of Projective Techniques and Personality Assessment, 34,* 375–387.

Fromm, E., & Shor, R. E. (Eds.). (1972). *Hypnosis: Research developments and perspectives.* Chicago: Aldine-Atherton.

Fromm, E., & Shor, R. E. (Eds.). (1979). *Hypnosis: Developments in research and new perspectives* (2nd ed.). New York: Aldine.

Furneaux, W. D., & Gibson, H. B. (1961). The Maudsley Personality Inventory as a predictor of susceptibility to hypnosis. *International Journal of Clinical and Experimental Hypnosis, 9,* 167–177.

Gardner, G. G. (1981). Teaching self-hypnosis to children. *International Journal of Clinical and Experimental Hypnosis, 29,* 300–312.

Gardner, G. G., & Olness, K. N. (1981). *Hypnosis and hypnotherapy with children.* New York: Grune & Stratton.

Gill, M. M. (Ed.). (1967). *The collected papers of David Rapaport.* New York: Basic Books.

Gill, M. M., & Brenman, M. (1959). *Hypnosis and related states: Psychoanalytic studies in regression.* New York: International Universities Press.

Gruenewald, D., Fromm, E., & Oberlander, M. I. (1979). Hypnosis and adaptive regression: An ego-psychological inquiry. In E. Fromm & R. E. Shor (Eds.), *Hypnosis: Developments in research and new perspectives* (2nd ed., pp. 619–635). New York: Aldine.

Hammond, D., Haskins-Bartsch, C., Grant, C. W., & McGhee, M. (1988). Comparison of self-directed and tape-assisted self hypnosis. *American Journal of Clinical Hypnosis, 31,* 129–137.

Hart, H. (1961). A review of the psychoanalytic literature on passivity. *Psychiatric Quarterly, 35,* 331–352.

Hatfield, E. C. (1961). The validity of the LeCron method of evaluating hypnotic depth. *International Journal of Clinical and Experimental Hypnosis, 9,* 215–221.

Hathaway, S. R., & McKinley, D. (1967). *Minnesota Multiphasic Personality Inventory.* New York: Psychological Corporation.

Hilgard, E. R. (1965). *Hypnotic susceptibility.* New York: Harcourt, Brace & World.

Hilgard, E. R. (1975). Self-induction of hypnosis by inexperienced subjects and self-deepening procedures of the highly hypnotizable. In L.-E. Uneståhl (Ed.), *Hypnosis in the seventies* (pp. 61–65). Örebro, Sweden: Veje Förlag.

Hilgard, E. R. (1977). *Divided consciousness: Multiple controls in human thought and action.* New York: Wiley.

Hilgard, E. R., & Bentler, P. M. (1963). Predicting hypnotizability from the Maudsley Personality Inventory. *British Journal of Psychology, 54,* 63–69.

Hilgard, E. R., & Lauer, L. W. (1962). Lack of correlation between the CPI and hypnotic susceptibility. *Journal of Consulting Psychology, 26,* 331–335.

Hilgard, E. R., Lauer, L. W., & Melei, J. P. (1965). Acquiescence, hypnotic susceptibility, and the MMPI. *Journal of Consulting Psychology, 29,* 489.

Hilgard, E. R., & Tart, C. T. (1966). Responsiveness to suggestions following waking and imagination instructions and following induction of hypnosis. *Journal of Abnormal Psychology, 71,* 196–208.

Hilgard, J. R. (1965). Personality and hypnotizability: Inferences from case studies.

In E. R. Hilgard, *Hypnotic susceptibility* (pp. 343–374). New York: Harcourt, Brace & World.

Hilgard, J. R. (1970). *Personality and hypnosis: A study of imaginative involvement.* Chicago: University of Chicago Press.

Hilgard, J. R. (1974). Imaginative involvement: Some characteristics of the highly hypnotizable and non-hypnotizable. *International Journal of Clinical and Experimental Hypnosis, 22,* 138–156.

Hilgard, J. R. (1979). *Personality and hypnosis: A study of imaginative involvement* (2nd ed.). Chicago: University of Chicago Press.

Hilgard, J. R., & LeBaron, S. (1984). *Hypnotherapy of pain in children with cancer.* Los Altos, CA: William Kaufmann.

Holt, R. R. (1965). Ego autonomy reevaluated. *International Journal of Psycho-Analysis, 46,* 151–167.

Holt, R. R. (1970). *Manual for the scoring of primary process manifestations in Rorschach responses.* New York: Research Center for Mental Health, New York University.

Horowitz, M. J. (1970). *Image formation and cognition.* New York: Appleton-Century-Crofts.

Jackson, D. N. (1974). *The Personality Research Form manual.* Goshen, NY: Research Psychology Press.

James, W. (1935). *The varieties of religious experience.* New York: Longmans, Green. (Original work published 1902)

Johnson, L. S. (1979). Self-hypnosis: Behavioral and phenomenological comparisons with heterohypnosis. *International Journal of Clinical and Experimental Hypnosis, 27,* 240–264.

Johnson, L. S. (1981). Current research in self-hypnotic phenomenology: The Chicago paradigm. *International Journal of Clinical and Experimental Hypnosis, 29,* 247–258.

Johnson, L. S., Dawson, S. L., Clark, J. L., & Sikorsky, C. (1983). Self-hypnosis versus heterohypnosis: Order effects and sex differences in behavioral and experiential impact. *International Journal of Clinical and Experimental Hypnosis, 31,* 139–154.

Johnson, L. S., & Weight, D. G. (1976). Self-hypnosis versus heterohypnosis: Experiential and behavioral comparisons. *Journal of Abnormal Psychology, 85,* 523–526.

Kahn, S., Fromm, E., Lombard, L., & Sossi, M. (1989). The relation of self-reports of hypnotic depth in self-hypnosis to hypnotizability and imagery production. *International Journal of Clinical and Experimental Hypnosis, 37,* 290–304.

Katz, E., Kellerman, J., & Ellenberg, L. (1987). Hypnosis in reduction of acute pain and distress in children with cancer. *General Pediatric Psychology, 12,* 379–394.

Kernberg, O. (1976). *Object relations theory and clinical psychoanalysis.* New York: Jason Aronson.

Kihlstrom, J. S., Diaz, W. A., McClellan, G. E., Ruskine, P. M., Pistole, D. D., & Shor, R. E. (1980). Personality correlates of hypnotic susceptibility: Needs for achievement and autonomy, self-monitoring, and masculinity–femininity. *American Journal of Clinical Hypnosis, 2,* 225–230.

Kihlstrom, J. S., Register, P. A., Hoyt, I. P., Albright, J. S., Grigorian, E. N., Heindel, W. C., & Morrison, C. R. (1989). Dispositional correlates of hypnosis: A phenomenological approach. *International Journal of Clinical and Experimental Hypnosis, 37,* 249–263.

Klein, M. (1940). Mourning and its relation to manic–depressive states. *International Journal of Psycho-Analysis, 21,* 125–153.

Kohen, D., Olness, K., Colwell, S., & Heimel, A. (1984). The use of relaxation–mental imagery in self-hypnosis in the management of 505 pediatric behavioral encounters. *Journal of Developmental and Behavioral Pediatrics, 5,* 21–25.

Kohut, H. (1971). *The analysis of the self.* New York: International Universities Press.

Kübler-Ross, E. (1969). *On death and dying.* New York: Macmillan.

Kunzendorf, R. G. (1985–1986). Hypnotic hallucinations as "unmonitored" images: An empirical study. *Imagination, Cognition and Personality, 5,* 255–270.

Laurence, J.-R., & Nadon, R. (1986). Reports of hypnotic depth: Are they more than mere words? *International Journal of Clinical and Experimental Hypnosis, 34,* 215–233.

Lavoie, G., Sabourin, M., & Ally, G. (1976). Hypnotizability as a function of adaptive regression among chronic psychotic patients. *International Journal of Clinical and Experimental Hypnosis, 24,* 238–257.

LeCron, L. M. (1953). A method of measuring the depth of hypnosis. *International Journal of Clinical and Experimental Hypnosis, 1,* 4–7.

Leuner, H. (1969). Guided affective imagery (GARI): A method of intensive psychotherapy. *American Journal of Psychotherapy, 23,* 4–22.

Liébeault, A. A. (1889). *Le sommeil provoqué et les états analogues* [Induced sleep and related states]. Paris: Doin.

Lindemann, E. (1944). Symptomatology and management of acute grief. *American Journal of Psychiatry, 101,* 1–11.

Lombard, L., Kahn, S., & Fromm, E. (1990). The role of imagery in self-hypnosis: Its relationship to personality characteristics and gender. *International Journal of Clinical and Experimental Hypnosis, 38,* 25–38.

Mahler, M., Pine, F., & Bergman, A. (1975). *The psychological birth of the human infant.* New York: Basic Books.

Maslow, A. H. (1968). *Toward a psychology of being* (2nd ed.). New York: Van Nostrand Reinhold.

Maupin, E. (1965). Individual differences in response to a Zen meditation exercise. *Journal of Consulting Psychology, 29,* 139–145.

McBain, W. N. (1954). Imagery and suggestibility: A test of the Arnold hypothesis. *Journal of Abnormal and Social Psychology, 49,* 36–44.

McConkey, K. M., Sheehan, P. W., & White, K. D. (1979). Comparison of the Creative Imagination Scale and the Harvard Group Scale of Hypnotic Susceptibility, Form A. *International Journal of Clinical and Experimental Hypnosis, 27,* 265–277.

Melges, F. T., & DeMaso, D. R. (1980). Grief resolution therapy: Reliving, revising and revisiting. *American Journal of Psychotherapy, 34,* 51–61.

Murray, H. A. (1938). *Explorations in personality.* New York: Oxford University Press.

O'Connell, D. N. (1964). An experimental comparison of hypnotic depth measured by self-ratings and by an objective scale. *International Journal of Clinical and Experimental Hypnosis, 12,* 34–46.

O'Grady, K. E. (1980). The Absorption scale: A factor-analytic assessment. *International Journal of Clinical and Experimental Hypnosis, 28,* 281–288.

Orne, M. T., & McConkey, K. M. (1981). Toward convergent inquiry into self-hypnosis. *International Journal of Clinical and Experimental Hypnosis, 29,* 313–323.

Palmer, R. D., & Field, P. B. (1968). Visual imagery and susceptibility to hypnosis. *Journal of Consulting and Clinical Psychology, 32,* 456–462.

Parkes, C. M. (1971). *Bereavement: Studies of grief in adult life.* New York: International Universities Press.

Perry, C. (1973). Imagery, fantasy, and hypnotic susceptibility: A multidimensional approach. *Journal of Personality and Social Psychology, 26,* 217–221.

Perry, C., & Laurence, J.-R. (1980). Hypnotic depth and hypnotic susceptibility: A replicated finding. *International Journal of Clinical and Experimental Hypnosis, 28,* 272–280.

Piccione, C., & Hilgard, E. R. (1987, October). *The Stanford Hypnotic Susceptibility Scale: The stability of scores over a 25-year period.* Paper presented at the annual convention of the Society for Clinical and Experimental Hypnosis, Los Angeles.

Pine, F., & Holt, R. R. (1960). Creativity and primary process: A study of adaptive regression. *Journal of Abnormal and Social Psychology, 61,* 370–379.

Pollock, G. H. (1961). Mourning and adaptation. *International Journal of Psycho-Analysis, 42,* 341–361.

Pollock, G. H. (1977). The mourning process and creative organizational change. *Journal of the American Psychoanalytic Association, 25,* 3–34.

Pollock, G. H. (1978). On siblings, childhood sibling loss, and creativity. *Annual of Psychoanalysis, 6,* 443–481.

Radtke, H. L., & Spanos, N. P. (1981). Was I hypnotized? A social psychological analysis of hypnotic depth reports. *Psychiatry, 44,* 359–376.

Radtke, H. L., & Spanos, N. P. (1982). The effect of rating scale descriptors on hypnotic depth reports. *Journal of Psychology, 111,* 235–245.

Rapaport, D. (1967a). States of consciousness: A psychopathological and psychodynamic view. In M. M. Gill (Ed.), *The collected papers of David Rapaport* (pp. 385–404). New York: Basic Books.

Rapaport, D. (1967b). Some metapsychological considerations concerning activity and passivity. In M. M. Gill (Ed.), *The collected papers of David Rapaport* (pp. 530–568). New York: Basic Books.

Richardson, A. (1969). *Mental imagery.* New York: Springer Publishing Company.

Richardson, A. (1972). Voluntary control of the memory image. In P. W. Sheehan (Ed.), *The function and nature of imagery* (pp. 109–129). New York: Academic Press.

Rønnestad, M. H. (1989). Hypnosis and autonomy: A moderator analysis. *International Journal of Clinical and Experimental Hypnosis, 37,* 154–168.

Rorschach, H. (1949). *Psychodiagnostics* (4th ed.) Bern, Switzerland: Verlag Hans Huber.

Rorschach, H. (1954). *Psychodiagnostic plates* (5th ed.) New York: Grune & Stratton.

Ruch, J. C. (1975). Self-hypnosis: The result of heterohypnosis or vice versa? *International Journal of Clinical and Experimental Hypnosis, 23*, 228–304.

Sacerdote, P. (1981). Teaching self-hypnosis to adults. *International Journal of Clinical and Experimental Hypnosis, 29*, 282–299.

Salter, A. (1941). Three techniques of autohypnosis. *Journal of General Psychology, 24*, 423–438.

Sanders, S. (1987). Styles of clinical self-hypnosis. In W. C. Wester II (Ed.), *Clinical hypnosis: A case management approach* (pp. 29–40). Cincinnati: Behavioral Science Center Publications.

Sanders, S. (1990). *Clinical self-hypnosis: The power of words and images.* New York: Guilford.

Schachter, S., & Singer, J. E. (1962). Cognitive, social, and physiological determinants of emotional states. *Psychological Review, 69*, 379–399.

Shapiro, S. S., & Wilks, M. B. (1965). An analysis of variance test for normality (complete samples). *Biometrika, 52*, 591–611.

Sheehan, P. W. (1979). Hypnosis and the process of imagination. In E. Fromm & R. E. Shor (Eds.), *Hypnosis: Developments in research and new perspectives* (2nd ed., pp. 381–411). New York: Aldine.

Shor, R. E. (1959). Hypnosis and the concept of the generalized reality orientation. *American Journal of Psychotherapy, 13*, 582–602.

Shor, R. E. (1960). The frequency of naturally occurring "hypnotic-like" experiences in the normal college population. *International Journal of Clinical and Experimental Hypnosis, 8*, 151–163.

Shor, R. E. (1962). Three dimensions of hypnotic depth. *International Journal of Clinical and Experimental Hypnosis, 10*, 23–38.

Shor, R. E. (1970). *The Inventory of Self-Hypnosis (Form A): Breaths version.* Unpublished manuscript.

Shor, R. E. (1978). *The Inventory of Self-Hypnosis (Form A)* (rev. ed.). Palo Alto, CA: Consulting Psychologists Press.

Shor, R. E. (1979). A phenomenological method for the measurement of variables important to an understanding of the nature of hypnosis. In E. Fromm & R. E. Shor (Eds.), *Hypnosis: Developments in research and new perspectives* (2nd ed., pp. 105–135). New York: Aldine.

Shor, R. E., & Easton, R. D. (1973). A preliminary report on research comparing self-hypnosis and heterohypnosis. *American Journal of Clinical Hypnosis, 16*, 37–44.

Shor, R. E., & Orne, E. C. (1962). *Harvard Group Scale of Hypnotic Susceptibility, Form A.* Palo Alto, CA: Consulting Psychologists Press.

Shor, R. E., Orne, M. T., & O'Connell, D. N. (1966). Psychological correlates of plateau hypnotizability in a special volunteer sample. *Journal of Personality and Social Psychology, 3*, 80–95.

Shostrom, E. (1972). *Manual for the Personal Orientation Inventory (POI): An inventory for the measurement of self-actualization.* San Diego: Educational and Industrial Testing Service.

Silverman, P. (1975). Widowhood and preventive intervention. *Family Coordinator, 8*, 9–27.

Singer, J. L., & Antrobus, J. S. (1972). Daydreaming, imaginal processes and personality: A normative study. In P. W. Sheehan (Ed.), *The function and nature of imagery* (pp. 175–202). New York: Academic Press.

Singer, J. L., & Pope, K. S. (1981). Daydreaming and imagery skills as predisposing capacities for self-hypnosis. *International Journal of Clinical and Experimental Hypnosis, 29,* 271–281.

Smith, S. J., & Balaban, A. B. (1983). A multidimensional approach to pain relief: Case report of a patient with systemic lupus erythematosus. *International Journal of Clinical and Experimental Hypnosis, 31,* 72–81.

Soskis, D. A. (1986). *Teaching self-hypnosis.* New York: Norton.

Soskis, D. A., Orne, E. C., Orne, M. T., & Dinges, D. F. (1989). Self-hypnosis and meditation for stress management: A brief communication. *International Journal of Clinical and Experimental Hypnosis, 37,* 285–289.

Spanos, N. P., & McPeake, J. D. (1975). The interaction of attitudes toward hypnosis and involvement in everyday imaginative activities on hypnotic susceptibility. *American Journal of Clinical Hypnosis, 17,* 274–282.

Spanos, N. P., Valois, R., Ham, U. W., & Ham, M. L. (1973). Suggestibility and vividness and control of imagery. *International Journal of Clinical and Experimental Hypnosis, 21,* 305–311.

Spiegel, D., & Bloom, J. R. (1983). Group therapy and hypnosis reduce metastatic breast carcinoma pain. *Psychosomatic Medicine, 45,* 333–339.

Spiegel, H., Fleiss, J. L., Bridger, A. A., & Aronson, M. (1975). Hypnotizability and mental health. In S. Arieti (Ed.), *New dimensions in psychiatry: A world view* (pp. 342–356). New York: Wiley.

Spinhoven, P. (1989). *Hypnosis and pain control.* Leiden, The Netherlands: University of Leiden.

Stolar, D., & Fromm, E. (1974). Activity and passivity of the ego in relation to the superego. *International Review of Psychoanalysis, 1,* 297–311.

Sutcliffe, J. P., Perry, C. W., & Sheehan, P. W. (1970). Relation of some aspects of imagery and fantasy to hypnotic susceptibility. *Journal of Abnormal Psychology, 76,* 279–287.

Swanson, G. E. (1978). Travels through inner space: Family structure and openness to absorbing experience. *American Journal of Sociology, 83,* 890–919.

Swenson, W. M., Pearson, J. S., & Osborne, D. (1973). *An MMPI source book: Basic item, scale, and pattern data on 50,000 medical patients.* Minneapolis: University of Minnesota Press.

Swirsky-Sacchetti, T., & Margolis, C. G. (1986). The effects of a comprehensive self-hypnosis training program in the use of Factor 8 in severe hemophilia. *International Journal of Clinical and Experimental Hypnosis, 34,* 71–83.

Tart, C. T. (1963). Hypnotic depth and basal skin resistance. *International Journal of Clinical and Experimental Hypnosis, 11,* 81–92.

Tart, C. T. (1966). Types of hypnotic dreams and their relation to hypnotic depth. *Journal of Abnormal Psychology, 71,* 377–382.

Tart, C. T. (Ed.). (1969). *Altered states of consciousness: A book of readings.* New York: Wiley.

Tart, C. T. (1970). Self-report scales of hypnotic depth. *International Journal of Clinical and Experimental Hypnosis, 18,* 105–125.

Tart, C. T. (1972). Measuring the depth of an altered state of consciousness, with particular reference to self-report scales of hypnotic depth. In E. Fromm & R. E. Shor (Eds.), *Hypnosis: Research developments and perspectives* (pp. 445–477). Chicago: Aldine-Atherton.

Tart, C. T. (1975). *States of consciousness*. New York: Dutton.

Tart, C. T. (1978). Quick and convenient assessment of hypnotic depth: Self-report scales. *American Journal of Clinical Hypnosis, 21*, 186–207.

Tart, C. T. (1979). Extended North Carolina Scale. In E. Fromm & R. E. Shor (Eds.), *Hypnosis: Developments in research and new perspectives* (2nd ed., pp. 567–601). New York: Aldine.

Tellegen, A., & Atkinson, G. (1974). Openness to absorbing and self-altering experiences ("absorption"), a trait related to hypnotic susceptibility. *Journal of Abnormal Psychology, 83*, 268–277.

Udolf, R. (1981). *Handbook of hypnosis for professionals*. New York: Van Nostrand Reinhold.

van der Hart, O. (1981). Symbolen en therapeutische rituelen [Dutch: Symbols and therapeutic rituals]. *Dth: Kwaartaalschrift voor Directieve Therapie en Hypnosis [Dth: Quarterly Journal for Directive Therapy and Hypnosis], 1*, 28–40.

Van Dijck, R. (1988). Future oriented hypnotic imagery: Description of a method. *Hypnos, 15*, 60–67.

Van Dyne, W. T., & Stava, L. J. (1981). Analysis of relationships among hypnotic susceptibility, personality type, and vividness of mental imagery. *Psychological Reports, 48*, 23–26.

Wagman, R., & Stewart, C. G. (1974). Visual imagery and hypnotic susceptibility. *Perceptual and Motor Skills, 38*, 815–822.

Wakeman, R. J. (1988). Hypnotic desensitization of job-related heat intolerance in recovered burn victims. *American Journal of Clinical Hypnosis, 31*, 28–32.

Wark, D. M. (1989). Alert self-hypnosis technique to improve reading comprehension. *Hypnos, 16*, 112–121.

Watkins, J. G. (1971). The affect bridge: A hypnoanalytic technique. *International Journal of Clinical and Experimental Hypnosis, 19*, 21–27.

Watkins, J. G. (1987). *Hypnotherapeutic techniques*. New York: Irvington.

Weitzenhoffer, A. M. (1957). *General techniques of hypnotism*. New York: Grune & Stratton.

Weitzenhoffer, A. M. (1989). *The practice of hypnotism* (Vol. 1). New York: Wiley.

Weitzenhoffer, A. M., & Hilgard, E. R. (1959). *Stanford Hypnotic Susceptibility Scale, Forms A and B*. Palo Alto: Consulting Psychologists Press.

Weitzenhoffer, A. M., & Hilgard, E. R. (1962). *Stanford Hypnotic Susceptibility Scale, Form C*. Palo Alto, CA: Consulting Psychologists Press.

Weitzenhoffer, A. M., & Hilgard, E. R. (1967). *Revised Stanford Profile Scales of Hypnotic Susceptibility, Forms I and II*. Palo Alto, CA: Consulting Psychologists Press.

Wilson, S. C., & Barber, T. X. (1978). The Creative Imagination Scale as a measure of hypnotic responsiveness: Applications to experimental and clinical hypnosis. *American Journal of Clinical Hypnosis, 20*, 235–249.

Winnicott, D. W. (1958). *Collected papers: Through pediatrics to psychoanalysis*. New York: Basic Books.

Winnicott, D. W. (1965). *The maturational processes and the facilitating environment: Studies in the theories of emotional development.* New York: International Universities Press.

Winnicott, D. W. (1971). *Playing and reality.* London: Tavistock.

Yanchar, R. J., & Johnson, H. J. (1981). Absorption and attitude toward hypnosis: A moderator analysis. *International Journal of Clinical and Experimental Hypnosis, 24,* 375–382.

Young, M. H., & Montano, R. J. (1988). A new hypnobehavioral method for treatment of children with Tourette's disorder. *American Journal of Clinical Hypnosis, 31,* 97–106.

Zlotogorski, Z., Hahnemann, L. E., & Wiggs, E. A. (1987). Personality characteristics of hypnotizability. *American Journal of Clinical Hypnosis, 30,* 51–56.

Author Index

Subject Index

Absorption, 6, 20, 21, 23, 59, 60, 62, 73, 75, 88, 95, 96, 98, 99, 116, 119, 148, 164, 178–180, 182
  definition, 57, 96, 98, 99, 126, 127, 160
  scales, 160, 161
  as structural component of self-hypnosis, 64, 66, 68, 79, 80, 95, 96, 104
Affect bridge, 203, 204
Age progression, 119, 120
Age regression, 15, 16, 33, 35, 77, 78, 90, 91, 106, 109, 110, 118, 119, 204, 205, 226, 227
Altered states of consciousness, 5, 9, 44, 50, 52, 53, 56, 73, 75, 78, 108 (*see also* Hypnosis)
  daydreaming, 5, 6
  meditation, 5–7, 78, 81
Attention, 18, 20, 21, 33, 34, 56, 59, 60, 62–64, 76–80, 88, 92, 96, 97, 108
  concentration, 6, 7, 33, 34, 59, 60, 76, 79
  concentrative, 117, 121
  expansive, 117, 118, 121
  as structural component of self-hypnosis, 64, 68, 79, 80, 95, 96, 104
Automatic writing, 33

C

Cognitive psychological theory, 50

Content components of self-hypnosis, 20, 21, 116
  age regression, 20, 21, 116, 232
  dreams, 20, 21, 116
  imagery, 20, 21, 97, 116, 170, 171, 174, 178, 179
    and trance depth, 170, 171, 177, 179
  personal memories, 20, 21, 116
  strong affect, 10, 15, 17, 18, 20, 78, 116, 227, 232
  suggestion of motor phenomena, 20, 21, 116
  suggestion of sensory phenomena, 20, 21, 116
  working on problems, 20, 21, 116

E

Ego modes, 122–124, 160, 161
  ego activity, 18, 19, 22, 28–30, 117, 122–124, 164, 226, 227, 232
    definition, 22, 123, 164
  ego inactivity, 123, 124
    definition, 22, 123
  ego passivity, 28–30, 122–124
    definition, 22, 123
  ego receptivity, 18–25, 33, 79, 96, 98, 99, 108, 109, 117, 118, 122–124, 164, 226–228, 232
    definition, 22, 123, 164
    importance in self-hypnosis, 24, 25, 174, 175, 178, 179

251

Structural components of self-hypnosis,
    95, 96, 116
  absorption, 64, 68, 79, 80, 95, 96, 104
  attention, 64, 68, 79, 80, 95, 96, 104
  fading of Generalized Reality Orien-
    tation, 64, 68, 79, 80, 95, 96, 104
  trance depth, 64, 68, 79, 80, 95, 96,
    104, 164

T

Time distortion, 21, 90, 114, 226
Trance, 3, 7–9, 11–19, 29, 96, 97, 121
  deepening, 4, 8, 17, 29–31, 81, 117

  depth, 14, 29–31, 60, 61, 64, 68, 79,
    80, 95, 97, 104
    fluctuations in self-hypnosis versus
      heterohypnosis, 97
    self-report measurements, 147–159,
      164
  induction, 4, 8, 9, 17, 30–32, 37, 38,
    78
    techniques for self-hypnosis: arm
      levitation, 34, 38, 47, 106; counting
      breaths, 105, 108; elevator image,
      105; relaxation, 17, 105; staring at
      a target, 105
Transference, 54, 78, 110